THE IDEOLOGIES OF TAXATION

LOUIS EISENSTEIN

The Ideologies
of Taxation

Foreword by David A. Weisbach

HARVARD UNIVERSITY PRESS

Cambridge, Massachusetts, and London, England

2010

The Ideologies of Taxation by Louis Eisenstein was originally published in 1961 by The Ronald Press Company.

Foreword by David A. Weisbach copyright © 2010 by the President and Fellows of Harvard College

Library of Congress Cataloging-in-Publication Data

Eisenstein, Louis, 1915–
The ideologies of taxation / Louis Eisenstein ; foreword by David A. Weisbach.
   p.   cm.
[Originally published: New York, Ronald Press Co. 1961]
Includes bibliographical references and index.
ISBN 978-0-674-04611-5 (pbk.)
1. Taxation—United States.   I. Title.
HJ2381.E35 2010
336.200973—dc22   2009036429

Contents

Foreword

We can probably count the number of truly great books about taxation on our fingers. By almost any measure, Louis Eisenstein's *Ideologies of Taxation* would be on the list. Written almost fifty years ago, it anticipates many of the most important arguments about tax policy made since then. Indeed, what strikes me most is how little has changed. Eisenstein's specific examples are dated and the names of the prominent individuals have changed, but the arguments and the rhetoric of the tax world of the 1950s and today's are strikingly similar. And, uniquely for a tax book, it is a great read, combining wit with wisdom. It is not easy to think of another book about taxation that so well combines these qualities.

Eisenstein's thesis is straightforward. Arguments about taxation, he maintains, are merely rhetorical devices to cover up fierce efforts by interest groups to avoid taxation. Our taxes, he says, reflect a continuing struggle among contending interests for the privilege of paying the least. This view, although a challenge to standard tax thinking, was based on long-discussed views of legislation as resulting from factions and self-interest. These ideas have roots in the writings of James Madison and others, and they were percolating in academia, with seminal publications by Kenneth Arrow, Anthony Downs, James Buchanan, Gordon Tullock, and Mancur Olson all appearing around the time *Ideologies of Taxation* was published. While perhaps it should not be surprising that taxes reflect interest group struggles, tax arguments are almost always made as if the goal of the tax system is to benefit the public overall.

Eisenstein's unique take—different from the standard public-choice fare—is his focus on the rhetoric and the argumentation rather than on the mechanics of interest group formation and influence. In a democratic society, Eisenstein observes, claims for reduced taxes based on naked self-interest will not suffice. Instead, public-regarding reasons must be given for proposals made by various groups or factions to reduce their taxes. Eisenstein does not speculate on why this is so. It is perhaps because most interest groups do not have the votes to use naked self-interest and therefore must convince others to go along with their proposals. Covering self-interest with a veneer of the public good may make it more difficult for the public to organize and oppose transfers. For example, imagine how much more difficult it would be for the wealthy to argue successfully that their taxes should be cut because they want more money to spend on private jets or bigger yachts rather than because cutting their taxes will improve the economy. Even if they are going to spend the money on private jets and yachts, they will argue that this very spending improves the economy. Factions therefore develop rationales for reducing their own taxes, which are skillfully elaborated into systems of belief or ideologies. Eisenstein's book is an exercise in debunking these belief systems or ideologies.

Eisenstein focuses on three ideologies: the ideology of ability, the ideology of barriers and deterrents, and the ideology of equity. The ideology of ability holds that taxes should be based on ability to pay, and that this means we should have a progressive income tax and a progressive estate tax. The ideology of barriers and deterrents focuses on the disincentives to work and save caused by the tax system. Taxes that are too high or taxes on particularly desirable activities create disincentives to work or save that hurt everyone, not just the individual or activity bearing the tax. The ideology of equity holds that similarly situated individuals should be similarly taxed. Eisenstein then argues that each of these ideologies is merely a cover for attempts by various groups to have their own taxes reduced.

The ideology of barriers and deterrents has since been renamed supply-side economics. It has been elevated from mere ideology to the semiofficial religion of the Republican Party. The party has purged heretics who do not sufficiently profess the faith, requiring loyalty oaths in the form of pledges not to raise taxes on anyone under any circumstances. Even tax law changes that do not increase net revenues are cast as tax increases, because, inevitably, somebody somewhere has their taxes increased by the change. Moreover, any attempt to even consider the distributional effects of the tax cuts for the wealthy is immediately labeled class warfare, as if this were Russia in 1917. Picking up directly from Eisenstein's ideology of barriers and deterrents, reducing taxes is now even said to increase tax revenues—individuals will work harder and save more, thereby sufficiently increasing the amount available for taxation to offset the effect of lower tax rates. These arguments are hardly new. As Eisenstein explains, "large tax savings for the few will provide prosperity for the many." Although no politician would use those precise words, the basic message could be part of a standard stump speech today. The ideology of barriers and deterrents is not the sole province of the Republicans, but as Eisenstein noted in 1961—and it is surely even truer today—Republicans are able to speak of barriers and deterrents with a distinguished monotony that Democrats are unable to acquire.

Eisenstein's dissection of the ideology of barriers and deterrents is better than any I have seen. He traces its history back to the beginnings of the income tax and to proponents of the ideology such as Andrew Mellon. Although not an economist, Eisenstein makes a persuasive case that there is no correlation between tax cuts on the wealthy or on particular favored activities and the performance of the economy. We have had periods of high economic performance with high tax rates and poor economic performance with low tax rates. For example, during the 1950s, immediately before the original publication of the book, the top marginal tax rate was 91 percent, yet we experienced phenomenal growth. And at times of low tax rates, we have had low growth and even recessions. The same is true for tax rates on capital gains. There appears to be no correlation between capital gains rates and economic performance. Modern day economists have roughly confirmed this claim; it is very difficult to correlate marginal tax rates or capital gains rates with economic growth. To be sure, many questions remain. We do not yet know with any confidence labor supply or savings elasticities, and estimates vary, with some on the high side. Nevertheless, Eisenstein's views have been confirmed: broad and certain claims of enormous disincentives because of taxes are more rhetoric than reality.

As Eisenstein notes, however, ideologies are stubborn things. An ideology is not a body of truth but a system of belief. It continues to command allegiance as long as it serves some purpose. Since the affluent will remain unreconciled to high taxes, the ideology will persist, regardless of what the facts may periodically disclose. Ideologists will, of course, challenge the facts—there remain debates about the effect of high rates on the economy. But, ideologists support the necessary result despite the facts. For example, faced with high rates and high economic performance, the ideologists of barriers and deterrents added a new twist to their arguments: taxes must be cut during recessions to pull us out of the recession, and they must be cut when economic performance is high to reduce the chance of a future recession. Eisenstein notes that, under the old view, prosperity is impossible if taxes in the upper brackets are too high. Under the new view, no matter how well the economy is doing, a recession is always possible. A reduction in the upper brackets will avoid this danger by inducing their occupants to be more energetic in their efforts and more daring in their investments. The virtue of such reasoning is that it never ends. After every reduction, a recession is still possible.

If he were writing today, Eisenstein might make a similar comment about modern claims that low tax rates do in fact correlate with high economic growth. Advocates can always show a correlation by adding appropriate time lag between the lowering of rates and the economic growth or by dismissing contrary data as outliers explained by some other factor. For example, Clinton increased tax rates in the early 1990s and we saw phenomenal economic growth. Although one might reasonably conclude that higher tax rates and growth are compatible, this growth, we are told, was instead due to the tax rate cuts by Ronald Reagan in the 1980s and was in fact dampened by the Clinton tax increases. As Eisenstein says, ideologies are stubborn things.

The favored ideology of liberals, the ideology of ability, receives equal criticism. Basing taxes on ability to pay sounds very nice, and it is difficult to object to such a pleasant-sounding phrase. Who, after, all, would want to impose taxes on those who do not have the ability to pay them? The belief is often traced back to Adam Smith, showing that even free-market economists should support the idea. It was prominent among academics during Eisenstein's time, and modern day tax academics still largely subscribe to the idea. As I write, the Barack Obama administration seems likely to propose tax increases on the wealthy based almost entirely on the ideology of ability.

Eisenstein points out, however, that the term *ability to pay* has no intrinsic meaning. It cannot be used to decide any remotely difficult tax problem. Given any difficult set of circumstances, one can always use ability to pay to argue for a tax reduction for the favored group or a tax increase for the disfavored group. For example, those who receive tort damages for physical injury might be said not to have an increased ability to pay because the damages merely compensate them for the harm they suffered. But of course, laborers receiving wages are merely compensated for the harm they suffer from having to work. We cannot decide whether to tax tort damages based on ability-to-pay logic. The same holds true for almost any comparison, including, most importantly, the comparison of someone with wage income to someone with capital income. Ability-to-pay adherents almost invariably support an income tax and high taxes on capital income over a consumption tax. The argument is simply that those with high incomes, no matter the source, have a higher ability to pay taxes than those with low incomes. So a person with, say, $1 million of income from clipping coupons has a higher ability to pay than someone with $100,000 or $50,000 of wage income. Only an income tax ensures that the wealthy coupon-clipper pays a higher tax and therefore comports with the ability-to-pay principle.

The ideology of ability to pay cannot support the weight income tax advocates would place on it. If two people each earn $50,000 and one spends it all this year while the other spends half and saves half, the saver will face a higher tax than the spender because the interest income from his savings will be taxed. Can we say that the saver has a higher ability to pay than the spender, or should we instead say that the two individuals have simply made different choices? Eisenstein would say, and I agree, that we are best off not asking this question—the answers it yields will reveal more about the person asking the question than about good tax policy. We must decide tax problems based on the underlying allocative and distributional effects of the tax at stake rather than on empty phrases. To quote Eisenstein, "it is useless to condemn distinctions [in tax treatment] for failing to abide by the standard of ability. If a response is to be effective, it must openly do battle on the questions of policy that are involved. To speak forcefully of ability to pay is merely to indulge in evasive rhetoric."

Eisenstein was far ahead of his time in making this argument. The theme was famously echoed by Boris Bittker in the late 1960s when he criticized Stanley Surrey's argument that we could define a "normal" tax base and measure deviations from this base. Surrey argued that deviations from a normal tax base should be treated as equivalent to cash expenditures by Congress on favored programs. Bittker responded that there is no notion of a normal tax base; deviations from this imaginary concept are entirely made up by the analyst. He showed that Surrey's normal tax base includes a large number of policy decisions that must be defended rather than assumed; these policy decisions are no different from the deviations that Surrey condemns. Bittker's article is justly famous, but Eisenstein got there first. Bittker's arguments follow directly from Eisenstein's dissection of the ideology of ability.

Eisenstein's argument was taken up again in the 1980s and 1990s by such scholars as Louis Kaplow and Tom Griffith. These scholars published a number of articles arguing that notions such as ability to pay are entirely empty of content. Notwithstanding these precedents, however, legal scholars today still believe in ability to pay. We still have much to learn from Eisenstein.

Eisenstein's discussion of the ideology of equality is equally prescient and equally ignored by many modern tax scholars. He argues that the idea of equity is meaningless because it fails to define the underlying criteria by which individuals are to be measured as equal. It is nothing more than a vague noise. For example, Eisenstein compares the equity arguments for an income tax and a sales tax. One may argue that an income tax is equitable because those with similar incomes pay similar taxes. Alternatively, one may argue that a sales tax is equitable because those who consume more pay more taxes. Equity supports both taxes equally. Similarly, equity can be used to support a special dispensation for any group one desires. For example, if one is arguing for a lower tax burden on an activity, advocates merely need to show that the activity at stake is different from other activities and therefore deserves a lower tax burden. An alternative but equally attractive approach is to find some other activity with a lower tax burden and argue that it is inequitable to be taxed higher than the other activity. Regardless of the approach chosen, equity provides a handy argument that anyone can use to support lower taxes on a favored group.

This argument was taken up in 1981 in a famous article about constitutional law by Peter Westen, "The Empty Idea of Equality." It reappears in tax literature in discussions of "horizontal equity" by Louis Kaplow in the 1990s. As with Eisenstein's criticisms of ability to pay, the argument is compelling: without a prior view of who should be treated equally, a claim of equality is meaningless. But once we have a prior view, there is no reason to separately resort to equality as an argument because it has no independent power. And once again, the argument has not stopped advocates from using equality liberally to support their claims. This reason is clear: as Eisenstein notes, it would be unpatriotic to oppose equality, which means that this rhetoric is always useful. I think Eisenstein would not be surprised by the survival of such an empty idea. As he notes, "[i]ts power to persuade hinges largely on its failure to enlighten. As Oscar Wilde remarked, nothing produces such pleasing effects as a good platitude."

Eisenstein's dissection of the three ideologies is the main part of the book, but it is also full of smaller delights for students of the tax law. His discussion of loopholes is a good example. Tax loopholes are a perennial problem, no less today than in 1961. Many have argued in recent years for eliminating corporate welfare and have complained bitterly that it is perfectly legal for large corporations and wealthy individuals to avoid taxes through loopholes. Tax shelters are pervasive. The Justice Department has convicted several professionals working at a large accounting firm and at a law firm for marketing fraudulent tax shelters, Congress has held repeated hearings, legislation is pending, reporters have won Pulitzer Prizes exposing shelters, academic conferences abound, and many lawyers and bankers have become wealthy peddling the schemes.

The problem then and today is that nobody seems to be able to determine exactly what a loophole is. As Eisenstein argues, "loopholes are repeatedly disapproved with persuasive vehemence. But we should not assume that what is roundly condemned is always clearly perceived. It is usually easier to deplore sin than to explain its content." He goes on to criticize the arguments made by Stanley Surrey about the unfairness of the special provisions and exemptions that erode our tax base. As noted, Surrey maintained that we should treat deviations from a broad income tax as expenditures (so-called tax expenditures), just like cash expenditures made through the appropriations process. Eisenstein argues against this view by showing that Surrey's definition of a loophole is entirely dependent on Surrey's preferred tax base. There is no independent notion of a loophole. The argument is essentially the same as the arguments about ability to pay and equity. If one wants to argue against a provision, one needs to make arguments based on the allocative or distributive consequences of the provision rather than merely calling it a loophole. Claiming something is a loophole is merely a vague but nice-sounding phrase that substitutes for actual reasoning. As Eisenstein puts it, "[m]y inquiry into loopholes confirms anew a familiar truth. Better answers require wiser questions." Ultimately dispensations for certain taxpayers are condemned, not because they conform to some definition of a loophole, but because they are considered undesirable for various reasons. Eisenstein's observations on loopholes remain as insightful as any made today about tax shelters. The numerous articles and legislative attempts to define them fail and were all destined to fail. Whether a transaction should be taxed depends on independent criteria, not on a preconceived definition of a loophole or shelter. Better answers require wiser questions.

While I have complained that much academic discussion has failed to absorb the lessons of Eisenstein's book of almost fifty years ago, I should not overstate the point. There is some new light being shed on tax problems. The best academic articles attempt to directly measure the effect of taxation on individuals and to weigh the burden on different individuals through explicitly stated criteria. At least two Nobel Prizes have been awarded in part for work in the field (the prize to William Vickrey and James Mirrlees and the prize to Joseph Stiglitz), and no serious tax scholar today (at least in my view) would base his arguments on ability to pay or horizontal equity. Instead, the best arguments about taxation are now based on direct analysis of how taxation affects individual welfare. A cost of this is that academic discussions are now far more removed from public discourse than they previously were, but I believe an advantage is that we have learned a lot.

For example, we have a far better understanding of the choice between income and consumption taxes now than we did when Eisenstein wrote. We now know that in their ideal form they are very similar in that they both tax labor income and rents. The only difference between them is that income taxes tax the risk-free rate of return. Due to work by scholars such as Bill Andrews, David Bradford, Alan Auerbach, Michael Graetz, and others, we have a better understanding of the different ways of implementing each type of tax so that we can compare not only the tax base, but the tax base implemented in various ways. Due to efforts by Arnold Harberger and many others, we have measures to think about the social or deadweight losses from taxation of various kinds. And thanks to Mirrlees, we have a far more rigorous method of thinking about progressivity than we did forty years ago. All of these understandings come from explicitly modeling how taxes affect individuals and how we should aggregate or weigh the total of the effects. We can now think about all these issues by explicitly examining the consequences rather than relying on slogans.

The particular details of the analysis of many tax issues remain disputed. Solid, broad-based empirical truths on which to base the analysis remain elusive. Even the most complex models are greatly simplified versions of reality. Individuals and the economy may not behave as predicted. The mathematical style in fashion today often seems designed to confuse more than enlighten. A modern scholar with Eisenstein's stiletto pen could have fun with this scholarship. One can imagine a fourth ideology—that of mathematics. These ideologists prefer to be precisely wrong rather than approximately right. Ronald Coase noted that when he was a child, it was said that what is too silly to be said may be sung; in modern economics, it is put into mathematics. Even with elaborate mathematics that few can understand, the models make gross simplifications and often fail to capture central elements of behavior. Data are poor because we cannot run experiments on people, which leads to ever more elaborate techniques for extracting information from what we do have. Modern tax scholars might be glad that because of the lapse of time they are not Eisenstein's target.

Nevertheless, the best papers using modern approaches to taxation avoid relying on slogans or empty phrases. The assumptions are (most often) explicit and the arguments subject to principled dispute. We still have much to learn, but what I view as the best scholarship has possibly been able to move beyond the mere ideologies criticized by Eisenstein. And there is no other option; traditional arguments about ability to pay and about equity remain as problematic today as they were in Eisenstein's time.

No discussion of *Ideologies of Taxation* would be complete without mention of Eisenstein's rhetoric and cynicism, so I will address both. It is not easy to write a review of this book, because any attempt at style would pale in comparison, and a review without any style would be dull to read indeed, particularly when the reader is going to flip the page and start reading Eisenstein's prose. A short quote should suffice. The issue Eisenstein addresses here is whether our tax law represents the collective choice of the American people, and he argues that it does not, because most people do not understand the tax law. He first considers whether this is because tax law is too dull but dismisses this suggestion: "Anything that involves human beings and money cannot be dull." He then turns to the second reason:

> The second reason given is that taxes are too difficult for the man in the street—or the man in the subway as Jerome Frank called him. Concededly, a good deal of tax law is exceedingly technical and abstruse. But no one claims that voters can be magically transformed into tax experts in several easy lessons. The question rather is whether they would grasp the basic essentials of tax policy if the issues were adequately presented to them. The real difficulty, I suspect, is that they might understand too well.

I will close with a discussion of cynicism. The reviews of *Ideologies* after it came out almost uniformly accused Eisenstein of undue cynicism. Walter Blum accused him of writing with a heavy mixture of cynicism, humor, and bitterness. The book, according to another, was said to have a caustic and cynical tone. These reviews are interesting, because they did not generally dispute his arguments. Instead, they complained that he did not provide an answer, a view of how the tax system should properly be structured. The same criticism has been made of public choice literature.

Eisenstein's response came at the end of a New York University Law School panel discussion of the book. I give him the final word:

> Several people have taken me to task because I failed to propose a so-called solution for our tax situation. There are two simple answers I could give. In the first place, my book is an essay in understanding, not an effort to convert. Professor Cahn has reminded me that Morris R. Cohen was once confronted with a similar complaint. He replied, 'It is enough for the present that I have cleansed the Augean stables.' In the

second place, there are already enough tax programs around to suit everybody's taste. I should add, however, that some of my friends who offer programs have very flexible notions of tax policy. As soon as they go into the government, they seem to change their minds.

However, there is still a more thorough answer. A society like ours is inevitably one of economic conflict. Hence there are no final solutions that will make everyone happy. Why should we expect more of tax policy than of policy in other areas of conflict, such as the tariff, the farm program, or public housing? And so, to those who are looking for a Santa Claus to make us all fiscally happy, I can only say that the tax laws must always be quite messy as long as they represent an uneasy compromise among contending groups and interests with different purposes and values.

Justice Holmes stated that taxes are the price we pay for civilization or for civilized society. I do not find this statement very informative. It begs all the questions to be resolved in evaluating a tax system. I would prefer to revise the statement to say that the taxes we impose may seriously affect the civilization that we have. For tax law, like all law, is a means to an end, and that end, as always, is the kind of world we want to live in.

Let me be a little more specific without being precise. In so far as taxes are concerned, every society must resolve its problems within a framework consisting of two basic elements. The first is ethical. How is one man to be treated in relation to another? What do we mean by justice in taxation? The second is economic. How does the tax fit with the presuppositions of our economic system in regard to such matters as incentives and acquisitiveness? Or perhaps, should those presuppositions be changed by taxes or otherwise? A tax system must operate within an economic framework, but it can also alter the framework.

Obviously, everyone will answer such questions in the light of his own philosophy of the good life. And so there are no ideal solutions to suit everybody. Any intelligent thinking on taxes eventually reaches the ultimate purpose of life on this planet as each of us conceives it.*

* Louis Eisenstein, Edmond Cahn, Thurman Arnold, and Robert J. McDonald, "A Discussion of *The Ideologies of Taxation*," *Tax Law Review* 18, no. 1 (1962): 21–22.

THE IDEOLOGIES OF TAXATION

Preface

Usually I am inclined to think that a book should stand on its own without the aid of preliminary observations. In view of the nature of the present work, I am prepared to make an exception in my own behalf.

This book is an essay on the intellectual content of an emotional subject—the distribution of our so-called progressive income tax among the American people. It is concerned with the systems of reason and rhetoric which groups and interests devise in order to obtain a distribution responsive to their pecuniary desires. These systems are distinct ideologies—complexes of ideas and attitudes suitably equipped with the necessary vocabulary. Of course, like all ideologies, they are presented as bodies of objective truth which only the prejudiced or benighted can fail to approve. Americans generally regard an ideology as some sinister mental activity of alien origin. However, we are no less prone to ideologies than others, though we may prefer to use a different word. Where ideologies are involved, too many of us are akin to Moliere's untutored hero, who was surprised to learn that he had been speaking in prose for some time.

A venture into tax ideologies is beset by two difficulties. The first is that ideologies are replete with platitudes which are designed to cheer and reassure without the intrusion of any meaningful message. This is as we should suppose it to be. Taxation is a political process, and we should not expect the clichés to be more illuminating than they are in other areas of political contention. Political wisdom today is largely the

1

art of making meaningless statements. The second difficulty is equally formidable. A good deal of tax discourse, both in and out of Congress, is a steady barrage of epithets and other excited observations which confuse verbal violence with rational analysis. It is more important to be indignant than thoughtful.

Despite the two problems which I have just mentioned, certain distinct clusters of ideas emerge which have made this book possible. Since my purpose throughout is to summarize and analyze these ideas, I have refrained from importing any of my own preferences into the discussion. Otherwise I would have wandered beyond the limits which I carefully set for myself. The reader is left entirely free to draw any conclusion he sees fit without the least suggestion or exhortation from me. As authors go, I am quite undemanding. I should add that those who are unversed in the esoteric intricacies of taxation have nothing to fear. Though I manage to qualify as a tax lawyer, I have sternly resisted any temptation to display a technical grasp of the Internal Revenue Code. In the first place, I would like to be understood. And in the second place, if I indulged in any such effort, I might inadvertently illustrate that tax lawyers often earn their keep in a state of bewilderment. Such confessions are unbecoming in public even if they were desirable in private.

In the spring of 1959 I had the honor of delivering the Julius Rosenthal Lectures at the School of Law of Northwestern University. This volume slowly derived from those lectures amid the pressures of a busy legal practice. As originally prepared for oral delivery, the manuscript was shorter, for those who listen can endure only so much at a time. The written word, however, seems to enlist more patience and fortitude. I would surely be remiss in my efforts as an author if I failed to take advantage of this difference.

Once again I am happy to express my appreciation to Dean John Ritchie, III, Professor Willard H. Pedrick, Professor Vance N. Kirby, and the many others who made my visit to their Law School a memorable occasion. I also wish to thank the students whose lot it was to sit through the lectures. To me their warm and generous response was an extraordinary compliment. They vividly confirmed my view that an audience can stay awake even though the topic is taxation. Joseph A. Pechman and my colleagues Carolyn E. Agger and Julius M. Greisman were good enough to make helpful suggestions. They did all they could to safeguard me from error. If they have not been entirely successful, the fault is mine. I am also indebted to Louis D'Amico, who patiently checked quotations and footnotes, and to my secretary, Jane M. Davis, who stoically deciphered one revision after another. Finally, I should acknowledge the prolonged tribulations of my family, who had the unhappy task of living with a lawyer who was attempting to be a scholar at the same time.

Louis Eisenstein
Washington, D.C.
May, 1961

CHAPTER 1

Groups, Interests, and Ideologies

We are about to consider the unpleasant subject of taxes. Few things are viewed with as much distaste and distress as these coerced contributions to our general welfare. Even in time of war, when civilization itself trembles in the balance, we are expected to part more readily with our lives than our money—which Alexander Hamilton described as "the precious metals, those darling objects of human avarice and enterprise." Hence the evasion of the draft is usually deemed less dignified and respectable than the evasion of taxes. Indeed, amid the last world war a select group of Republicans sternly warned that there is little reason "to do and die" if income taxes are too high. For then those who may perish will suffer in vain though in the end they survive. Their way of life, for which they have offered life itself, will have disappeared during their absence.[1] As an ancient Roman rightly remarked, "Nothing stings more deeply than the loss of money."

At times there is much to be said for stating the obvious. And so I start with what seems beyond dispute. Our taxes reflect a continuing struggle among contending interests for the privilege of paying the least. I am not unaware that others have a loftier view of the matter. They prefer to believe that our tax laws are usually inspired by more generous motives which are then insidiously subverted for some unworthy purpose. The triumph of a special interest is considered an unfortunate deviation from the general rule. However, if we are to discuss taxes intelligently, we should gracefully abandon such pleasing illusions. In the words of an admirable conservative, we must clear our minds of cant. Tax legislation commonly derives from private pressures exerted for selfish ends.

4

Of course, others have also paid their respects to the obvious. It seems enough to quote James C. Carter and Dr. T. S. Adams. Carter was a noted lawyer who enjoyed the rare distinction of presiding over the American Bar Association. "In every community," Carter declared, "those who feel the burdens of taxation are naturally prone to relieve themselves" from their fiscal discomfort. "One class struggles to throw the burden off its shoulders. If they succeed, of course it must fall upon others. They also, in their turn, labor to get rid of it, and finally the load falls upon those who will not, or cannot, make a successful effort for relief." Carter ungraciously added that the "struggle" is a "one-sided" affair, "in which the rich only engage"—and "in which the poor always go to the wall."[2] These observations were made some sixty years ago. While they must now be tempered in the light of later events, they are still instructive. Adams was a prominent economist who had served as a high official of the Treasury and closely participated in the formulation of tax policy. His experiences in Washington led him to conclude that "modern taxation or tax-making in its most characteristic aspect is a group contest in which powerful interests vigorously endeavor to rid themselves of present or proposed tax burdens. It is, first of all, a hard game in which he who trusts wholly to economics, reason, and justice, will in the end retire beaten and disillusioned. Class politics is of the essence of taxation."[3]

Mr. Justice Holmes tried to make taxes less disagreeable by means of a definition. Taxes, he wrote, "are what we pay for civilized society." He even said, "I like to pay taxes. With them I buy civilization."[4] Yet a skilful definition can only accomplish so much and no more. We may cheerfully concede that taxes are an inevitable overhead of civilization, and that civilization is well worth having and saving. But it hardly follows that everyone should be happy to bear his allotted share of the overhead. For the question always remains whether the cost is properly allocated among the many beneficiaries. A taxpayer may readily wonder whether he is paying too much of that cost. If he regards his burden as excessive, he may even infer that civilization is in a very sorry state. Holmes also overlooked another difficulty in his effort to be helpful. Various groups are firmly persuaded that their functions are peculiarly vital to the progress of civilization. And so they easily reason that since their contributions are exceptional, their taxes should be small. Holmes' aphorism on civilization is more quotable than meaningful.

Usually Holmes was more penetrating. He viewed society as an aggregate of diverse interests busily competing for legislative dominion. The "tacit assumption of the solidarity of the interests of society," he stated, is "very common" but "false." Whatever groups possess "the supreme power for the moment" are "certain to have interests inconsistent with others which have competed unsuccessfully. The more powerful interests must be more or less reflected in legislation," for legislation is a conventional mode of placing "burdens which are disagreeable to them on the shoulders of somebody else." Holmes had little patience with those who condemn legislation because "it favors one class at the expense of another; for much or all legislation does that; and none the less when the *bona fide* object is the greatest good of the greatest number." The sensible objection to class legislation "is not that it favors a class," but that "it fails to benefit" the intended class, or dangerously ignores the desires of "a competing class," or "transcends the limits of self-preference which are imposed by sympathy."[5]

Holmes himself applauded a tax philosophy that cannot be explained by a mere devotion to the virtues of civilization. In the spring of 1924 he informed his friend Sir Frederick Pollock that he had read "a good little book" on taxes by Andrew Mellon, who was then Secretary of the Treasury. Holmes regretfully added, "I believe Congress has turned him and his ideas down," though "they seemed right to me."[6] Mellon was a dedicated apostle of low taxes for high incomes. His ideas on taxes were "right" only as his concern for the affluent was "right."

Whether taxes are high or low, they are a constitutional means of appropriating private property without just compensation. The power to tax is the power to confiscate. In short, taxes are distinctly disagreeable burdens, and so there is a constant striving to place them on the backs of others. The tax laws record the terms of the uneasy peace which happens to prevail at a particular moment. The terms periodically change as the contentions continue. I am not suggesting that taxes raise only questions of how they are to be distributed among those disinclined to pay them. The elected statesmen and the appointed experts who labor over taxes are troubled by other questions as well. They have to decide how much money is to be collected and how much money is to be spent. They have to say whether it is better to try for a surplus or to acquiesce in a deficit. They have to consider economic effects and political consequences. But so far as taxpayers are concerned, all such questions are subsidiary to the critical issue of distribution. As our tax hearings repeatedly reveal, it is usually assumed that other problems may be best resolved by shifting the burdens elsewhere. And there is no lack of ingenuity in providing the necessary rationalizations for the desired results.

I have been pursuing the thought that our tax laws reflect the fiscal aspirations of classes or groups. The time has come to be more precise. What do I mean when I speak of a "class" or "group"? Here, as on other occasions, we may return with profit to the Founding Fathers.

In the days of the Fathers a class or group was called a "faction"— which Madison defined as "a number of citizens, whether amounting to a majority or a minority of the whole, who are united and actuated by some common impulse of passion" emanating from self-interest. "From the protection of different and unequal faculties of acquiring property," he wrote, "the possession of different degrees and kinds of property immediately results; and from the influence of these on the sentiments and views of the respective proprietors, ensues a division of the society into different interests and parties." Madison recognized that there are other sources of factions, but he concluded that "the most common and durable source" is "the various and unequal distribution of property. Those who hold and those who are without property have ever formed distinct interests in society. Those who are creditors, and those who are debtors, fall under a like discrimination. A landed interest, a manufacturing interest, a mercantile interest, a moneyed interest, with many lesser interests, grow up of necessity in civilized nations, and divide them into different classes, actuated by different sentiments and views." Madison, unlike Karl Marx, had no desire to remove "the *causes* of faction." He sought the more modest relief "of controlling its *effects*."[7]

I am content to follow in the footsteps of the formidable Fathers. For present purposes I generally define a class or group as a number of persons who are animated by a common economic concern in their own behalf. I would be glad to speak of "factions," for the distinct interests in society still have their special sentiments and views. But, unfortunately, we have lost the capacity to be as frank as the Fathers, and we no longer speak of factions. Apparently the word is considered too indecorous. It has connotations of immoderate combativeness which should be more politely expressed. Perhaps the word "class" will soon disappear as well, because it is too closely associated with Marx. Already we rarely speak of "the poor." Instead we refer with due detachment to "the low income groups." While the word "class" does not make me shudder, many others prefer to do without it. Hence the accepted terminology now consists largely of "groups" and "interests"; and usually these approved nouns are preceded by the adjective "special."

Not every change is a change for the worse. A good deal can be said for the present vocabulary, apart from its respectability. The words "groups" and "interests" are much more flexible and adaptable than the word "class." A class is rather rigidly conceived in terms of some basic economic function or attribute. The customary categories are relatively few. They consist of such ultimate divisions as wage earners, farmers, businessmen, and capitalists. These categories are very useful when properly applied. But they are not useful enough for tax purposes because they do not adequately illuminate the variety of pressures from which the tax laws derive. "Groups" and "interests" more aptly describe the many voices that are heard and the many influences that are felt. The pressures that normally count are effectively exerted by smaller clusters of those who would pay less. As Madison pointed out, there are different interests, "with many lesser interests."

The words "groups" and "interests" are admirably versatile. They enable us to understand all sorts of distinctions that Congress has made. As a matter of principle, for example, it is generally assumed that all who are engaged in a trade or business are entitled to be treated as kindred souls. Since they are companions in risk, their tax liabilities should not invidiously vary. Businessmen, no less than others, may rightfully expect the equal protection of the laws. However, there are businessmen and businessmen, and some are considered more deserving than others. If a businessman grows and sells grain, his profit is ordinary income. But if he grows and sells timber, his profit may be capital gain. If he raises and sells poultry, his profit is ordinary income. But if he raises and sells livestock, his profit may be capital gain. If he buys and sells real estate, his profit is ordinary income. But if he buys and sells stock, his profit may be capital gain. If he produces steel, he can only deduct his actual costs. But if he produces oil, he may also deduct imaginary costs known as percentage depletion.

The variations do not become less interesting as we continue our way through our Internal Revenue Code. If a royalty is received from an iron mine, it is ordinary income. But if a royalty is received from a coal mine, it may be capital gain. If an employee resides in this country, his earnings are taxable. But if he resides abroad, his earnings are not taxable. And if he resides here but works abroad, his earnings may be exempt up to $20,000. Needless to say, there are also scrupulous distinctions between one corporation and another. If a domestic corporation does business here, it pays 52 per cent on income over $25,000. But if it does business elsewhere in the Western Hemisphere, it pays only 38 per cent. The arts and sciences, too, are not ignored. Income from the sale of a book is ordinary income. But income from the sale of an invention may be capital gain. Composers and painters are regarded as no better than writers.

In listing these distinctions, I am not implying that they were necessarily conceived in error. Distinctions which are so delicately drawn may well reflect an estimable wisdom, though that wisdom may not be immediately apparent. The examples which I have given merely illustrate that "groups" and "interests" are more fitting nouns than "classes." They do a much better job of describing the beneficiaries of Congressional solicitude. Moreover, "groups" and "interests" serve another use which is not to be slighted. An increasing number of statutes are narrowly designed to relieve just a few select taxpayers. A good many, in fact, are carefully drawn to assure the salvation of only one or two. A familiar example is the special statute devised for a Hollywood executive who was quite dissatisfied with his prospective burden.[8] "Groups" and "interests" are pliable enough to explain the rewarding results in these cases also. While one taxpayer is too solitary to be a "group," he may still qualify as an "interest."

One other refinement is in order before we move further afield. Those who deplore the triumph of groups and interests repeatedly suggest that the Treasury is benevolently animated by different purposes. According to these unhappy observers, the Treasury is assiduously devoted to the public welfare as distinguished from private profit. This view of the Treasury is overly generous. It is an understandable effort to find comfort amid unpleasant circumstances.

The Treasury is not a neutral which is happily removed from the war of interests. On the contrary, it is intimately involved in their efforts to have their way. As Andrew Mellon disclosed, the precise sympathies of the Treasury will vary with those who are authorized to speak in its name. In the forties the Treasury was concerned with the burdens of small taxpayers. In the fifties it was comparably anxious on behalf of others. The spokesmen for the Treasury, however, cannot always be as sympathetic as they would like to be. As custodians of the exchequer, they are troubled slaves to duty. Regardless of their compassion for certain groups and interests, they are obliged to gather the necessary revenues. Collections must correspond to expenditures. To a Secretary of the Treasury a deficit may be the proverbial fate worse than death. The Secretary who is especially worried over taxpayers in the upper brackets is also the Secretary who is most disturbed by an unbalanced budget. Much as he may wish to alleviate their distress, he must weigh their suffering against the pain of diminished receipts. Even Mellon suggested higher estate taxes in the early thirties, when he was suddenly overtaken by the disaster of deficits. Finally, the Treasury must always evaluate the political effects of what it says and does. Whenever it lends its aid and comfort to a particular group or interest, it must do so with measured restraint. An undue display of enthusiasm may be condemned as a reckless failure of responsibility.

Taxes, then, are a changing product of earnest efforts to have others pay them. In a society where the few control the many, the efforts are rather simple. Levies are imposed in response to the preferences of the governing groups. Since their well-being is equated with the welfare of the community, they are inclined to burden themselves as lightly as possible. Those who have little to say are expected to pay. Rationalizations for this state of affairs are rarely necessary. It is assumed that the lower orders will be properly patriotic.

As political democracy comes upon the scene, complications soon emerge. Taxes can no longer be imposed without public consultation and debate. Those who have less property have more votes. Since heads are to be counted, they must first be persuaded. Reasons have to be given for the burdens that are variously proposed or approved. In time the contending reasons are skilfully elaborated into systems of belief or ideologies which are designed to induce the required acquiescence. Of course, if an ideology is to be effective, it must convey a vital sense of some immutable principle that rises majestically above partisan preferences. Except in dire circumstances, civilized men are not easily convinced by mere appeals to self-interest. What they are asked to believe must be identified with imposing concepts that transcend their pecuniary prejudices.

While ideologies invoke lofty abstractions, they are sensitively adapted to practical needs. In our fiscal system today these needs are set by the progressive income tax and the progressive estate tax. The income tax arrived in 1913 and the estate tax in 1916. Though both taxes have significantly changed over the years, one basic question has remained intact. How are progressive taxes to be reconciled with an economic system which places a premium upon private initiative and the accumulation of wealth? The system presupposes that men should be busily engaged in adding to their worldly goods. But a progressive tax presupposes that as they add more and more, they should keep less and less. This apparent incongruity has inspired various ideologies which are diligently elaborated and urgently pursued.

I turn to what I regard as the three primary ideologies. For convenience I refer to them as the ideology of ability, the ideology of barriers and deterrents, and the ideology of equity. These three provide a framework of reason and rhetoric within which classes, groups, and interests assert themselves. Others who have looked into these weighty matters may feel that my selections might have been more wisely made. I can only plead that the three which I have chosen seem to me the most impressive and the most effective. As a further excuse I add that I have not tried to be exhaustive. My attempt to be informative is at best an essay, and an essay is a studied effort to be incomplete.

The ideology of ability declares that taxes should be apportioned in accordance with the ability to pay them; and that ability to pay is properly measured by income or wealth. Therefore, the ideal levies are a progressive income tax and a progressive death tax. The ideology of barriers and deterrents takes a dim view of this conclusion. It embraces three related precepts that point to the inevitable disintegration of private enterprise if the precepts are disregarded. Progressive taxes dangerously diminish the desire to work; they fatally discourage the incentive to invest; and they irreparably impair the sources of new capital. Our economic system must come to an untimely end if private capital cannot accumulate and private initiative is destroyed. The three precepts merge into a more general perception of impending disaster. Progressive taxes are critically viewed as barriers and deterrents to the economic growth and stability of the nation. Even if the system is not on the verge of collapse, the barriers and deterrents must be rapidly removed. Otherwise the system must eventually decline and decay, since neither capital nor ambition will be available to sustain it. Finally, we have the ideology of equity. This ideology is closely concerned with the eloquent theme of equality among equals. It maintains that those who are similarly situated should be similarly treated, and those who are differently situated should be differently treated.

Ideologies necessarily have their ideologists. In the realm of taxation the function of the ideologist needs little elaboration. His task is to explain, in the light of appropriate principles, why specific measures should be wisely approved or wisely rejected. The ideologists of taxation may be divided into three groups: those who believe through interest, those who believe through compensation, and those who believe through principle. These distinctions do not in the least impugn the sincerity of a particular conviction. One may truly believe what it pays to believe.

The first group consists of those who directly gain from the application of their ideology. They speak as taxpayers, and their heart is where their treasure is. The Chamber of Commerce and the American Mining Congress are among the many examples that may be cited. However, this group is by no means confined to organizations that express common pecuniary interests. It includes as well individual taxpayers whose burdens are directly involved. As long as these taxpayers are active adherents of the ideology, they qualify for membership in the group. The controlling criterion is not whether they are adequately informed in the details of the ideology, but whether they are sufficiently dedicated to its realization and utter the customary words and phrases. The second group consists of those who are devoted because they are paid for their exertions. The range of compensation varies. They may be well paid or poorly paid. Usually these ideologists are lawyers, economists, retired Congressmen, and others who are especially equipped to provide the necessary rationalizations. The third group consists of those who believe without any immediate pecuniary inducements. They are largely statesmen, scholars, and professional experts.

I have identified three ideologies and divided the ideologists into three groups. Now a caveat is advisable. My categories are not mutually exclusive. They are merely modest efforts to classify belief and behavior in the universe of taxation. Since belief and behavior are flexible, discrepancies should be expected. Consistency is not always conducive to agreeable results. And so we find that while the ideology of ability and the ideology of barriers and deterrents are hostile to each other, now and then an adherent of ability may be induced to worry over barriers and deterrents. Members of Congress are especially adaptable when a shift in ideology is required. Or, again, the adherents of one ideology may skilfully borrow the language of another in order to be more persuasive. In tax law, too, the devil knows how to quote scripture with a display of conviction. To complicate matters further, the adherents of ability and the adherents of barriers and deterrents have something in common. Each group invokes the ideology of equity as the occasion warrants. This situation is scarcely surprising; for, of the three ideologies, equity is easily the most accommodating. It supplies the desired answer to almost any prayer.

The ideologists are also nicely flexible as they move from one group to another. The American Bar Association is an impressive illustration because this eminent organization is replete with energetic ideologists. When they speak for the Association in tax matters, they usually do so as believers through principle. Their marked devotion to a particular project does not derive from direct interest or compensation. But at times this general rule gives way to an exception. An individual member may resort to the Association as a means of easing the lot of his clients. Since he is then stimulated by monetary rewards, he is a believer through compensation as well as conviction. Finally, the members of the Association may also be directly concerned as troubled taxpayers in search of relief for themselves. When they are so personally involved in their own behalf, they are believers through interest. One of the major achievements of the Association is that it enables the tax lawyers to serve in several capacities without fear of embarrassment.

CHAPTER 2

The Troubled Creed of Ability

The ideology of ability to pay speaks with the voice of dispassionate justice, as a good ideology should. According to its adherents, taxation on the basis of ability is an ideal principle of fiscal policy that is immaculately aloof from the pressures of warring contentions. It is the principle to which all understanding legislators should wisely aspire, for it is inherently impeccable like the Forms or Ideas of Plato. At the very least, the ideology continues, the principle calls for a progressive income tax which universally applies without special favor or exception. Such a levy is intrinsically just, regardless of class, group, or interest. Deviations from the principle are an unseemly surrender to selfish pressures.

This view is undoubtedly attractive, but it unduly ignores history. Our income tax, like our estate tax, was deliberately devised as a partisan measure against specific segments of American society. It was born of class politics and on the wrong side of the street. We need not forget its unpleasant origin in order to applaud its present virtues.

Except for one aberration during the Civil War, Congress carefully refrained from imposing an income tax until the close of the nineteenth century. The prevailing taxes were levies on consumption—customs duties and various excises, such as taxes on tobacco and the more potent beverages. This lingering situation conformed to the expectations of the Founding Fathers. The Fathers confidently assumed that for a long time to come the revenues would derive from imposts, excises, "and, in general, all duties upon articles of consumption."

What they expected they also deemed desirable. Hamilton had nothing but praise for taxes on consumption. "The amount to be contributed by each citizen," he explained to all who might be disturbed, "will in a degree be at his own option, and can be regulated by an attention to his resources. The rich may be extravagant, the poor can be frugal; and private oppression may always be avoided by a judicious selection of objects proper for such impositions." "It is a signal advantage of taxes on articles of consumption, that they contain in their own nature a security against excess."[1] The poor can protect themselves by refusing to buy.

Eventually this fiscal attitude provoked a good deal of unkind criticism. As individual income rises, relatively less is spent and more is saved. Therefore, in terms of income, the taxes of the well-to-do were much lower than the taxes of the not-so-well-to-do. Those who found it difficult to make ends meet were unable to understand why income spent should be taxed while income saved is exempt. The solution proposed was a tax on income, whether it was spent or saved. Many who were dissatisfied came to a more daring conclusion. Laborers in the East and farmers in the West ominously proposed that glaring inequalities in wealth should be reduced by heavier taxes on higher incomes. It was not enough to impose a tax on income as distinguished from consumption. The tax, they argued, should also be progressive; the rates should increase as incomes increase. With malice aforethought they sought to reverse the existing situation, so that the more prosperous would pay a relatively larger tax than the less prosperous. In the language of today, they requested a redistribution of income.

In 1894 Congress at last yielded and imposed an income tax of 2 per cent.[2] By current standards the rate was mild and inoffensive; indeed it seems a poor excuse for any intense monetary agitation or any related intellectual efforts. But those who abhorred the tax refused to be so complacent about the matter. They were deeply concerned with principle rather than rates. In their view the tax was clearly an attempted subversion of civilization. And so the powers of rhetoric rose to the occasion. As usual, members of the Senate were especially eloquent. Senator John Sherman described the tax as an insidious venture in "socialism, communism, devilism." Senator David B. Hill anxiously explained that the tax was devised by "the professors with their books, the socialists with their schemes," and "the anarchists with their bombs" in "the midst of their armed camps between the Danube and the Rhine." A Tammany statesman protested against the "betrayal of our ancient principles," and "this treason to our faith, to our platform, to our tradition, to our heroes." A respectable economist announced that the tax was "a system of class legislation, full of the spirit of communism."[3] Today these impassioned observations may appear overly exuberant. But as Chief Justice Warren recently reminded us, when President Taft proposed an income tax on corporations, even he was accused of advocating socialism.[4]

The Supreme Court soon came to the rescue. The Court held, in the remarkable *Pollock* case,[5] that the newly imposed tax gravely offended the Constitution. That decision is only one of many that make constitutional law an easy route to an enviable reputation for critical scholarship. For present purposes, however, the important point lies elsewhere. No attempt was made to persuade the Court that the tax reflected some transcendent concept of justice divorced from the mundane differences of men concerned with their economic lot. Instead the tax was shamelessly defended as an assault by the poor on the rich. Since the rate was a flat 2 per cent, no matter how large the income, why was the tax regarded as class legislation? The answer is supplied by the personal exemption. Congress set the exemption at $4,000, and the result was obvious discrimination. Those with more income were burdened, while those with less income were relieved. Any effort to disguise the class character of the tax was useless. Though the tax was only 2 per cent of income, the taxpayers were only 2 per cent of the population.[6] Hence the defenders of the tax fully agreed that it was an essay in deliberate discrimination. They even informed the Court that an income tax is "preëminently a tax upon the rich."[7]

The most sensitive response to the exemption of $4,000 came from the legal luminary Joseph H. Choate. Though it has often been quoted, it may with profit be quoted once more. The tax of 2 per cent, Choate declared, was "communistic in its purposes and tendencies," and was "defended" on "principles as communistic, socialistic—what shall I call them—populistic as ever have been addressed to any political assembly in the world." Then Choate cogently asked the Court, "If you approve this law, with this exemption of $4,000, and this communistic march goes on and five years hence a statute comes to you with an exemption of $20,000 and a tax of 20 per cent upon all having incomes in excess of that amount, how can you meet it in view of the decision which my opponents ask you now to render?" Having asked this searching question, he promptly replied: "There is protection now or never." For once it is settled that the many can tax the few, "it will be impossible to take any backward step." The exemption might even be set at $100,000, and then the unfortunates above that minimum would be completely helpless.[8]

Mr. Justice Field shared this disquieting view. He also feared that if an exemption of $4,000 were allowed, a majority might freely draw the line at any figure which placed their own number beyond the reach of the levy. The tax, he asserted, was "class legislation." It was no better than "the English income statute of 1691," which taxed Protestants "at a certain rate," Catholics "at double" that rate, and Jews "at another and separate rate." The Justice combined his distaste for class legislation with a sociological observation. "Whenever a distinction is made in the burdens a law imposes or in the benefits it confers" on the basis of "birth, or wealth, or religion, it is class legislation, and leads inevitably to oppression and abuses, and to general unrest and disturbance in society." He contrasted such an unsettling tax with "wise and constitutional legislation" which requires everyone to "contribute his proportion, however small the sum, to the support of the government." It was misguided kindness, he reproachfully added, "to urge any of our citizens to escape from that obligation."[9]

James C. Carter was among the defenders of the tax, and he made the unkindest cut of all. There was "clamor," he stated, that the tax was "class legislation" because it made "a distinction between the rich and the poor." The accusation was correct. The tax was "class legislation in that sense. That was its very object and purpose." And such distinctions, he continued, "should always be looked to in the business of taxation." In the past, unfortunately, the distinction had "been observed in the wrong direction," and the "poorer class" had been "prodigiously overburdened." On the other hand, it is "the very nature of an income tax" to discriminate against the affluent. All this failed to disturb Carter because history had yet to record "an instance in which governments have been destroyed by attempts of the many to lay undue burdens of taxation on the few."[10]

The language of Carter is no longer fashionable in our more discreet times. Illuminating candor is now deplorable crudeness. But the history of the income tax speaks plainly for itself, despite the changes in verbal manners. The tax originated as class legislation of the most obvious kind. It derived from the pressures of self-interest exerted against a small minority. I am not unaware that those who desired the tax were presumably in the majority. Undoubtedly they felt that the tax served the greatest good of the greatest number. But legislation is no less selfish because it faithfully expresses the self-interest of the majority.

Regrettably, the matter cannot end here. Regardless of its class origin, the income tax is now intimately associated with the concept of ability to pay. And the ideologists of ability firmly assume that this concept provides a principle of taxation which is happily unmarred by selfish interest or bias. If their appraisal is correct, then an income tax which conforms to this principle is inherently just, despite the partisan passions of the past. By the same token, the tax is no longer a mere instrument of class or group. It has been purified by principle.

This view of the income tax is prominently displayed in official observations. When the tax reappeared in 1913, it was formally approved on the basis of ability and equality. An income tax, the Ways and Means Committee explained, responds to "the general demand for justice in taxation." The consumption taxes of an individual are determined, "not by his ability to pay tax, but by his consumption of the articles taxed." But an income tax "is levied according to ability to pay" and secures "to the largest extent equality of tax burdens." The Committee concluded that it is difficult to devise a fairer tax.[11]

As these statements indicate, the income tax is identified with "ability to pay," which in turn is associated with "equality of tax burdens." Both phrases are designed to contrast consumption taxes and an income tax. Consumption taxes are imposed on income spent as distinguished from income saved. The poor spend proportionately more than the prosperous, because saving is a luxury which they can ill afford. Hence consumption taxes take a greater share of small incomes than large incomes. Or, as the Ways and Means Committee once observed, "such taxes bear most heavily upon those least able to pay them."[12] On the other hand, an income tax is imposed on income as a whole, whether it be spent or saved. In either event the income is an economic accretion which confers a capacity or ability to share the costs of civilization.

The statements which I have quoted yield three conclusions. First, a tax in accordance with ability to pay is a tax based on "equality" and "justice." Second, a taxpayer's ability to pay is properly measured by his entire income rather than a select portion. Third, an income tax qualifies as a levy of "equality" and "justice" if it corresponds with ability as so conceived. For the moment I look beyond the problems that lurk in the concept of ability and focus on the theme of equality. The principle asserted is that an income tax proportioned to ability is untainted by partiality for any class or group. It treats everyone equally, and so is a sturdy neutral among contending interests.

This notion of neutrality is often heard. I cite a random example. In the spring of 1941 the Secretary of the Treasury appeared before the Ways and Means Committee in order to obtain a needed increase in taxes. His program, he declared, was "designed so that all sections of the people shall bear their fair share of the burden." He particularly noted that "one group may urge that new taxes be imposed on labor but not on business; while another group may urge that the rich and prosperous can afford to bear the whole load." The appropriate answer to these divergent requests, the Secretary continued, was the principle of ability to pay. "Both kinds of advice should be disregarded. The job before us is so big that all the American people must help to carry it out, in proportion to their ability to pay. It is unsound, especially at a time like this, to proceed on the assumption that any group of our people should be penalized or that any section should be exempted from sharing in the common task."[13] Evidently the Secretary had no doubt that ability to pay is the sure way to equality for all and partiality toward none.

In the light of these views an elementary question emerges. If equality and neutrality are cardinal virtues, and if these virtues depend on taxation in accordance with ability, how do the ideologists of ability justify progressive rates? I need hardly add that such rates have been repeatedly rationalized under the auspices of ability to pay. It has been authoritatively stated that "the principle of ability to pay" is "the principle underlying the entire system of progressive income taxation in effect in this country." For that matter, it has been assumed that an individual income tax does not conform to the principle of ability unless the rates are progressive.[14] We may safely say that in the absence of progressive rates, there would be little interest in ability. Yet the very essence of progressive rates is that taxpayers are not treated equally and neutrally. Different incomes are taxed at different rates. At present the rates for the various brackets start at 20 per cent and end at 91 per cent. Can such disparities in rate be reconciled with equality and neutrality? Or have the ideologists of ability taken on an impossible task?

These questions have evoked various answers, but it seems enough to state the one that is usually considered the most compelling. Briefly put, the reasoning is that a larger income confers a relatively greater ability to pay taxes than a smaller income. As income rises, it moves from necessities to luxuries. If it continues to rise, it moves from the smaller luxuries to the larger luxuries. Each additional increment of income moves further away from the minimum requirements of a decent existence. As income increases beyond the area of necessities, it can more easily be spared. Another $100 means one thing to a taxpayer earning $100,000, and something else again to a taxpayer earning $1,000. Under a system of progressive rates more is taken where more can be afforded. As a Secretary of the Treasury summarized this analysis many years ago, "ability to pay increases in much more than arithmetical proportion as the amount of income exceeds the limit of reasonable necessity."[15]

The position which I have just outlined rests on a plain-spoken premise. While the ability to pay taxes consists of units of income, the same ability does not inhere in each unit. Despite their arithmetical equivalence, units of income do not have a uniform value. The ability which each dollar bestows depends on the wants that it may satisfy. Wants vary in significance, and the dollars available for the least important can be foregone with the least difficulty. Since the ability to pay is the ability to do without, the more dispensable dollars are the more taxable dollars.

This reasoning, however, does not persuade everybody. Professors Blum and Kalven, of the Chicago Law School, are especially troubled. "To get progression under an income tax," they say, "out of notions of ability to pay requires the thesis that ability increases more rapidly than income."[16] This position, they contend, cannot be sustained because we have no objective criteria for measuring the importance of particular wants to particular taxpayers. I doubt that this response is wholly correct, but in any case it seems irrelevant. The question is not whether wants can be scientifically classified as if we were weighing and comparing different quantities. The point, rather, is that wants may be socially evaluated. Those that are customarily satisfied with additional income may be deemed of diminishing importance. Larger incomes can bear relatively heavier taxes because the basic amenities of life are less seriously disturbed.[17]

The same two critics have argued that this reply will not do. It presupposes a "moral scheme of consumption," and such schemes are "distasteful." In "a free society" men should be "free to maximize their satisfactions according to their own hierarchy of preferences." They should not be told that certain wants are more significant than others, and then be coerced into agreement through differential rates.[18] However, an abstract plea for individual liberty to maximize satisfactions is an argument for no taxes whatever. All taxes, including those imposed in a free society, disturb this freedom to choose, for they leave less to be spent or saved. A proportional tax on income also reflects a moral scheme of consumption. Though a single rate is uniformly imposed, no tax is payable until income exceeds the personal exemptions. In this way the tax distinguishes between the income required for necessaries and the income available for other things. But if this distinction is concededly proper,[19] little reason remains to censure progression for imposing a moral scheme of consumption. Graduated rates may be regarded as only further refinements of the distinction already made. The exemptions draw a line between the more basic needs and other wants. The graduated rates then draw further lines that mark the variations in desires as income moves upward in the realm of luxuries. In short, the rates may be viewed as an ascending series of diminishing exemptions.

Even sales taxes intrude on a personal hierarchy of preferences or the freedom to maximize satisfactions as one sees fit. They discriminate in favor of satisfactions obtained by investing income, since they tax only those secured by spending income. Or they may express a moral scheme of consumption through special exceptions for various items. If Blum and Kalven are correct, sales taxes should never tolerate the least exemption, whether of food, lodging, or anything else. For such exemptions also disclose a moral judgment that certain expenditures should be better treated than others. I see no escape from what another professor wrote: "Taxation must affect the distribution of income, whether we will it so or not; and it is only sensible to face the question as to what kinds of effects are desirable."[20]

The essential difficulty with the effort to derive progression from ability to pay is quite different. Whether or not the attempt proceeds on a correct view of ability, it scarcely indicates that progressive taxes are equal and neutral taxes. Let us compare the burdens of two husbands. One has an income of $100,000 and the other an income of $5,000 before exemptions for himself and his wife. I further assume that neither of the two has capital gains or any other kind of income which is delivered from the progressive rates. One pays a tax of $52,776, the other a tax of $760. Before tax the income of the first is 20 times as large as the income of the second. After tax it is only about 12 times as large. The effect of progression is still greater if our two taxpayers are single. The tax on the first is then $66,798, and the tax on the second $944. After tax the income of the first is only about 8 times as large instead of 20. To speak of equality and neutrality in such circumstances is to indulge in a strange use of English.

Here, again, we may profit from history. Originally the principle of ability to pay was synonymous with proportional taxation—the same single rate on all incomes. Adam Smith summarized this initial understanding when he enunciated his famous canons or maxims of taxation. The first of the canons was equality of burden. "The subjects of every state," Smith wrote, "ought to contribute towards the support of the government, as nearly as possible, in proportion to their respective abilities; that is, in proportion to the revenue which they respectively enjoy under the protection of the state. The expence of government to the individuals of a great nation, is like the expence of management to the joint tenants of a great estate who are all obliged to contribute in proportion to their respective interests in the estate. In the observation or neglect of this maxim consists, what is called the equality or inequality of taxation."[21]

The admonitions of Smith consist of several interrelated propositions. Each and every citizen, rich and poor, should pay taxes. The burdens that are imposed should be as equal as possible. The required equality exists if the burdens are proportioned to abilities. The true measure of each taxpayer's ability is his income. Finally, everyone should pay taxes in proportion to his income because the government is akin to "a great estate," and the diverse incomes reflect the "respective interests in the estate."

It is not difficult to understand why these precepts are perennially admired. They articulate the principle of equality before the law. Everybody should bear the same rate of tax. If the poor are not to be treated worse than the rich, neither are the rich to be treated worse than the poor. All are similarly burdened though they are differently blessed. As economist F. A. Hayek puts it, proportional taxation expresses "the basic tradition that a law, to be just, must mete out equal treatment to all."[22] Next, the propositions have an appropriate air of neutrality. Under a proportional tax everyone who pays is left in relatively the same position in which he was found. There is no attempt to disturb the dissimilar rewards of the market place. If one taxpayer has an income of $100,000 and another an income of $2,000, the higher income is still 50 times as large as the lower income after both bear a tax of 20 per cent. The tax does not alter the ratio.

Others have sought to restate Smith's precepts more effectively. They have compared a progressive income tax to "common thievery." John Stuart Mill condemned it as "a mild form of robbery."[23] Two of our Civil War statesmen charged that the tax is "a punishment of the rich man because he is rich," and is defensible "on the same ground the highwayman defends his acts."[24] Many kindred observations may be quoted which reveal similar powers of description. Progression is considered either a form of legalized theft or a penal code devised for the offense of being successful. As income increases the offense increases, and so the penalty increases, too. The worst offenders, therefore, pay the heaviest fines.

Yet not even Adam Smith was entirely faithful to the principle of equality as he understood it. After arguing that tax burdens should be strictly proportioned to incomes, he stated in matter-of-fact fashion, "It is not very unreasonable that the rich should contribute to the public expence, not only in proportion to their revenue, but something more than in that proportion."[25] Smith made this remark while discussing a tax on house-rents payable by tenants. The tax was a percentage of the rent. In practical effect, the relative burden of the levy increased with the tenant's income. Smith agreed that the results departed from the canon of equality, but then he added that the deviation was no cause for alarm.

When a revered master says the wrong thing, his devoted disciples usually prefer to assume that the mistake was never made. It is easier to forget than to forgive. And so Smith's analysis of the tax on rent is quietly ignored by those who echo him with the utmost enthusiasm.[26] In an effort to compensate for this discreet silence, I now quote the neglected part of his analysis. "The proportion of the expence of house-rent to the whole expence of living," Smith explained, "is different in the different degrees of fortune. It is perhaps highest in the highest degree, and it diminishes gradually through the inferior degrees, so as in general to be lowest in the lowest degree. The necessaries of life occasion the great expence of the poor. They find it difficult to get food, and the greater part of their little revenue is spent in getting it. The luxuries and vanities of life occasion the principal expence of the rich; and a magnificent house embellishes and sets off to the best advantage all the other luxuries and vanities which they possess. A tax upon house-rents, therefore, would in general fall heaviest upon the rich; and in this sort of inequality there would not, perhaps, be any thing very unreasonable." To make matters worse, Smith quoted, without disapproval, a proposed rule of taxation that inequality of wealth should be remedied "as much as possible, by relieving the poor and burdening the rich."[27]

Smith's analysis is still instructive, though others think that he sadly nodded when he should have been wide-awake. He carefully reasoned that a tax is equal in impact only if it appropriates the same percentage of all incomes, whether they be large or small. The precise subject of the tax is immaterial. The controlling criterion of equality is the relation of the amount paid to the taxpayer's income. Yet while Smith cherished equality, he also felt that at least one exception is permissible. If equality is important, so is a sensitivity to differences in fortune. Inequalities in wealth justify inequalities in tax—as long as it is the well-to-do who are required to pay relatively more. When Smith made his unpleasant exception, he was speaking of selective taxes on consumption that are weighted against the affluent. But if his exception is allowable, it applies just as well to a general tax on income. If we may distinguish between expenditures for "necessaries" and expenditures for "luxuries and vanities," we may also distinguish between income available for "necessaries" and income available for "luxuries and vanities." And an easy way of doing so is to impose an income tax whose rate increases as income increases.

One other item remains to be mentioned, and it is the most important of all. Smith approved heavier taxes on the wealthy, but he did not try to excuse them in the name of ability to pay or equality of treatment. To Smith a tax was equal only if it was proportioned to ability; and it was proportioned to ability only if it was proportioned to income. He frankly indicated that a higher rate on the affluent subjected them to unequal treatment. He made no attempt to disguise the obvious. But the ideologists of ability are unable to be so commendably candid. They find it necessary to insist that heavier taxes are also equal taxes. They anxiously dissemble where Smith was honest and at ease.

Why, then, are the ideologists of ability so insistent on identifying progression with equality? Two causes seem to be at work. In the first place, the ideologists of ability are usually those who are known as liberals; and it is now the custom among liberals to avoid any charge or suspicion that their beliefs are partisan preferences. The liberals of today like to regard themselves as neutralists, whose convictions are dispassionately conceived and intrinsically right. This state of mind has simply been extended to the tax field. Most ideologists of ability firmly believe that the dominant purpose of progression is to reduce economic differences. They are dedicated to their ideology precisely because they desire to control the accumulation of wealth through the power to tax. But what they believe is one thing; what they say is another. A tax cannot reduce the spread between a larger income and a smaller income unless it discriminates against the larger income. But the adherents of whom I speak cannot concede that they favor discriminatory taxes. Somehow the desire for taxes that are unequal must be reconciled with the precept that taxes should be equal. The required peace of mind is obtained by saying that the affluent, no less than others, are being taxed in accordance with ability to pay. If everyone is taxed according to ability, everyone is treated equally.

Twenty years ago the economist Henry Simons well-nigh apologized for arguing that the function of progression is to mitigate disparities in wealth. In his view the matter had become too settled for further debate. "Indeed," he wrote, "we tend now toward relative overemphasis, both in our talk and in our action, upon this particular objective." Simons was overly optimistic. At present honesty is not the best policy. Though we still have progression, it is no longer prudent to say in so many words that the primary purpose of graduated rates is to diminish the economic differences that characterize our economy. To speak in this manner is to sound subversive. It is much wiser to say, as Edwin Seligman used to say, that "the function" of progression is "to apportion the burden more equally among the taxpayers." At the very least the language of ability to pay renders three services. It provides a means of appearing duly respectable while the same disreputable thoughts are retained. Many who approve progressive rates are enabled to feel more comfortable, while others who might disapprove are enabled to be less disturbed. And, in Holmes' phrase, references to ability help "to beautify what is disagreeable to the sufferers."[28] They may be consoled by the thought that the larger privations they endure promote the cause of equal treatment.

The intense preoccupation with equality is also induced by something else—the relentless pressure of fear. The ideologists of ability are constantly concerned that if they advocate inequalities in treatment, others will do the same. All sorts of distasteful discriminations will then be justified, and eventually little will remain of ability to pay as a standard of taxation. It is easy to sympathize with this abiding anxiety over the future. But the fear of disaster does little to avert the disaster that is feared. While the ideologists of ability are busily espousing equality, others are successfully doing without it. As we will shortly see, the forebodings that disturb the adherents of ability serve only to restrain them.

Since the ideology of ability professes to be dispassionate, it is even evasive where it purports to be most informative. The ideology declares that he who can afford to live much better can afford to pay much more. This rationalization tacitly assumes that incomes should be evaluated solely in terms of the personal consumption they command. Income available for luxuries is less important than income required for necessities. But an avowed premise of our economic system is significantly different. It asserts that possessors of large incomes should not be appraised as mere consumers, whether conspicuous or subdued. Their principal function is to furnish investment capital, which in turn keeps the system going. As this function is conventionally described, the well-to-do benefit society by saving their income and "providing the wherewithal for economic growth." In order to save they "must overcome an obstacle and make a sacrifice"—they must "undergo the penalty of foregoing the pleasure of current consumption of their income."[29] In brief, we have here two evaluations of large incomes, and the two are in overt conflict. On the one hand, the possessor of a substantial income is considered a potential consumer who can do with much less. On the other hand, he is deemed a potential investor who cannot do with much less if he is to discharge his special function after making the required sacrifice. The ideology of ability makes no effort to explain why the first view should be preferred over the second.

Again, the ideology insists that the rates be progressive, but beyond this admonition it offers no aid. Where should progression begin? How rapidly should it proceed? Where should it end? If the rates are to mitigate inequalities of wealth, how drastic should they be in pursuit of this objective? At best we can only surmise that inequalities are to be reduced, not removed. The rates are to be effective, but not too effective. Simons proposed that the rates should "correct excessive economic inequality" and "preclude inordinate enduring differences among families or economic strata in wealth, power, and opportunities."[30] But this advice only changes the form of the question. At what point do economic inequalities become excessive and enduring differences inordinate?

The answer is that there is no answer—if the only one that will do is one that is dispassionately ascertainable. Some will be concerned over the fate of the middle income groups, and urge a moderate degree of progression in their behalf. Others will be disturbed by the burdens of the lower income groups, and favor a more thorough progression in the brackets above. Still others will be worried over the lot of the upper income groups, and try to halt the march of progression as soon as possible. Everyone who meditates on such problems will respond in the light of his own views on inequality. And these views usually change as one moves upward from one tax bracket to another. Notions of proper progression are the creatures of economic preference— whether they be our own and therefore well reasoned, or someone else's and therefore uninformed.

The ideology of ability is necessarily reticent in the face of more basic questions. On the one hand, the pursuit of gain and the accumulation of wealth are proclaimed supreme virtues which are to be fostered

and cherished. On the other hand, those who prove to be the most virtuous are singled out for the largest burdens. The ideology does not
try to give answers to such questions. For answers would require the
adherents to concede that they are no more dispassionate than others.
And this they will not do.

CHAPTER 3

The Dissolution of an Ideal

A large question must now be considered. How well has the ideology of ability fared in the hard world of politics? In order to obtain an informative answer, we must first examine the concept of ability as its adherents usually understand it. The success or failure of a creed should be appraised in the light of its aspirations.

The ideology states that burdens should be apportioned in accordance with ability to pay, and that ability to pay is properly measured by income. The elder La Follette described these two canons of taxation as "principles" and "truths" that are "self-evident."[1] Over the years they have received the tribute which such principles and truths rightfully deserve. Ability to pay, then, is a matter of arithmetical quantity—the amount of income realized by the individual taxpayer.[2] As the adherents often assert, individuals with equal incomes have equal abilities, and so they should bear equal burdens. The two self-evident precepts are joined by a third. While ability is measured by income, one dollar of income is not necessarily the same as another. As income increases, ability increases even more. Therefore, an income tax should also be a progressive tax.

At this point we come to another refinement on which the adherents of ability usually insist. An individual lacks the necessary ability to pay until his income exceeds the cost of a decent existence. In response to this further perception it is now agreed that ability is affected by the number of mouths to be fed. Hence personal exemptions are allowed for the taxpayer and those whom he maintains. It was

not always so. The income tax of 1894 paid no attention to varying obligations to support others. An individual was allowed an exemption of
$4,000, whether or not he had a spouse or children. When an income
tax was next imposed in 1913, the exemption was $3,000 for single in-
dividuals and $4,000 for married couples. But again no exemption was
granted for offspring.[3] Congressional views on children have since
changed for the better. It has been conceded for some time that the
support of offspring, as well as a spouse, affects the ability to pay taxes.
Congress has, indeed, gone much further. For the present it is settled
that many other relatives, and even non-relatives who reside with the
taxpayer, are to be taken into account.

We need not pause to inquire whether a particular relative or non-
relative should be regarded as a dependent. Another matter seems
more important as we appraise the ideology of ability. Initially the personal exemptions were designed to assure an ample standard of living
before the tax applied. As I have indicated, in 1913 the exemption was
$4,000 for a married couple and $3,000 for a single individual. By 1939
these exemptions had become $2,500 and $1,000, and the additional
exemption for dependents stood at $400.[4] Today the exemption is
$1,200 for a married couple, $600 for a single person, and $600 for
each dependent.[5] In other words, the exemptions for a married couple and two children total $2,400 as compared with $4,000 at the outset and $3,300 twenty years ago. Meanwhile the cost of living has risen
200 per cent since 1913 and over 100 per cent since 1939. Moreover,
the essentials of a civilized existence are now more generously conceived. Obviously, a per capita allowance of $600 hardly purports to
keep pace with these changes. By the same token, this meager allowance sheds a strange light on the view that the income tax is "the most
sensitive and powerful instrument of social justice in the fiscal field. It
classifies people both according to size of income and according to
family obligations, the two factors most widely recognized as determining one's ability to pay."[6]

The personal exemptions have come to serve a purpose which is
quite removed from a concern for ability to pay and social justice.
They are essentially a means of determining how much revenue is to
be obtained from the mass of taxpayers at the bottom. A change in exemption significantly affects the yield of the tax. If the current exemptions were merely raised $100 per head, the loss in revenue would be

about $2.8 billion.[7] As a result, the exemptions are kept as low as politically feasible. What began as a criterion of ability to pay is now a convenient device for collecting as much as possible from those with the least ability. The late Senator Walter George of Georgia, who was rarely impressed by the ideology of ability, called the present exemptions "a very cruel method by which the tax upon the people in the low-income brackets has been constantly increased."[8] This new function for the exemptions is reinforced by another factor—the problem of inflation. The vast bulk of consumer spending is among the lower income groups. The taxes which they pay are considered an apt method of controlling inflation through the diversion of excess purchasing power. Since the threat of inflation has become a continuing condition, the exemptions must generally stay as they are. Nor can any aid be expected from the ideologists of ability. By and large they concur in this conclusion, and so they have silently abandoned their prior view of the exemptions in the equation of ability.[9]

The adherents of ability are more troubled by another kind of misfortune that has overtaken their precepts. The exemptions which I have noted are general in nature. They make no attempt to measure ability in terms of the special needs of the particular taxpayer or his dependents. The same amount is allowed for everyone, whether he is newly born or well advanced. However, in the last two decades Congress has sporadically developed a scheme of more sensitive allowances. In 1942 it provided a special deduction for medical expenses. In 1944 it granted a special allowance to the blind. In 1948 it conferred an additional exemption on the elderly. Soon Congress became still more concerned over the problems of old age. In 1951 it enlarged the medical deduction for the elderly. In 1954 it gave them a "retirement income credit." In 1958 it expanded the medical deduction for those who are both elderly and disabled. Then, in 1960 it increased the medical deduction for elderly parents who are dependents of their children.

The allowance for medical expenses is hedged by refined rules and limitations. Generally speaking, a taxpayer may deduct the expenses paid for himself, his spouse and his dependents, to the extent that they exceed 3 per cent of his adjusted gross income. Only the excess is deductible because only the excess is considered so burdensome as to impair his ability to pay. But if the taxpayer or his spouse is over 65, then the expenses of the two are deductible, whether or not they exceed 3 per cent of income. The same is true of payments for the care of dependent parents who are over 65. The allowable amounts, in turn, are subject to different ceilings. Usually the limit is $5,000 if the taxpayer is single, and $10,000 if he is married or head of a household. But the limit is $15,000 each for the medical care of a taxpayer or a spouse who is over 65 and disabled.

The allowance for blindness is an extra exemption of $600 for a taxpayer or a spouse with that disability. This special exemption is supposed to cover additional expenses due to the disability, such as the cost of readers and guides. The allowance for old age is a further exemption of $600 for a taxpayer or a spouse who is over 65. The retirement credit is a benefit generally bestowed on taxpayers over 65 whose income derives from investments, annuities, and pensions. At current rates the credit provides a tax reduction up to $240 a year.

All these special allowances were enacted with little debate, except the exemption of $600 for those over 65. That deduction, on the other hand, emerged amid a heated dispute. The differences were so serious that even the Republicans and Democrats disagreed.[10]

The adherents of ability have been profoundly distressed by the growth of special allowances. Professor Stanley S. Surrey, formerly of the Harvard Law School and now Assistant Secretary of the Treasury, illustrates the concern that is repeatedly expressed. He would promptly eliminate the exemptions for old age and blindness because they are "distortions of the exemption provisions of the income tax."[11] It is easy to understand why the allowance for old age is so disturbing to adherents of ability. Let us compare the taxes of two married couples. In one case husband and wife are 25; in the other case, 65. Both have the same income of $2,400 before exemptions. The first couple pays a tax of $240. The second couple pays no tax at all. For that matter, if the income of the older couple consists entirely of dividends and other investment income, they may receive as much as $6,100 without paying any tax. This pleasant result is the combined effect of the exemption for old age, the retirement credit, and special dispensations devised for those who receive dividends.

The adherents of ability are puzzled as well as perturbed by the exemptions for old age. Why, they ask, is a successful investor, entrepreneur, executive, or professional in peculiar need of another exemption as soon as he or his spouse celebrates a sixty-fifth birthday? In any event, why should age make a difference if incomes are the same? Needless to say, their criticism does not stem from any callous disregard for elderly taxpayers and their spouses. It reflects, rather, a stern adherence to their basic precepts. A taxpayer's age, they declare, is irrelevant to his ability to pay. It is no more significant than the color of his hair or the shape of his nose.

The ideologists are troubled and bewildered because ability to pay does not mean the same to them as to others. They persistently assume that the one true measure of ability is the amount of income realized. They fail to grasp that others have a new view of ability, as revealed by the special exemption for old age. Under this new view the criterion of ability is not only the income which a taxpayer is able to realize, but also the additional income which he is unable to obtain. Hence equal incomes may be variously taxed. The exemption for the elderly faithfully applies this revised canon of ability. It draws a distinction on the basis of age because older persons are less able to cope with high prices and high taxes than younger ones. As the Republicans stated in behalf of the exemption, the elderly have "suffered with unusual severity." Unlike their younger compatriots, they cannot alleviate their financial plight by earning more income "at prevailing high rates of wages." The additional exemption is a means of mitigating their special difficulties by easing their tax burden. It helps those who cannot help themselves.[12]

I doubt whether this thoughtful explanation can satisfy the adherents of ability. At the risk of seeming disrespectful to our elders, they will remain disturbed by several matters. Many taxpayers over 65 fare very well despite taxes and inflation. As for the elderly with fixed incomes, their requirements are generally less than those of younger taxpayers. Even if their needs are as great, why should their taxes be less? If younger individuals are better able to earn more income, they also pay more taxes when they do. At any rate, practically everyone is afflicted by a varying incapacity to earn more income. Why should the extra exemption be granted only to a select group of elderly taxpayers? Questions like these obviously suggest that the exemption for the elderly has no relation to ability to pay. It is simply a special reduction for certain taxpayers, and all the allusions to ability are merely designed to make the reduction seem more urgent. When the reduction was increased in 1954 through the retirement credit, Congress did not even bother to justify its action in the language of ability to pay.

However, the legislative custodians of tax policy are still impressed by their new view of ability as applied to elderly taxpayers. In their opinion the inability to acquire more income is ample reason for imposing less tax on the income that is actually acquired. And, of all taxpayers, those over 65 are regarded as most unable to improve their lot. The fact that a taxpayer within this group may be doing well enough without improvement is beside the point. As soon as he becomes 65, his ability to pay presumptively declines, though his income may remain the same or even increase. Indeed, Congress has carefully curtailed or denied the retirement credit to those who continue to earn too much. The credit is reduced if the taxpayer's wages or other earnings exceed $1,200 for the year; and it is entirely withdrawn if his earnings are as much as $2,400 for the year.[13] True, the credit remains fully available to those who receive dividends and other investment income, no matter how large that income may be. Hence if a taxpayer over 65 receives dividends of $100,000, he is entitled to a tax saving of $240; but if he receives a salary of $2,500, he is not equally deserving. This distinction between earned income and investment income may at first seem incongruous. But the difficulty should disappear once the new view of ability is firmly grasped.

According to Surrey, the special exemption for the blind is scarcely better than the special exemption for the elderly. The income tax, he states, "is not the vehicle for relief to special groups handicapped by physical ailments."[14] Evidently this adverse conclusion stems from the ideology of ability for which he speaks. However, there is more to be said than he has mentioned.

Ability to pay, as customarily conceived by its adherents, does not appear until income exceeds the cost of providing the basic decencies of life. The personal exemptions are supposed to represent the required expenses. But if ability to pay is the residue of income left after taking care of essential needs, then the exemptions may be more meticulously refined for special difficulties that add to the cost. The medical deduction, which Surrey reluctantly accepts,[15] is in effect a further exemption for the undue expenses of illness. If a burdensome illness strikes a taxpayer, surely his ability to pay is less than the ability of one who is not similarly weighed down. Why, then—apart from revenue needs and administrative considerations—should Congress be less attentive to other expenses imposed by marked physical disabilities? Very little is contributed by disparaging the allowance for blindness as an example of relief to special groups. Tax law, like all law, proceeds on the basis of distinctions. When distinctions are drawn, groups are inevitably recognized and differently treated. A more meaningful question is whether a particular distinction was properly made. Certain married couples are much less heavily taxed than single individuals, and to that extent relief is similarly bestowed on a special group. Yet Surrey and other adherents of ability have cheerfully approved the differences in tax. Even the general exemptions are a special treatment of special groups. They distinguish those who are married from those who are single, and those who have children from those who do not. It seems just as reasonable to distinguish between those who are blind and those who can see—assuming that the physical difference significantly affects the cost of living.

Surrey's strictures derive from an embarrassing difficulty which exceeds the expenses of illness and blindness. It is the problem of personal deductions. The ideologists of ability agree that the expenses of earning income should be taken into account in measuring ability to pay. But they are disinclined to approve the deduction of personal expenses, such as mortgage interest and property taxes on a home, sales taxes on domestic purchases, and the cost of medical care. There is a perennial fear that such allowances will erode the concept of ability. The tax will no longer be a general levy on income, regardless of how the income is used. Instead it will be narrowed by various deductions which provide the largest benefits in the upper brackets.[16] Hence Surrey is even troubled by the modest allowance to working wives and widowers for the care of children under 12, as well as any other dependent who is physically or mentally unable to care for himself. He is not consoled by the fact that the deduction is granted only if the expenses are paid so that the taxpayer may be gainfully employed. Yet at the same time Surrey indicates that the problem of personal deductions cannot be resolved by a rigid adherence to ability to pay. Even he concedes that such allowances may be tolerable if they serve some worthy purpose. For example, he approves the deduction for charitable contributions until a better "way is found of encouraging private philanthropy." It makes no difference that the deduction provides relief for a special group who are well-to-do. But once such concessions are made, not much remains of the basic objection. The issue, then, is not whether personal deductions impair the concept of ability to pay, but whether the impairment is justified by adequate reasons. On such questions the ideology of ability is scarcely instructive.[17]

The special allowances for the elderly illustrate a larger wisdom which extends well beyond them. Ability to pay, as Congress now conceives it, depends not only on the amount of income that is realized, but also on the particular person who realizes the income. Therefore, the same income represents less taxable capacity in the hands of an older person than in the hands of a younger person. A wisdom which is so discerning cannot be exhausted with one application. It must be equally sensitive to further distinctions between one taxpayer and another. And so we should not be surprised that Congress has detected a more significant difference—between those who are married and those who are single. A married couple is now entitled to what is known as "income splitting." Their total income is cut in half, and the tax on each half is separately computed. The net result is that progression comes to a halt midway and then starts all over again. In effect, the tax brackets for husband and wife are twice as wide as the brackets for bachelors and spinsters.

This strange mode of computing an income tax came as the solution to a venerable problem. For many years the well-to-do in the community property states paid much less tax than their equivalent brethren in the common law states. The Supreme Court reasoned that a wife in a community property state earns or owns half of the income which would otherwise be taxable to her husband as the source of the income.[18] Since half was attributed to each spouse and the rates were progressive, the sum of their two taxes was smaller than the tax on the same income paid by a husband in a common law state. The disparity appeared as soon as the income passed beyond the first bracket, and the extent of the disparity depended on the size of the income and the rate of progression. In 1947 the tax on $25,000 was 29 per cent more in New York than in California, and the tax on $100,000 was 20 per cent greater. Ability to pay was determined in the light of the supposed dictates of property law. A California husband had less taxable capacity than a New York husband, though both produced precisely the same incomes. Actually there is hardly a difference in dominion and control between the two groups of husbands. A California husband spends his earnings as freely as a New York husband. Whatever restraints their wives may exercise in their individual ways have little to do with variations in property law.

This situation led to two proposals. The first was that income earned or controlled by a husband in a community property state should be taxed entirely to him. The second was that incomes of husband and wife should be added together and taxed as one on a compulsory joint return. Neither remedy obtained the needed number of votes. The solution for community income displeased the prosperous in the community property states.[19] The solution of joint returns displeased the prosperous in all the states. Each proposal was defective, for it would have increased the taxes of those affected. Of course, various arguments were heard which spoke of other things. Joint returns, for example, were condemned as an insidious incitement to divorce or a renewed degradation of married women. Amid all the rhetoric it rarely occurred to anyone that these observations might be incompatible. Eventually it became clear that the required remedy would have to avoid all these unhappy results. The answer was resourcefully found. In 1948 Congress authorized "income splitting" in the fashion of community property. Husband and wife are now permitted to pay tax as if each earned half of their total income. In view of the difficulties involved this solution was quite admirable. Those who had suffered from the discrimination were enabled to pay less, and those who had profited were not obliged to pay more. The relief was nicely confined to the married couples for whom it was designed. Only 22 per cent of all married couples were benefited, and 97 per cent of the benefits went to 5 per cent of the beneficiaries.[20]

Income splitting proceeds on the tacit premise that the same income does not necessarily reflect the same ability to pay tax. Married men are distinguished from the single variety. When distinctions are drawn in tax law, nothing is so informative as arithmetic. On $20,000 a husband pays $5,280 and a bachelor $7,260. On $50,000 a husband pays $20,300 and a bachelor $26,820. On $100,000 a husband pays $53,640 and a bachelor $67,320.[21] As a result of income splitting, husbands with incomes between $10,000 and $50,000 are now paying less than they paid in 1941.

Despite such interesting incongruities, many adherents of ability have bestowed their approval on income splitting. They are more impressed by the fact that splitting prevents distasteful inequalities among married couples. Besides, they say, no other solution was politically possible. Yet even these rationalizations apparently leave them uneasy and disturbed. Such explanations unfortunately imply that the removal of one discrimination justifies the creation of another. Hence still another attempt has been made to rationalize the present differences between the married and the single. It is vaguely suggested that marriage entails increased expenses that call for a lesser tax. As between the married and the single, equal incomes do not represent equal abilities because the financial responsibilities are different.[22]

This further effort is marred by at least three difficulties. First, the essential living expenses of taxpayers and their dependents are supposedly handled by the personal exemptions. According to the traditional views of ability, beyond the exemptions equal incomes signify equal abilities. Second, the rationalization is a precarious essay in pure reasoning. The basic living expenses of a married couple are less than twice as much as the expenses of a single person. Actually the present exemptions are more inadequate for single people than for married people.[23] Third, and more important, income splitting does not reveal any rational distinction between the single and the married on the basis of living expenses. The tax reduction enjoyed by married couples varies haphazardly with the size of their incomes. It is 7.3 per cent at $5,000; 16.7 per cent at $10,000; 28.9 per cent at $24,000; 24.3 per cent at $50,000; 20.3 per cent at $100,000; and 7.4 per cent at $400,000. Or, to amplify the comparison, at $5,000 the reduction is $80, and at $100,000 it is $13,680. The couple with 20 times as much income saves 171 times as much tax. On the other hand, income splitting evinces no interest whatever in the household expenses of married couples with incomes of $2,000 or less, after exemptions. They are taxed at the same rate as single people. Over 50 per cent of the married couples filing taxable joint returns fall within this lowly category. The substantial beneficiaries of income splitting are concentrated at the upper levels. At the same time the over-all revenue loss is now about $4 billion a year.[24]

While my appraisal of income splitting is necessarily brief, it suffices for my limited purpose. In an effort to explore the ideology of ability to pay, I started with a simple notion that is often proclaimed with suitable enthusiasm. Individuals with equal incomes should pay equal taxes, because equal incomes reflect equal abilities. This notion was then refined by a further perception. An individual does not have the required ability to pay unless he first has the capacity to sustain himself and his dependents. Ability to pay became the amount of income realized by a taxpayer less allowances for an adequate standard of living. At this point, however, my learning began to dissolve. It turns out that the personal exemptions are little related to the cost of providing the decencies of life. Moreover, certain allowances are merely devices designed to reduce the taxes of certain groups. Their function is not to measure the ability that exists before taxes, but to increase the income that remains after taxes. Then I came to income splitting, which cogently confirmed what had already become clear. Ability to pay depends not only on the amount of income received, but on the person who receives the income. Hence in the end equal incomes do not reflect equal abilities.

The ideologists of ability are naturally unhappy over this state of affairs. To quote a typical response, Surrey describes the special allowances for the elderly as "aberrations" from ability to pay—"a windfall for many above the lowest brackets."[25] Yet the lucrative benefits for the married above the lowest brackets fail to inspire similar observations, though income splitting departs even more drastically from the ideology of ability as its adherents usually understand it. How, then, are we to account for these varying views emanating from the same sources? The answer is not too difficult if we look past the rhetoric. The troubled ideologists are merely applying the ancient maxim that the end justifies the means. If the end is desirable, Congress may deviate from the customary criteria of ability to pay. It so happens that Surrey disapproves of special allowances for the elderly and approves of income splitting for the married. Therefore, he calls one group of benefits a windfall and the other something else.[26]

A more delicate question still lingers on. If I may return to an earlier inquiry, why are the ideologists of ability unable to be more candid about their views? Why do they fear to state, in so many words, that their criteria of taxation may be abandoned in pursuit of a higher end? Here, too, there are several contributing causes which have made candor inappropriate. As I previously noted, ideologists of ability are largely liberals; and liberals are very reluctant to concede that the end may justify means which otherwise seem undesirable. Again, as ideologists they are understandably hesitant to announce that their system of belief may from time to time be abandoned. Cherished principles cannot tolerate too many exceptions if they are to remain principles. Finally, there is the pragmatic consideration that if ability to pay may be disregarded in behalf of higher ends, the necessary ends will be amply supplied by others.

The adherents of ability are fearful in vain. For revealing evidence that their concern is fruitless, I turn to another aspect of ability—the source or origin of income. As an illustration, let us compare the situations of two individuals. One has an income of $10,000 derived from personal services. The other has an income of $10,000 produced by investments of $250,000. I add the further fact that both are married and have the same personal exemptions. Are the abilities of the two equal because their incomes are equal? Or, to generalize beyond my example, should earned incomes be taxed to the same extent as incomes that are derived from investments?

If we look for wisdom among the adherents of ability, the answer seems clear. I quote two typical statements. "A sound and just tax system," the younger La Follette wrote, "should apply the ability-to-pay standard to the individual taxpayer regardless of the source of his income." More recently the Joint Economic Committee declared that "all taxpayers with equal taxpaying ability" should be equally treated, "without reference to the particular circumstances out of which the taxpaying ability arises."[27] If such assertions mean what they apparently say, the source of the income is irrelevant. It is the amount of the income that counts.

In contrast, tax experts who would hardly pass as devoted adherents of ability have proposed a lesser tax on earned income than investment income. Among them the most celebrated is Andrew Mellon. As Secretary of the Treasury, Mellon strongly urged a tax differential of 25 per cent in favor of earned income.[28] Perhaps stranger still, those who have advocated the differential have justified it on the basis of ability to pay. As the argument has been simply stated, the taxpayer who receives earned income "must each year save and set aside a portion of his income in order to protect him in case of sickness and in his old age, and in order to provide for his family upon his death. On the other hand, the person whose income is derived from investments already has his capital and is relieved of the necessity of saving to establish it. He may spend each year his entire income, and at the same time have sufficient capital to protect him in old age and to provide for his family upon his death. In most cases the person whose income is derived from investments is able to pay a greater tax than the one whose income is the result of personal effort."[29]

Under this analysis the ability to pay taxes involves savings as well as earnings. Just as the concept of ability must recognize the need to provide for present wants, so must it take into account the need to set aside for future wants. From this point of view an individual whose income flows from capital necessarily has more ability than an individual whose equivalent income stems from services. To the extent of the capital the savings are already there. The less the need to save, the greater the ability to pay; and if the ability is greater, the tax should be larger. It seems difficult to quarrel with this conclusion once it is agreed that ability must allow for the varying compulsion to save. Nor do I detect any reason why the need to save is necessarily irrelevant to the concept of ability. Of course, the income tax was designed to remove the prior discrimination between income saved and income spent. But it does not follow that the relative need to provide for the future must be ignored in appraising the relative ability to pay in the present.[30]

Yet the firmest adherents of ability to pay have shown the least interest in a lesser tax on earned income. With few exceptions they are wedded to the belief that the source of the income is immaterial. This situation is quite interesting; for the warmest ideologists of ability qualify as liberals, and liberals are normally prone to favor those who work for their income. As an explanation for this peculiar condition, I can only offer what I have already said on the subject of progression. The disinclination to distinguish between earned income and investment income is induced by a desire to appear properly neutral and a fear of unfortunate consequences. There is the same reluctance to seem partial to any class or group. And there is a constant concern over the discrimination that others will justify if incomes can be distinguished in the light of their source. Nothing looks so dispassionately aloof as a simple arithmetical notion of ability.

But the supposed neutrality and the genuine fear are largely wasted. Despite the abundant talk of ability, Congress has provided more and more special exceptions for income from selected sources. Interest on certain loans is tax-exempt. Profits from the disposal of certain assets are taxed at a lower rate reserved for so-called capital gains. Compensation through certain devices is similarly taxed at the same rewarding rate. Profits from certain businesses are reduced by deductions for imaginary costs. The exceptions are rarely justified under the alleged authority of ability to pay. When reasons are given, each exception is usually rationalized in terms of some economic benefit that it will bestow. The argument is almost always the same. Unless the few who are chosen are allowed to pay less, the many who are passed over will seriously suffer. The reduced taxes of the few are only the means to a generous end—the welfare of everybody. As Dr. Pangloss repeatedly observed to Candide, it is all for the best even when we fail to understand it. At any rate, to insist that taxes should be measured by ability, while others are promising to improve our lot, is to indulge in question-begging. When the oil and gas industry lauds percentage depletion for the blessings it brings, the praise cannot be dissipated by resounding declarations that percentage depletion departs from the sovereign principle of ability to pay.

True, at times Congress justifies its good works on the basis of ability to pay. But even when it does so, the adherents of ability must remain unhappy. For on those occasions Congress methodically resorts to its new view of ability—that certain taxpayers are entitled to pay less because they are unable to earn more.

This new view, for example, was helpfully applied in behalf of those who derive royalties from leases of coal properties. The tax committees discovered that relief was urgent because many of these taxpayers were in a sorry predicament. They had leased their properties to coal operators under long-term arrangements which no longer produced a sufficient rate of return. Specifically, the royalties payable to the lessors were a stated number of cents per ton rather than a percentage of the value of the coal taken from the mine. As a result, the lessors were unable to share in rising prices through an automatic increase in royalties. While the operators received more for their coal, the royalties remained the same. Under the new view of ability the required remedy was as obvious as the unfortunate difficulty. The inability to obtain larger royalties had to be compensated by the benefit of lower taxes.[31] It was immaterial that the taxes of others were simultaneously raised because of the Korean war. The problem was easily handled by declaring that coal royalties are taxable as capital gains. Therefore, the tax cannot exceed 25 per cent, no matter how ample the royalties may be.

To the adherents of ability this solution is inexcusable. But if the elderly merit the special relief bestowed on them, why are the receivers of coal royalties less deserving? We may even say that the case for coal royalties is the better of the two, for the receivers of such income are sadly imprisoned within improvident contracts from which they cannot escape. Congress has truly helped those who cannot help themselves. Of course, in the process others have also been helped. Precisely the same relief is given to lessors whose royalties automatically rise with increases in the price of coal. However, anyone who is troubled by this discrepancy is unnecessarily perturbed. Congress was unwilling to indulge in complex distinctions between one coal lessor and another. By helping all of them without discrimination, it avoided the need of writing an elaborate statute. Simplicity should not be deplored.

My survey would be too brief if I failed to mention the most respectable departure from ability to pay—the corporate mode of doing business. Corporations are not subject to the individual tax rates. They have a separate schedule of their own, which now consists of two rates. The first $25,000 of income is taxable at 30 per cent, and all additional income at 52 per cent. The combined effect of the individual rates and corporate rates is to emasculate the scheme of taxation which the ideology of ability so carefully rationalizes.

If an individual does business as a proprietor, his earnings are taxable at the usual progressive rates. But if he does business as a corporation, the earnings are only taxable at the corporate rates, except as he withdraws them through salary or dividends. Since the corporation may deduct his salary, he will try to compensate himself as much as possible until his individual rates threaten to exceed the corporate rate at 52 per cent.[32] This dangerous situation comes to pass when his individual income reaches $36,000 if he is married, or $18,000 if he is single. Since the corporation may not deduct his dividends, he will generally refrain from distributing any to himself. As an organization devoted to the problems of businessmen has stated, "paying dividends is clearly a tax waste."[33] Corporations, then, are a recognized sanctuary from the upper brackets, and progression commonly ends at 52 per cent. But corporations produce other benefits as well. If the stockholder later sells his shares, the profit on the retained earnings of the corporation is a capital gain taxable at no more than 25 per cent. And if the shares are sold after he dies, the profit on the earnings accumulated at his death is entirely exempt from income tax.

A special penalty has been devised for those who fail to pay dividends to themselves in order to avoid the progressive rates. It consists of an additional corporate tax on undistributed earnings that are not required for "the reasonable needs of the business." This penalty, however, is as effective as Prohibition. Everyone is aware of it, but few are attentive to it. Though corporate hoarding is widespread, the penalty is rarely paid. In many cases the risk of incurring the penalty is deliberately assumed, for at worst the penalty is only 38½ per cent as compared with individual rates rising to 91 per cent. Even if the penalty is paid, one may still be ahead. The tax savings increase with the individual rates which would otherwise apply if dividends were withdrawn. And so the penalty is least effective where it should be most effective— in the upper brackets. As a Congressional study concluded, the prudent failure to distribute earnings is "a broad highway to avoidance of personal surtax." The "inadequate penalty" invites the very behavior which it is supposed to prevent.[34]

But we should not rashly infer that Congress is distressed by this mode of avoidance. On the contrary, the sustained reluctance to pay dividends is considered a venerable practice which should not be unduly impaired. Businessmen would be too preoccupied with taxes if their corporate accumulations were more thoroughly penalized. Indeed, for fear of the penalty they might timorously distribute excessive dividends and deprive their corporations of sorely required funds. A mild sanction persuades Congress that it has done its duty, and reassures businessmen that they have little to fear.

If tax policy should start from the principle of ability to pay, it need not end there. Otherwise we would not have the many discrepancies which even the adherents of ability apparently approve. If an individual receives compensation for services, his gain is taxable. If another individual receives the same amount as a gift, his gain is not taxable. While their arithmetical abilities to pay are equal, almost everyone seems satisfied that their tax liabilities should be different. For reasons wholly divorced from ability, it is agreed that gifts should not be subject to income tax. Those who labor are treated less tenderly than those who live off the benevolence of others.[35] Or, to consider two narrower distinctions, if a student works his way through college, his earnings are taxable. But if he is maintained there by a scholarship, his means of support is not taxable. Again, if an author receives a monetary prize for a novel submitted in a literary contest, his gain is taxable. But if he receives the same sum in later recognition of his literary achievement, his gain is not taxable. In these cases, as in many others, equivalence of ability to pay is not regarded as an adequate reason for similar treatment. Significant distinctions are made in terms of the source from which the gain derives, and at times there is scarcely a difference in source.

My reflections lead on to a broad conclusion. The most ardent adherents of ability do not contend that their faith excludes other considerations in the formulation of tax policy. Gifts to charity provide as good an example as any. If a taxpayer contributes to an eleemosynary institution, his gift is deductible from his income. If he gives the same amount to his son, the gift is not deductible. The difference is justified on the ground that philanthropy should be encouraged through a reduction in tax. A taxpayer will donate more to charity if he may pay less to the Government. The problem is basically similar when the issue is whether income from one source should be more sparingly taxed than income from another. Whatever the answer may be, little is gained by arguing over the true content of ability to pay. If ability is simply a matter of amount, as its adherents usually believe, it may still be desirable to impose diverse burdens on equal incomes for reasons quite apart from ability. The question is not whether some exception departed from the concept of ability. The question is whether the departure was nevertheless appropriate.

"Everything's got a moral," a famous Duchess said, "if only you can find it." What, then, in the end are we to make of the ideology of ability? The ideology, as we know it today, was born of a desire to justify progressive taxes on income and wealth. It contemplated that the middle and upper levels of society would bear most of the burdens, and it invoked the rhetoric of ability in order to absolve the intended discrimination. The language of ability enabled the adherents to identify a progressive tax with equality and neutrality. A *rara avis* like Professor Simons would impatiently deny that graduated rates are impartial rates, and would candidly praise progression as a deliberate means of mitigating economic inequalities.[36] But his was a voice crying in the wilderness.

The results have not been entirely as expected. A class tax has become a mass tax. As late as 1939 only 4 million people paid income taxes. Today about 46 million enjoy the privilege of doing so. In 1913 the initial rate was 1 per cent on the first $20,000 of taxable income after personal exemptions. Today the initial rate is 20 per cent on the first $2,000 of a single person and the first $4,000 of a married couple. For the fiscal year 1913 the taxes on individual and corporate incomes yielded slightly over $35 million. For the fiscal year 1960 the tax on individual incomes alone produced almost $41 billion. Of this tremendous total, about 86 per cent comes from the initial rate which all must pay. The progressive rates contribute only the balance of 14 per cent.

However, it is not enough to focus on the individual income tax. There are also state and local taxes, as well as other federal levies. When all taxes are put together, the picture is rather different from what was hopefully anticipated. According to Professor Richard Musgrave, the over-all tax system in the United States is only barely progressive for incomes up to $10,000—which account for about 90 per cent of all family units. The total effective rate creeps from 26.9 per cent on the first $2,000 of income to 33 per cent on incomes between $7,500 and $10,000. For all incomes over $10,000 the combined effective impact is about 40 per cent.[37] Or to restate Musgrave's revelations, despite the repeated allusions to ability and progression, the burden is essentially proportional on incomes up to $10,000, and mildly progressive on incomes beyond. For most taxpayers the progression of the income tax does little more than offset the regression of other taxes, state and federal.[38]

Meanwhile it has become apparent that the ideology of ability cannot bring us to the land that was promised. The ideology initially assumes that all gains should be treated alike. But then many distinctions are made—at times with the approval of the most faithful among the adherents. As a rule, the distinctions are ultimately justified on some ground of economic or other social policy. Hence, in any event, it is useless to condemn distinctions for failing to abide by the standard of ability. If a response is to be effective, it must openly do battle on the questions of policy that are involved. To speak forcefully of ability to pay is merely to indulge in evasive rhetoric.

CHAPTER 4

The Ideology of Barriers
and Deterrents

The ideology of barriers and deterrents is a doctrine steeped in gloom. For the most articulate expression of its content and mood I go to its confirmed believers. As a mere bystander I cannot adequately summarize its precise mode of thought and the related sense of urgency. Only the true believers have the capacity to convey the required fear of calamity that hovers over us. While many believers may be quoted, I must be satisfied with but a few. Fortunately, the omissions are not too serious, for all the observations generally sound alike.

The so-called Special Tax Study Committee, headed by Roswell Magill, does well as a first example. This group served the House Ways and Means Committee in an advisory capacity in 1947. Its stated function was "to insure" that tax problems "would be approached in a thoroughly nonpartisan fashion." Representative McCormack, of Massachusetts, has described the Special Committee as a group of "prominent industrialists, bankers, and tax lawyers."[1] His appraisal seems somewhat inaccurate, for one of the members was an executive of the American Federation of Labor. Therefore, I prefer the Special Committee's own view of itself as "a representative group of citizens qualified to perform a difficult technical task." In the process of bestowing the benefit of its "advice and practical experience," the group, other than the labor official, carefully meditated on barriers and deterrents.

After reflecting at length the Special Committee produced a report both melancholy and ominous. "Our country has grown great," the Committee stated, "by the chances we have offered to every country boy and workingman to build himself up by his industry and thrift to as good a position as his capabilities justify. Our great productivity results from the work of men who have made their own ways to the top." But with the "present scale of tax rates," the Committee mournfully continued, "we have put the brake on men's incentives to a dangerous degree by piling heavier and heavier burdens on them as they try to climb up the ladder. Not only is this stultifying to the kind of dynamic long-term growth that has characterized this country in the past, but—to the extent that it impedes production—it is an element in our inflationary pressures today." Taxpayers simply refuse to be as productive as they would be if taxes were lower. And so we now have the "builder who doesn't build the extra house, the farmer who doesn't market the extra carload of cattle or grain, the wage earner who doesn't put in the extra day, because doing so would put him in a higher tax bracket and multiply his tax."[2]

Our dangers hardly end there. "Another trouble with the Federal income-tax system is that it is so designed that it makes thrift difficult. Men cannot save much money when taxes and prices are both very high. This is true all up and down the income scale. At one end of the scale the white-collar man (except perhaps some who have had substantial increases in income) is able to set aside little or nothing for the 'rainy day' after paying the rent and other expenses and settling with the tax collector. The young man starting out on his career is prevented from building up the nest egg of savings that will enable him to start a business of his own." The situation is just as bad at "the other end of the scale." Our "men of substantial means, who in the past have supplied a large share of the venture capital for starting new enterprises and expanding existing ones, find little or no margin of saving left for this essential role after paying taxes." The supply of capital is so inadequate that "even the strongest corporation finds it impossible to raise additional funds through offerings of share capital except on terms so costly as in many cases to necessitate deferment of plans or financing through borrowings, with consequent increase of debt."[3]

As these gloomy reflections indicate, the ideology of barriers and deterrents dwells on the alarming theme that the economy is deteriorating because the rates are too high. The rates are gravely diminishing the desire to work, the ability to save, and the inclination to invest. The resulting curtailment of production is so serious that it breeds in-

flation by denying us the goods that we eagerly want. Even wage earners are not as energetic as they should be, for higher wages subject
them to higher rates. Many would rather earn less income than pay
more tax. However, the ideology of barriers and deterrents is primarily interested in the plight of others as they make their perilous way
amid the disconcerting rates. Businessmen must be made happier with
lower taxes lest their ambitions sag and the nation suffer. Investors
must be similarly heartened so that corporations are no longer in dire
need of capital. These propositions have the authoritative sanction of
Adam Smith, who was also troubled by the problem of enervated businessmen and depleted investors. Taxation, he cautioned, may subtract
more from the economy than it adds to the Treasury. It "may obstruct
the industry of the people, and discourage them from applying to certain branches of business which might give maintenance and employment to great multitudes. While it obliges the people to pay, it may
thus diminish, or perhaps destroy, some of the funds which might enable them more easily to do so."[4]

The observations on barriers and deterrents are customarily combined with a further notion of good and evil. Industry is inherently
productive while government is inherently wasteful. Income taxes and
estate taxes foolishly shift our economic resources from the thrifty ant
to the irresponsible grasshopper. Adam Smith may again be cited as a
respectable ally. Smith specifically criticized death taxes because they
"tend to diminish the funds destined for the maintenance of productive labour." In his view they were "all more or less unthrifty taxes that
increase the revenue of the sovereign, which seldom maintains any but
unproductive labourers; at the expence of the capital of the people,
which maintains none but productive."[5] This contrast between productive industry and unproductive government continues to evoke
profound convictions and melancholy misgivings. But the alleged difference is now more vividly stated. While high rates may diminish
financial incentives, they may also enhance the powers of expression.

The noted lawyer George Wharton Pepper illustrates the current
mode of distinguishing between the contributions of government and
the achievements of business. He first states that the income tax, with
the aid of Prohibition and "New Deal regulations," has undermined
our constitutional liberties. Then he becomes more precise. "The
present federal income tax policy," he declares, "virtually prohibits the

citizen from putting his surplus earnings into productive enterprise and, instead, first appropriates them and then pipes them into the treasury. Thence they are pumped out and made to flow into channels the direction and destination of which is determined by men who themselves may never have been able to earn more than a precarious living." Pepper, obviously, considers the power to tax and the power to spend as an unfortunate system of plumbing. Alexander Hamilton's "darling objects of human avarice and enterprise" are constantly moving in the wrong direction and into the wrong hands. "This process," Pepper concludes with understandable emotion, "cannot long continue. Either productive enterprise will be starved to death or the piping, pumping and diversion of earnings will have to be brought within reasonable limits." The power to tax and the power to spend are no less than the power to convey our resources from "the competent" to "the incompetent." The Government is "a miscellaneous collection of men few of whom, as individuals, are competent to launch or run any sort of business." It has "only what these men by taxation and borrowing can take from those who have the ability and energy to do what they themselves cannot do."[6]

Given the problem and the diagnosis, the answer seems clear. Congress must drastically reduce the rates so that they are no longer too high for the ambitious and the thrifty. But how high is too high? Over the years the ideology of barriers and deterrents has fluctuated from one response to another. In late 1916 Representative Rainey announced, with the usual confidence of statesmanship, that the individual income tax had reached "the very highest notch."[7] When this statement was made, the top rate was 15 per cent on net income over $2 million. In the twenties Secretary Mellon was sure that the tax should not exceed 25 per cent. The American Bar Association agrees with Mellon that 25 per cent is about right. The National Association of Manufacturers is inclined to be more generous. It has suggested a top rate of 35 per cent, which is to be reached in several stages.[8] The corporate income tax has also inspired various responses that are sensitive to barriers and deterrents. Two illustrations should suffice. In 1942 Representatives Treadway and Knutson, of the Ways and Means Committee, vigorously objected to a proposed increase above 40 per cent. Mr. Treadway firmly believed "that 40 per cent is as high as we can safely go in taxing normal corporate profits." Mr. Knutson despondently added that small corporations would be put out of business, and predicted a resulting unemployment "beyond calculation." Eight years later other members of the Committee echoed the same views. If the corporate tax were raised to 41 per cent, "a contracting" economy would inevitably follow.[9]

Despite these and other predictions of disaster if certain limits are ignored, high taxes have continued for some time and the system has survived fairly well. The top rate of the individual income tax is now 91 per cent. Since 1942 it has been as high as 94 per cent and never below 82 per cent. For almost ten years the tax on corporate incomes over $25,000 has stood at 52 per cent. Nevertheless we have not had the unemployment "beyond calculation" that Congressman Knutson grimly prophesied. I am not saying that high employment has been due to high taxes. My point is that there has been high employment together with high taxes. People have continued to produce and invest although their ambitions should have languished. We have discovered what many of us have suspected all along—that the system does not grind to a halt because the rates far exceed those which suit the ideology of barriers and deterrents.

Are we then to infer that the ideology will soon pass quietly away into oblivion? The answer, of course, is no. An ideology is not a body of truth but a system of belief. It continues to command allegiance as long as it serves some purpose. Since the affluent will remain unreconciled to high taxes, the ideology will persist, regardless of what the facts may periodically disclose. And so we will continue to hear what we have often heard before—that "the most serious threat to the growth and vitality of the American economy" is "the steeply progressive rate of personal income taxes."[10]

We already have ample proof that the facts are immaterial. Perhaps the best evidence is supplied by Secretary of the Treasury Mellon. According to the gospel of Mellon, "the prosperity of the middle and lower classes depended upon the good fortunes and light taxes of the rich."[11] The rich, he reasoned, would be unable to save and reluctant to invest if their taxes were too high. And if they failed to save and invest, the economy would finally perish. In order to keep the system going, the rich had to be taxed at a rate they would be willing to pay. On their happiness hinged the happiness of everyone else.

These conclusions were expressed in the familiar verbalisms peculiar to the ideology of barriers and deterrents. High taxes, he cautioned, were "gradually destroying business initiative." They "kept capital out of ordinary productive business." They were "discouraging industry and threatening the country's future prosperity." If a "man of energy and initiative" is denied "the right to receive a reasonable share of his earnings, then he will no longer exert himself and the country will be deprived of the energy on which its continued greatness depends." "Any one at all in touch with affairs knows of his own knowledge of buildings which have not been built, of businesses which have not been started, and of new projects which have been abandoned, all for one reason—high surtaxes." "The spirit of initiative may still be there, but the present high surtaxes are driving it into idleness. America will become a nation of followers, not leaders." If "the country is to go forward in the future as it has in the past, we must make sure that all retarding influences are removed." The "only way to save the situation is to put the taxes on a reasonable basis that will permit business to go on and industry to develop." Taxes "must be cut far enough to free capital for new enterprises" and "new investments." The rates must be reduced, not "to relieve the wealthy," but "to relieve the country." Mellon even hoped "that some day we may get back on a tax basis of 10%, the old Hebrew tithe, which was always considered a fairly heavy tax."[12]

When Mellon took office in 1921, the top income tax rate was 73 per cent on net incomes over $1 million and the top estate tax rate was 25 per cent on net estates over $10 million. Mellon proposed two ways of keeping the affluent in the required state of contentment. The first was a generous reduction of the income tax; the second was a complete repeal of the estate tax. The Secretary finally concluded that the highest income tax compatible with the least discouragement to business was 25 per cent. The estate tax he regarded as wholly irreconcilable with private enterprise, whether the rates were high or low. It destroyed the "values which we call wealth" by forcing executors into sales at a loss in order to pay the Government. "This has the effect of dropping the price at which securities can be sold and results in bringing down not only the values of such property and securities but values everywhere." "No tax can be more illogical," he counselled, "than that which is destructive of the very values upon which the tax is based." The estate tax was pernicious for still another reason. It "destroyed" capital in order to cover the "current operating expenses" of the Government; and "the cumulative effect of such destruction cannot fail to be harmful to the country." With substantial rates, "the result would be not that the Government had absorbed the wealth of the country, but that the wealth had been spent and none was left." In any event, he reasoned, the tax should not be levied in order to break up large estates. Otherwise we would violate the "theory upon which the country was founded"—"equality of opportunity." But whatever the motive for the estate tax, he insisted that a top rate of 25 per cent was "very heavy."[13]

After a few frustrating experiences Mellon finally had his way with the income tax. He was not entirely successful with the estate tax, but in the end he did fairly well. Through the heroic efforts of Mellon the ideology of barriers and deterrents enjoyed a Golden Age of about seven years. Between 1925 and 1932 the highest rate of income tax was 25 per cent. It did not apply until income exceeded $100,000. In the same period the highest rate of estate tax was 20 per cent. It did not apply until an estate exceeded $10 million. At no time since have the income and estate taxes been so pleasantly low as in the Mellon era. The ability to save and the incentive to produce were thoroughly released from the burden of oppressive taxes. The "country boy" who wished "to climb up the ladder" was told that even if his income was over $100,000, he would still keep 75 per cent of the excess. He was also informed that even if his accumulations were over $10 million, his family would still receive 80 per cent of the excess. Even the "builder who doesn't build the extra house" because of income taxes had little reason to refrain from further effort. He was assured that the modest rates were "a permanent peace-time tax structure."[14] Yet before the Mellon era came to a close, private enterprise collapsed. The lack of barriers and deterrents had failed to keep it going. Low taxes on the well-to-do had not assured prosperity for the others.

Now if facts were relevant, the ideology of barriers and deterrents would soon disappear. Very low rates were followed by unparalleled disaster. Very high rates have been accompanied by unprecedented growth. Despite Mellon's qualms over the estate tax, values are higher than ever. But since the facts are irrelevant, the ideologists of barriers and deterrents courageously carry on with the same words and phrases. Though they naturally hesitate to cite Mellon as an oracle, they faithfully echo his words and follow in his footsteps.[15] If imitation is the sincerest kind of flattery, no higher tribute can be paid.

I am not implying that the ideologists in question are wilfully closing their eyes to disagreeable facts. No other alternative is available to them. They are simply doing as well as they can. The constant objective has been small taxes on large incomes. Conceivably, the ideologists might argue that when a rate passes beyond a certain point, it becomes unethical and hence unworthy of enactment. In the light of experience, however, they realize that a resort to ethics is an essay in futility. The only available course is to speak of failing incentives and dwindling savings. This approach has the unmistakable virtue of selflessness. By relieving the larger incomes, we will safeguard all incomes. As the National Association of Manufacturers puts it, the "bulk" of the desired tax reduction will "flow to the energetic and ambitious," but those who are not so "energetic and ambitious" will profit even more—through "better jobs" and "standards of well-being yet to be achieved."[16] If the prosperous are taken care of, they will take care of the rest of us. There are those who unkindly describe such rationalizations as "the 'trickle-down' theory of taxation"—"if economic advantage is given to those taxpayers at the top, the rest of the people will eventually receive through a 'trickle down,' some undefined and unknown economic advantage."[17] Critics who indulge in such unfriendly comments are inexcusably harsh. They fail to understand that the ideologists have no choice but to speak of barriers and deterrents if they are to rationalize what they seek. They are the helpless captives of their own ideology.

The ideology has a related virtue which should not be overlooked. Our statesmen are akin to lawyers. They like to repeat what others have said. The ideology provides an abundant vocabulary to which they may regularly repair when tax reductions are to be justified. This extensive arsenal of words was amply displayed in the Republican observations preceding the reduction of 1948. In selecting this example I do not mean to slight the verbal capacities of the Democrats. They also know how to speak of barriers and deterrents when the need arises. But the Republicans are able to do so with a distinguished monotony that the Democrats are unable to acquire. In 1920 the Republicans announced that "one of the chief needs of the country is the revision of taxation as one way to lower the cost of living, restore business confidence, and stimulate enterprise."[18] From this program the Republicans have never departed. Nothing can shake their assumption that what has once been said is worth saying forevermore. Such a firm regard for the past is often referred to as an admirable adherence to principle. The precise content of the principle seems unimportant.

After many lean years the Republicans finally obtained control of Congress in 1946. As the ideology of barriers and deterrents prescribed, one of the first orders of business was a tax reduction in the higher brackets. The ideology also supplied the necessary words and phrases which Mellon would have readily appreciated. I now dip into the large assortment of sentences that may be found in the reports of the House Ways and Means Committee and the Senate Finance Committee.[19]

High taxes are "a real threat to the initiative and new investment essential to a high level of employment." They are "a serious obstacle" to the necessary "increase in production." They discourage the desire to earn more "by new investment, or by increased salary from acceptance of added responsibility." They deter "the opening of bottlenecks by management" and the "maintenance of a high level of business activity." "If the investors of the country are unwilling to take the risks of developing new enterprises and the managers do not have the incentive to put forth increased effort, the level of business activity will decline, to the detriment of all persons in our society." The "taxes of individuals in the middle and upper brackets" must be reduced in order to "stimulate investment and managerial incentive." "This stimulus consists primarily of the knowledge that from now on the net return allowed on a successful venture and the net reward paid for outstanding managerial achievement is going to be substantially greater than in the past." "The availability of sufficient risk capital to meet the needs of business is a significant factor in increasing production in the immediate future, and the paramount consideration for the long run." Because of high taxes there is an "inadequate supply of this risk capital." "The savings of the middle and upper bracket income recipients are the principal sources of the venture capital for business expansion." The "bulk of the relatively speculative business investments are made by individuals with incomes of $10,000 and over." But "today" these individuals "are for the most part seeking relatively riskless investments." In contrast, those "with smaller incomes not only save relatively little, but are apt to keep what they do save in cash, Government bonds, insurance policies, savings accounts, etc." What they do invest in enterprise "is likely to be invested in old, well-established business. Such persons have neither the information nor the time to examine the possibilities of making investments in new ventures, and cannot afford to assume the risks involved." A tax reduction will increase the willingness to invest of those who have the necessary income to do so. In addition, it will encourage "business managers to take on added responsibilities and work harder to make their businesses a success." "The decisions of the executives who receive relative [sic] large salaries are of greatest importance with reference to the development of industrial production."

It is difficult to find a better statement of the creed of barriers and deterrents among authoritative sources. All the usual verbalisms of the ideology are carefully collected, such as initiative and incentive, effort and risk, savings and investment, production and responsibility, risk capital and venture capital, obstacle and stimulus, bottlenecks and obstructions. Though the quoted portions are mere excerpts, I have tried to preserve the distinct effects of the originals by including a number of sentences that may seem mere repetition. Sustained reiteration is one of the important ingredients in the recipe, and I have no desire to alter the flavor. If something is said often enough, it may eventually become indisputable. As the Bellman cried while hunting for the Snark, "I have said it thrice; what I tell you three times is true." The various sentences yield the same familiar message. Private enterprise cannot keep going successfully because the high rates deter effort and investment. Taxes in the middle and upper brackets must be eased so that the system will function as it should. All this is stated as if we were in the presence of undeniable facts which sternly insist on one obvious conclusion.

Let us begin with the allegation that the rates are debilitating the desire to work and produce. If taxes are high, we are informed, ambitions inevitably falter. The situation is so serious that managers of enterprise are conspicuously refusing additional responsibilities with more income. The rates must be sharply reduced if our business executives are "to work and to grow."[20] In making these assertions the ideologists speak with a confidence that experts on incentives are unable to muster. I refer with profit to Professor Dan T. Smith, of the Harvard

Business School, who is also a prominent adherent of the faith. After looking into the matter, even Smith concluded that the efforts of executives are generally unaffected by high rates. Their "primary motivation," he reported, is not financial gain, but "the satisfactions which some men find in business activity and achievement." Happily, executives are not too different from other people. Many factors besides taxes influence their efforts and condition their behavior. "Other countries," Smith noted, "have had unimaginative business leadership without high taxation; we have thus far avoided stagnation in spite of high taxes." And, he added, "it is still true that in business activities one can get a higher level of economic welfare than in any other type of career."[21]

The empirical knowledge at our disposal indicates that managerial efforts are not sagging. Professor Thomas H. Sanders has found, on the basis of carefully accumulated data, that executives are not prone to lose interest in their work if their taxes are high. The common observations about declining incentives are at odds with the evidence. Taxes "are not sufficient to quell adventurous and vigorous spirits." Executives are working as hard as ever because their motives are much more entangled and varied than a simple aversion to taxes. Their efforts are sustained by a complex of "non-financial incentives to work, as well as the compulsions of administrative organization and disciplines." "The evidence is overwhelming that the business executive is putting a full measure of work and energy into his regular job." All the "grumbling at the taxes he pays" and the "wry allusions to working most of the time for the government" should not be taken seriously. There are no signs of lethargy. Executives have adjusted themselves to high rates and are "still going full blast." When their taxes were substantially reduced in 1948, they did not suddenly become more ambitious and energetic. On the whole, high taxes make them work even harder.[22]

Professor Challis A. Hall has made a related study of executives, and his conclusions are also reassuring. He emphasizes that the effect of taxes on incentives must be distinguished from their effect on efforts. Though monetary incentives have been reduced, executive exertions have not been impaired. There are two reasons for the persistence of managerial effort in the face of pecuniary adversity. First, "nonfinancial incentives or rewards" significantly determine "the level of executives' morale and effort." Among these stimulants are a desire for power and prestige, a need for security, a duty of loyalty, and a sense of achievement. Second, a "considerable monetary incentive" remains despite high taxes. Another finding is still more interesting. Even when executives receive compensation under an arrangement enabling them to pay less tax, their efforts and efficiency are not particularly increased. A number of executives interviewed by Professor Hall confided to him that "nonfinancial rewards are more closely related to efforts than financial rewards."[23]

The heartening views of Professors Sanders and Hall are fortified by Crawford H. Greenewalt, the president of Du Pont. Greenewalt doubts that high personal taxes have seriously affected "the performance of present-day management people." They are "reasonably immune" to adverse effects because one who "has reached a position of eminence within his organization" is "influenced importantly by his sense of loyalty, his sense of obligation, a preoccupying interest in the work, or, as has been unkindly suggested, by conditioned reflex." Greenewalt himself is the very model of a modern executive. Since he has a large income from investments, his entire compensation is taxed at the top rate of 91 per cent. "I think," he states, "that if I were motivated solely by what I put in my pants pocket I would quit around January 2." Yet he hastens to say, "I still work."[24] And he works just as hard after January as during January.

Nevertheless Greenewalt cannot refrain from worrying. While he is not troubled by the reduced monetary rewards of "the executive of today, or even of the immediate future," he fears that eventually high taxes will take their toll. It will be "more difficult than heretofore to persuade young men with real ability to enter the rank of business." It will also be harder to convince those "who have risen to the point where they are in sight of reaching their top capacity to keep on going rather than to rest on their oars." And, as our supply of executives dwindles, "all of us will face a bleak and static future." Here, of course, Greenewalt is in the realm of speculation. His vision of the future is dark because he yields to a pessimistic assumption. He sadly supposes that business will be at a competitive disadvantage in an environment of high taxes. It will be unable to attract or inspire sufficient talent, since it cannot offer the nonpecuniary satisfactions that other fields provide. Executives have little more to look forward to than money. To quote Greenewalt once again, "For businessmen there are few medals, prizes, degrees, uniforms, patriotic citations, or grandiose honorifics." They do not even enjoy the pleasures of being a celebrity. "With few exceptions executives of great ability remain relatively unknown. A player of even minor roles in the films, a leader of a jazz orchestra, or a writer of only average accomplishment may be far better known than many leaders of industry."[25] While these somber observations may be correct, they overlook the power, prestige, and influence that automatically attach to executives in the higher echelons of business. The eager pursuit of gain is our most respected activity. And the so-called ability to meet a payroll is one of those few things that make one an authority on all other things. Hence a successful career in business has been a prime qualification for appointment to the Cabinet.

If I may revise a familiar comment of President Cleveland, the ideology of barriers and deterrents confronts us with a theory—not a condition. More accurately, it is a dogma rather than a theory, for the relevant ascertainable facts are unimportant. At best we have a bare assumption on executive behavior which is then transformed into an authoritative doctrine not to be sullied by doubts. Nor is the assumption sustained by any apparent compulsion of deductive reasoning. If it be argued that high taxes make our managers work less because they retain less, it can also be argued that high taxes make them work more so they may have more. We may easily reason that a heavy tax bolsters incentives which might otherwise falter. It keeps people at work by reducing their ability to accumulate. As an expert who "detests" the income tax points out, "the people who are doing the hard work are increasingly the people in the upper-income brackets; the business and professional groups."[26] Or it can be urged that high taxes make people neither lazier nor busier because in the end they are more concerned with power, prestige, and achievement than with income after taxes. Business is their pleasure. Human nature, in the world of business as elsewhere, is more complex and adaptable than the ideology of barriers and deterrents assumes. The desire to make money is not the one key that unlocks the door of human behavior. Men are driven by other hopes and aspirations, of which they are often unaware. Since executives are like other human beings, they are not moved by bread alone.

Let us suppose, however, that Professors Sanders and Hall are too optimistic; that some executives have failed to adjust themselves to high rates and are disturbed by a tax neurosis. Let us further suppose that they would rather cease to be energetic businessmen than put up with an offensive tax burden. Even these assumptions would scarcely call for the bleak outlook of the ideology of barriers and deterrents. Managerial effort is not a faucet which the average executive can turn on or off as the rates are revised. Or, to alter the figure of speech, the mere fact that an executive is unhappy over taxes does not enable him to go off and sulk like Achilles in his tent. Secondly, private enterprise is not necessarily impaired by hastened departures from business. Earlier retirements may produce a net social gain, as younger individuals with fresher insights move into positions of authority. And those who retire may profit, too, for they may then enjoy the fruits of leisure. Economists Pechman and Mayer have noted that the "substitution of leisure for remunerative work may not be a dead loss from the economic standpoint. Home-owners, for example, may use their time at home to do their own plumbing and electrical work, carpentry, housepainting, or gardening."[27] While this statement seems beyond reproach, it does not go far enough. Why should leisure be justified solely in economic terms, as if the only relevant criteria are those prevailing in a society of industrious ants? A gross national product that increases from year to year is not the ultimate test of a worthy civilization. Much may be said for a tax system which induces people to do things other than work.

We may even ask a more subversive question. Is society necessarily the loser if taxes encourage the able to enter fields other than business? As I have just suggested, our well-being consists of more than the contributions of industrial enterprise. Very likely we would not have profited less if various executives had chosen to write or paint instead of producing or selling commodities. If we must think solely as economists, we may still conclude that the future of the economy does not depend only on the efforts of businessmen. Scientists, engineers, and others also serve in their own special ways. Dan T. Smith has suggested that our economic welfare might well be enhanced if the tax rates induced talented individuals to pursue careers in government rather than business.[28] Businessmen, too, have long felt that we should have more businessmen in government, though in the last few years they may have revised their views. So far, however, the high rates have not deterred many from deserting government for business. They stubbornly refuse to be discouraged from earning more money.

The dogma of declining effort is by no means confined to harried executives. It generously embraces everyone who labors for a living and sadly finds himself in the middle or upper brackets. When the dogma is appraised in all its ramifications, the results are curious. The first impression is that the country is going to wrack and ruin. Almost everyone who counts is discouraged. If executives are increasingly listless at their work, so are small businessmen, professionals, and entertainers. Even painters, composers, and writers refrain from being as creative as they would otherwise be. Taxes are depriving us of enjoyable books, and aesthetic sights and sounds. The results become "curiouser and curiouser" as we continue to contemplate the dogma. One ideologist warns that high taxes will divert the ambitious and energetic from the large corporations to other fields where financial incentives are not so important. At the same time a second ideologist warns that high taxes will send the ambitious and energetic from other fields to the large corporations. The situation is so serious that some "will go to work for the Government." A third ideologist takes a third view. High taxes, says Roswell Magill, are biased "in favor of a business career as the finest that life offers," whether the enterprise is large or small.[29]

Despite his heartening appraisal, Magill qualifies as one of the gloomier ideologists. On the subject of incentives he speaks with peculiar sorrow and uneasiness. The "money incentive for choosing any particular career," he states, "is largely gone." One "can hardly pick an occupation which will ultimately produce a private yacht or a private car or a mansion on Fifth Avenue. Certainly some occupations are still much better remunerated than others, but in hardly any is there much prospect of making a million dollars." "The ancestral home in the country" has practically disappeared. "So a wise father will advise his son to choose an occupation that is congenial and promises an adequate living, not necessarily a great income." Magill, indeed, wonders whether taxes are not inducing "men of unusually high caliber" to enter the ministry. The situation is especially grave in the legal profession. A prosperous law firm "can no longer honestly assure promising young men that if they become partners they can save money in substantial amounts, build country homes and gardens for themselves like their fathers and grandfathers did, and plan extensive European holidays." Magill is moved to ask whether a lawyer today has any chance of building the kind of home that Elihu Root owned on Park Avenue. Yet somehow Magill manages to relieve the gloom somewhat. He concedes that it is still possible to become a millionaire.[30]

What are we to make of Magill's analysis? On the whole, the future which he paints seems dark and discouraging. In the light of the past we have entered a cheerless period. However, a poignant yearning for other days has apparently endowed the past with a deceptive charm. We may doubt that new members of affluent law firms were usually assured of country homes in the United States and extended holidays in Europe. If we set aside such reconstructions of the past, exactly what remains? At best, Magill has established that a large income no longer provides the standard of living to which Elihu Root was accustomed. This item of information hardly indicates that lawyers of today are therefore working less vigorously than their equivalents of other days. But we would be unreasonable if we expected any such proof. The ideology of barriers and deterrents derives from an intense desire to enjoy a standard of living which would be available in the absence of high taxes. This desire, in turn, is linked with the welfare of society. Hence it is easily inferred and readily argued that if the desired mode of existence is not available, ambitions and efforts must steadily decline. A dogma can do without proof.

The dogma of declining effort leads on to the dogma of diminishing risk. This second doctrine is concerned with the incentive to invest. It informs us that there is no incentive to invest unless the prospective returns sufficiently exceed the attendant risks. Since high taxes leave meager returns, the well-to-do are disinclined to assume the risks. Therefore, we are dangerously deprived of the new investments on which private enterprise depends.

Again the reasoning consists essentially of the same two elements—a simple notion of psychology combined with a brief exercise in logic. It is first assumed that taxes singularly determine the decision to invest or not to invest. It is then inferred that since taxes are high, the desire to invest must be low. Those who are less persuaded by the dogma need not speculate on their own. Professor J. Keith Butters and his associates, of the Harvard Business School, have carefully probed and analyzed the evidence. In response to their findings they have rejected both the psychology and the logic to which the dogma resorts. The evidence reveals that taxes are only one factor among many that determine the investment policies of individuals. And "more often than not" the other factors are more important. These include the individual needs of the investor, his customary attitudes, and the economic climate. Inflation, for example, has been particularly prominent in the complex of motives. On the logic of the dogma Professor Butters and his colleagues are equally clear. They agree that the investment policies of taxpayers in the upper brackets are of "overwhelming importance." But they "have uncovered little, if any, evidence of a so-called general investors' strike which, if ended, would unloose a large flow of funds seeking equity investment."[31]

Even if taxes are erroneously isolated as the critical factor, the dogma of diminishing risk reflects a will to believe rather than a desire for accuracy. The effect of taxes must be appraised against the background of objectives which induce individuals to invest. Generally speaking, investors divide into two groups: the security-minded and the risk-minded. The security-minded are interested in capital preservation and a proper return, while the risk-minded are intent on capital appreciation. The risk-minded include a majority of all investors with incomes over $25,000.[32]

When tax considerations operate, the two groups are differently affected. On the one hand, the security-minded are induced to become more conservative. They shift to "lower yield, less risky investments" because the prior return after taxes is deemed inadequate for the hazards involved. To this extent high rates are "an investment deterrent," but such switches are "relatively small." On the other hand, under the influence of taxes the risk-minded become even more venturesome. It is "overwhelmingly" clear that for them the vital factor is the capital gain rate as compared with the ordinary rates. "This differential has stimulated inherently venturesome individuals to seek out investments which offered prospects of capital gains rather than the receipt of ordinary income." They are impelled to move from conservative holdings to speculative listed equities, closely held companies, new ventures, real estate, and oil properties. The charm of oil is especially enhanced by the special dispensations provided for the industry. The combined effect, then, of the ordinary rates and the capital gain rate is to reinforce the individual traits of investors. The security-minded become more cautious and the risk-minded more daring.[33]

This conclusion is confirmed by a painstaking inquiry in two areas of investment—new issues of stock and new ventures. According to the findings, most investors have little interest in new issues, regardless of taxes. Only a small group are "favorably inclined," and their "dominant incentive" is capital appreciation. While a minority within this group is affected by taxes, on the whole there are no adverse effects. Some are deterred from investing in new issues, but others are stimulated to acquire them. The stimulating effects may exceed the deterring effects. In 1951, for example, investments in new issues were half again as large as in 1949. The report on new ventures is about the same. The tax-affected individuals are about equally divided between those who are deterred and those who are stimulated. Most of the deterred are conservative investors who are in any event disinclined to place sizable sums in a new business. Most of the stimulated are venturesome investors who are already disposed toward such risks. The capital gain rate "definitely" induces them "to invest a larger proportion of their funds in new ventures." All in all, "the facts do not justify the extreme statements often made with respect to the effects of taxes on the supply of venture capital. The tax incentives operate in both directions, and it may well be that those tending to channel funds to new ventures actually outweigh in significance those tending to divert funds from such investments."[34]

We come to the third dogma—the dogma of inadequate savings. Here the thesis is that we are suffering from a critical lack of capital because high taxes consume potential savings at the upper levels of income. There are strong suggestions that the United States is an underdeveloped country desperately in need of funds. To quote one of many statements of the dogma, the "equity capital necessary to finance an expanding economy and full employment" is "pitifully inadequate." Individual investors are unable to accumulate the funds that are so urgently required by new and growing businesses.[35] At this point the dogma becomes obscure. It speaks confidently of a shortage of savings, but what is the criterion of adequacy which is being applied? Is the dogma merely saying that the demand for savings has exceeded the supply? Or is it projecting a future rate of growth, and asserting that the necessary savings will not be available for the desired growth? Some of the believers, it seems, entertain the first notion of adequacy; others, the second; and still others, both the first and the second.

While it might be rewarding to clarify these ambiguities, some relevant facts are probably more informative. At the very least they indicate the scope of the problem on which the dogma dwells.

To begin with, if any problem exists, it is not so pervasive and ominous as the dogma suggests. Adolf Berle has estimated that from 1919 to 1947 the gross capital formation in the United States was about $770 billion. Of this total, merely 2 per cent, or $15 billion, derived from individual savings invested in new issues of common stock. And of this 2 per cent, only a portion was exposed to the hazards of new ventures. In short, "only a tiny fragment of risk capital is ventured by individuals."[36]

Even within its narrow province the dogma speaks too freely. The dogma assumes that new enterprises precariously depend on large savings accumulated by potential investors for their equity capital. The evidence, however, is much more restrained. The initial funds of a new business are usually provided by those who organize and operate it. They are reluctant to obtain equity capital from others because they are unwilling to share ownership and control. Of course, as the business develops, they may have to call upon others in order to expand. The individuals who respond to such requests for aid are usually investors in search of capital gains. But if the company can expand on retained earnings, it will forego outside capital. Retained earnings are preferred as a means of growth because, once again, outside capital will dilute ownership and control. As the company continues to prosper, outside capital becomes even less significant. And as the company matures, its ability to borrow increases. American business, then, has relied primarily on retained earnings rather than new capital to finance its growth. New capital, supplied by individual investors, is at most important in the earlier years of growth. Moreover, not all individual investors will furnish this capital. Generally, only those who are animated by a desire for capital gains will do so. The role of individual investors as a source of venture capital has been "greatly exaggerated."[37]

The next question is whether high taxes have left too little to invest as new capital. This question focuses on the small group of individuals with large incomes, for it is their capacity to invest with which the dogma is concerned. As Professor Butters and his associates have shown, the answer is clear. Taxes have not "wiped out, or anywhere nearly wiped out, the capacity of upper bracket individuals to accumulate new investable funds." Their savings "have been consistently large in postwar years, both in absolute amounts and as a percentage of the total accumulations by all individuals." The findings do not coincide with the "frequent" complaint that "existing tax rates practically preclude individuals with large incomes from saving." Personal savings were $8.5 billion in 1949. Despite tax increases over the next two years, savings were $12.6 billion in 1950, and $17.7 billion in 1951. Since 1950 personal savings each year have averaged 7 per cent of income after taxes, as compared with 5 per cent for 1929. No less important, annual accumulations are concentrated where the ideology of barriers and deterrents expects them to be. One per cent of all families—those with incomes over $15,000—has about 35 per cent of the savings.[38]

There are two basic reasons for the continuing capacity to save. First, individuals in the upper regions persist in the habit of accumulation. Each year at least half of those in the top 1 per cent save 20 per cent or more of their income before taxes. Second, many in the upper regions do not bear the burdens which the progressive rates supposedly impose. They enjoy the privilege of paying much less through special dispensations devised in their behalf.[39]

Facts, the saying goes, are stubborn things; but so are dogmas. Hence it is not surprising that the dogma of inadequate savings has come to full bloom in the least congenial circumstances. If the dogma is correct, the economy should have been in a sorry condition. Instead it has paid no attention to the dogma. The years since World War II have been a period of considerable growth. In the period 1946 to 1959 real income per capita increased by almost 20 per cent. In 1959 it was about 33 per cent more than in 1929, when the population was 55 million less.[40] Yet in 1929 the highest individual rate was 25 per cent, and now the lowest rate is 20 per cent. In 1929 the corporate rate was 12 per cent, while now it is 30 per cent on the first $25,000 and 52 per cent on the remainder.[41]

Though a dogma may be oblivious to disrespectful facts, the differences may eventually be too conspicuous to ignore. The dogma of inadequate savings is particularly susceptible to such difficulties. It was designed to satisfy those with smaller incomes that the economy must decay unless the progressive rates on larger incomes are greatly reduced. If the contradictions become obvious, as they have in recent years, the dogma may fail to be properly persuasive. The problem is not that the believers will begin to doubt, but that the doubters will refuse to believe. Even confirmed adherents of barriers and deterrents grudgingly admit that "our traditional system" has been successfully maintained "in spite of our tax laws." Various excuses have been offered. Some have strangely said, "Were it not for the full employment and great national prosperity of these present years, our tax burden might have braked the economy to a stop." As I understand this novel explanation, prosperity has prevented high taxes from causing a depression. Or, instead of relying on such reasoning, they may gravely observe, "It takes time for the symptoms of cancer to show, and, in the meantime one can be seemingly healthy and strong."[42] In such unhappy circumstances only one solution will do. The dogma must be bolstered by additional rationalizations which compensate for the noticeable discrepancies.

A crisis of this sort developed in 1947 and 1948, when the Republicans diligently reduced taxes in the upper brackets. In 1946 the gross national product was over $210 billion, or almost as much as the record output during the war. In the same year gross private domestic investment was over $28 billion, or almost $18 billion more than the record investment during the war. Corporate profits after taxes had never been so high since 1929. Amid such data it seemed odd to say that the economy was in dire need of additional capital for expansion. Evidently the Congressional adherents of barriers and deterrents also realized that the economy was not deteriorating for lack of capital. In 1948 they conceded, with some emphasis, that the output of goods and services had been steadily increasing. They even declared, "It is now quite generally agreed that for some time at least income levels not only will remain high, but will continue to rise."[43]

Yet the ideologists were not discouraged. To the usual observations on high taxes and inadequate savings they added others. They reasoned, for example, that output had not increased enough, and therefore inflation was becoming worse. The ultimate solution for inflation, the ideologists repeatedly explained, was production. Only "increased production" was "the most satisfactory answer to the high prices resulting from the pressure of pent-up demand on a limited supply." But high taxes were a serious obstacle to more production. They deterred "the productivity of labor, the breaking of bottlenecks by management, and the willingness of investors to assume risks." Reduced rates would soon provide the required incentives for greater output and the "removal of bottlenecks." They would improve "the productivity of labor," stimulate "the initiative of our business managers," and leave sufficient profits "to attract investors into risk-taking enterprise." In the end lower taxes would bring lower prices. However, the ideologists added, while it was necessary to encourage labor to be more productive, it was also necessary to distinguish between large incomes and small incomes. Too much relief for taxpayers in the low brackets would only increase the inflationary pressures, for these taxpayers "spend nearly all of their current income."[44]

The homilies on inflation enhance the ideology of barriers and deterrents in two respects. First, they make the ideology less embarrassing and awkward. One need no longer argue that the economy cannot function unless taxes are reduced. Instead one can argue that prices are too high because taxes are too high. Second, those in the bottom brackets are given a new reason why more relief should be bestowed in the upper brackets. If lower taxes are imposed on smaller incomes, prices will rise. But if lower taxes are imposed on larger incomes, prices will fall. A critic might charge that the ideologists have faltered where they should have been steadfast. In view of their reasoning, only the rates in the upper brackets should be reduced. Further reductions in the bottom brackets can only add to the perils of inflation by leaving more funds available for consumer goods. However, any such comments would be undeserved. Economic logic must yield to political expediency. There cannot be a reduction above without some reduction below. As a result, the same ideologists who feared that a reduction below would increase inflationary pressures, were also compelled to rejoice that it would increase purchasing power.[45] Consistency is not easily attained if everybody must be pleased.

The co-existence of high production and high rates produced another variation on the familiar theme of barriers and deterrents. The adherents began to reason that the rates in the upper brackets had to be pared in order to prevent a recession. They admitted that the prevailing levels of employment and output were high. But they also argued that the proposed reduction in the upper brackets would help maintain those levels by providing "a hedge against recession." It was immaterial that no recession had yet appeared. If Congress waited until it was upon us, the reduction would come too late. The reduction had to "be made now, since a considerable period must elapse before these tax-reduction measures achieve their full economic effects."[46]

This rationalization is a significant advance in the ideology of barriers and deterrents. It is a wise adjustment to conditions that were not anticipated. Under the old view prosperity is impossible if taxes in the upper brackets are too high. Under the new view the presence of prosperity is no longer disturbing. No matter how well the economy is doing, a recession is always possible. A reduction in the upper brackets will avoid this danger by inducing their occupants to be more energetic in their efforts and more daring in their investments. The virtue of such reasoning is that it never ends. After every reduction a recession is still possible. Though the new view seems an impressive response to a formidable problem, I must add that the ideologists themselves have not always been similarly impressed. In 1947 they maintained that taxes should be reduced because a recession might otherwise come. In 1958 they maintained that taxes should not be reduced though a recession had already arrived. Some may ungraciously suggest that a rationalization which is so easily discarded is not above suspicion.[47]

Finally, one other attempt has been made to adapt the ideology of barriers and deterrents to the unfortunate condition of high production with high taxes. It is not denied that the postwar era has been one of appreciable growth. But a vital distinction is drawn between "normal incentives" and other incentives. The Eisenhower Administration was especially enamored of this distinction as a happy solution to an unpleasant problem.

The year 1953 was a very difficult one for the ideology of barriers and deterrents. Everything seemed to go wrong. The gross national product, personal income, and business outlays all advanced to record levels. Economic activity and employment reached "new peaks" as private demand expanded. The year was "one of substantial achievements in terms of utilization of manpower and industrial resources, additions to productive capacity, higher consumer living standards, and over-all stability of prices."[48] Despite such trying data the Administration was not discouraged. In his Budget Message of 1954 the President announced that the tax laws must be revised "to restore normal incentives for sustained production and economic growth." He attributed the recent expansion to "recurring inflation," and then continued, "We must restore conditions which will permit traditional American initiative and production genius to push on to ever-higher standards of living and employment." The tax committees echoed the President. "The restrictive effects of the present law on economic growth," they declared, "have been obscured and somewhat offset during the past decade by the inflationary pressures of the war and postwar decades." Reforms are necessary "in order to create an environment in which normal incentives can operate to maintain normal economic growth." Treasury spokesmen resorted to the same newly discovered thought. "As one looks forward to normal growth," Dan T. Smith explained, "the importance of restoring normal incentives and removing punitive tax provisions becomes clear."[49]

I would like to admire this further rationalization but, unfortunately, in the realm of ideas I am unable to admire what I cannot understand. Of course, an ideology may be impressive precisely because it is incomprehensible. But since I lack the devotion of a believer, I am compelled to rely on the meaning which words supposedly convey. What are normal incentives as distinguished from presumably abnormal incentives? Are we to infer that incentives are never normal in a period of inflation? If inflationary pressures have only somewhat offset the restrictive effects of taxes on economic growth, how are we to account for most of the vast growth that has occurred? Amid all the observations, however, one thing seems clear. It is strongly implied that recent growth has not derived from normal incentives, and that only growth due to such incentives can be credited to American initiative and production genius. Yet this thought leaves me very troubled and uneasy. It suggests that American businessmen are not entitled to praise for the tremendous expansion of the economy. They have merely been the compliant instruments of a higher power known as inflation.

Although the facts have failed to cooperate, we need not fear that the rhetoric of barriers and deterrents will soon disappear. The same words and phrases will continue to march gaily along as if nothing had gone astray. If the ideology does not fit the facts, so much the worse for the facts. Therefore, if "employment, pay rolls, and industrial activity" rise to "the highest records ever known," a Secretary of the Treasury can take credit for the results, and then proceed to say that taxes "inhibit growth and incentive and deter initiative and development of a vigorous free economy." Another expert can write that "economic growth has, thus far, continued without deceleration," and then promptly warn that when tax rates pass beyond 50 per cent our "economic incentive" is eroded "at a rapidly accelerating rate." And a ranking member of the Ways and Means Committee can glowingly describe the Mellon era as the "greatest period of prosperity" ever "enjoyed by the people," but forget to add that the removal of barriers and deterrents was followed by the Great Depression.[50]

CHAPTER 5

By Incentives Possessed

I return to the *Pollock* case[1] for illumination and guidance. As the arguments in that case disclosed, both sides agreed that the tax of 1894 was designed for the pecuniary discomfort of the rich. The personal exemption of $4,000 was the chosen means of discrimination. And so the eminent counsel for the well-to-do condemned the levy as an act of "exaction and confiscation" rather than "taxation." A tax is truly a tax, they maintained, only if it is "equal and uniform and not of selected individuals or classes." Moreover, they argued, equality before the law is forever gone if the majority may tax the minority without taxing themselves. William D. Guthrie, one of the distinguished spokesmen, put it bluntly and urgently: "we are here to plead that Congress cannot sacrifice one—the lowliest or the richest—for the benefit of others."[2] At the precise moment of this impressive utterance, Guthrie may have been more interested in the richest than the lowliest, but the immediate cause of his anxiety does not obscure the basic question of principle that he raised.

His colleague Joseph H. Choate had another complaint. The exemption of $4,000 not only distinguished between rich and poor, but also discriminated among the prosperous. "Some exemptions," Choate stated, "are always defended as established in order to prevent grinding in the faces of the poor; to prevent taking the ordinary comforts, if you please, out of the mouths and off the tables of the mechanic and laborer; in a word, to admit of perfect comfort in every household in the land."[3] But the allowance of $4,000 was well beyond "that principle of public policy." It exempted people who enjoyed "perfect comfort" without working. On what ground, he asked, should an exemption be conferred on someone who lives "in idleness and in clover, drawing $4,000 a year net, from invested securities?" If an exemption of $4,000 is reasonable, then any larger exemption is no less rational. Hence if the line were drawn at $20,000, "a man with $666,000 at 3 per cent, or $500,000 at 4 per cent," would also be "a fit subject for exemption."[4]

The act of 1894 made still other distinctions which disturbed Guthrie and his brethren. While individuals had an exemption of $4,000, corporations had no exemption at all. While corporations for the pursuit of gain were taxable, savings banks, mutual insurance companies, and building and loan associations were tax-free. These differences were also assailed with appropriate words of reproach. Exemptions were equated with inequality, and inequality was spoliation.

"If exemptions are to be granted," the argument ran, "then such exemptions must be equally allowed to those who have their means invested in corporations and who derive their income from the corporate profits." Individual enterprise and corporate enterprise must be treated alike. Nor may Congress grant tax immunity to certain "favored private corporations and associations." As Guthrie stated, "If the business of an insurance company is conducted on the stock plan for the benefit of all shareholders, every dollar of profit is taxed; if it is carried on for the benefit of its members or policyholders, who are but another form of shareholders, it is wholly exempted." Guthrie granted, perhaps reluctantly, that the power to tax includes the power to exempt, but he insisted that an exemption must be justified by "some public interest." Though he was not too helpful in distinguishing "public" interests from "private" interests, of one thing he was sure. "Private enterprises for the primary benefit of their members can never be aided under the guise of the discretion to exempt." Choate was still bolder. He would not even condone the most hallowed of exemptions—those enjoyed by religious associations. "Take Trinity church" in New York, he declared, "with its hundreds of parcels of real property and stores and houses and millions of property, from which it receives a fabulous income. Is there any public policy in exempting that income at the expense of the poorer sections of the country?"[5]

The warm observations which I have quoted are undoubtedly

touched with ambiguity. But it is not unusual for large statements of principle to be indistinct. Otherwise they would not sound as effective as they often do. When a generality is carefully hedged with exceptions and refinements, its persuasive quality may be seriously impaired. Although we may wish that the statements in question were more lucid, they seem clear enough for present purposes.

The spokesmen for the well-to-do were rigidly opposed to special exemptions for special groups. Income was income. If equality was to be maintained, no distinctions could be drawn in terms of the amount, source, or receiver of the income. This rule of equality was subject to only one grudging exception. The income of certain recipients could be spared if the exemption reflected some "public interest." But this one exception was very narrowly confined. An exemption was not imbued with the necessary public interest if it was bestowed on an organization engaged in business for profit. Aside from the lonely exception, the controlling principle was equality. The rich were not to be distinguished from the poor, nor corporations from individuals. Even exemptions for churches were viewed with suspicion. An income tax must be a classless tax. Mr. Justice Field succinctly summarized the matter. Any personal exemption, he said, no matter how small, is pernicious "class legislation." Besides, he added, an exemption for the poor would only deprive them of "their manliness and self-respect."[6]

The plea for equality was a sensitive response to a practical problem. It was apprehensively assumed that before long the income tax would be exclusively reserved for the very prosperous. If equality prevailed, this distressing situation would be avoided. No one anticipated that the income tax would become a mass tax, as budgets swelled beyond the tax-paying capacities of the affluent. But once the Sixteenth Amendment was adopted and a progressive income tax was approved, the plea for equality died away. There was no use in continuing to insist, in the fashion of the earlier Senator Lodge, that the income tax was the "pillage of a class."[7] New problems called for new solutions, and the required rationalizations soon emerged. Instead of the vain talk of equality we now have what I conveniently call the ideology of barriers and deterrents.

If we scan the rates of the income tax, the ideology of barriers and deterrents seems a dismal failure. The rates rise to 91 per cent on taxable income over $200,000. Even if we allow for income splitting between husband and wife, the initial impression remains about the same. For married couples the rate on income exceeding $200,000 is at best only two points less than 91 per cent. The table of rates is a far cry from the schedule of 1913, when the top rate was merely 7 per cent on taxable income over $500,000.

But the ideology of barriers and deterrents cannot end with the rates. It is grimly concerned with the survival of investment and production. Its function is to shield private enterprise from destruction through progressive taxes on income and wealth. This significant service may be performed in two ways. One method, as we have seen, is to obtain a rate reduction for those in the upper brackets. The other method is to obtain a special dispensation for a particular class, group, or interest whose incentives are dangerously barred or deterred. The distinct advantage of this second method is that it leaves the progressive rates intact. As a result, taxpayers in the lower brackets continue to suppose that the pain above is much greater, while various taxpayers in the upper brackets are pleasantly aware that their suffering is exaggerated.

Under the ideology of barriers and deterrents, then, all incomes need not be treated equally. Special exceptions are appropriate in special situations. If so, what becomes of the plea for equality which the affluent made in the *Pollock* case? Income is income, they ably argued, and Congress cannot provide dispensations for favored groups that are engaged in the pursuit of gain. If I may repeat the eloquent words of Guthrie, an income tax must be "equal and uniform and not of selected individuals or classes." Those who would detect a contradiction here are too troubled by discrepancies. As Emerson indicated, it is foolish to indulge in "foolish consistency." The demand for equality was a means to an end—the prevention of an income tax on the well-to-do. Since the effort had failed, the demand for equality gives way to a demand for exceptions. Income may be income, but one income is not the same as another.

The exceptions vary, but they all have one thing in common. Each is designed to avert economic decay. True, certain taxpayers are the inevitable beneficiaries of the special exceptions, but the benefits which accrue to them are only incidental to the greatest good of the greatest number.

The most venerable exception is the familiar dispensation for investors—the special rate for capital gains. This dispensation distinguishes between "long-term" gains and "short-term" gains from the sale or exchange of stock or some other capital asset. A gain is long-term if the property is held for more than 6 months, and short-term if it is held for any shorter period. The tax on long-term gains is only half the tax that would otherwise be due on the same amount of income—subject to a significant limit. No matter how much income the taxpayer may have, the top rate on long-term gains is 25 per cent. The line between long- and short-term gains is drawn at 6 months in order to separate investors from speculators. Only investors deserve the special rate of 25 per cent. Speculators are treated no better than workers. They are fully subject to the ordinary rates.

Though taxpayers in the lowest bracket are asked to pay 20 per cent on their earned income, their brethren in the higher regions are expected to pay only 5 per cent more on their long-term capital gains. The taxpayers now enjoying this dispensation are married couples with taxable income over $36,000, heads of households with income over $24,000, and single individuals with income over $18,000. If a married man has a taxable income of $8,000 and receives a raise of $500, the tax on his additional earnings is 26 per cent. But if a married man has a taxable income of $100,000 and realizes a capital gain of $500,000, the tax on his additional profit is 25 per cent. In effect, the special rate for capital gains is a progressive tax reduction. The benefit increases as income increases. For married couples the regular rates are 59 per cent at $50,000, 75 per cent at $100,000, and 89 per cent at $200,000. The dispensation reduces the rates by 57.7 per cent at $50,000, 66.7 per cent at $100,000, and 72 per cent at $200,000. Adherents of ability to pay may find this situation strange and incongruous. If they do, they have only themselves to blame. They are inadequately attentive to the ideology of barriers and deterrents.

As the ideology instructively insists, there are good reasons for the small difference between the lowest rate on ordinary income and the special rate on capital gains. If the gains are more heavily taxed, we will foolishly kill the geese that lay the golden eggs. A higher rate will discourage those with substantial means from supplying capital to new and growing businesses. For it will make them unwilling to dispose of old investments in order to provide the necessary funds. An "excessive tax on capital gains freezes transactions"; it deters "the free flow of capital into productive enterprises." As the problem is currently stated, investments are "locked in."[8] The Ways and Means Committee has given us a simple example. "Suppose an individual with a large net income desires, as a matter of investment, to place some of his money in an airplane factory. It might be a new factory in which he is interested or he might come to the rescue of an existing factory which is desperately in need of capital. The usual way in which this is accomplished is for him to buy securities in the corporation. In order to do this, he will be compelled to sell certain of his property in order to raise money to make the investment. If the capital gains tax is too high, it will prevent him from undertaking the enterprise." As an unfortunate by-product of such paralysis, the Treasury will lose the revenue which it now obtains from capital gains.[9] If all these evils are to be avoided, investors must be kept content with the special dispensation. In enabling them to pay much less, we are wisely assuring our own future.

Until 1921 capital gains were taxed like other income. Between 1913 and 1919 the maximum rate rose from 7 per cent to 77 per cent, and from 1919 to 1921 it was 73 per cent. Yet somehow, private enterprise managed to survive. In 1921 this precarious situation came to an end. The top rate was reduced to 58 per cent, and a separate rate was fixed for capital gains. Initially the special rate was set at 12½ per cent. The Ways and Means Committe and the Finance Committee agreed that the dispensation was urgently required. "The sale of farms, mineral properties, and other capital assets," they reported, was "seriously retarded" because "gains and profits earned over a series of years" were "taxed as a lump sum" in the year of the sale at progressive rates. Since many such sales had been blocked, the revenue had suffered. "In order to permit such transactions to go forward without fear of a prohibitive tax," the lesser rate was clearly necessary.[10] Under the dispensation as granted in 1921, a gain qualified for the special rate if the investment was held more than 2 years rather than 6 months.

Some adherents of ability have persuaded themselves that the dispensation was originally designed as an averaging device. Before 1921 a profit accruing over an extended period was taxed as one lump sum in the year in which it was realized. Since the rates were progressive, the resulting burden was often much heavier than it would have been if the gain had been reported piecemeal from year to year. According to these adherents of ability, the special rate was devised as a fair equivalent of the lesser burden that would have been borne if the tax had been paid on that basis.[11] But a flat rate of 12½ per cent hardly purported to average annual burdens imposed by progressive rates ranging up to 58 per cent. Those who proposed the dispensation were disturbed by a problem quite different from averaging. They feared that if the tax on capital gains exceeded 12½ per cent, investors would refrain from shifting to new ventures in need of their capital. The controlling purpose was to remove "the decided interference with the normal course of business and commerce." High progressive rates were "a severe artificial restraint on sales at a profit."[12] The requirement that the property be held at least 2 years was added toward the end at the insistence of a few senators who did not want short-term speculators to pay less tax than individuals engaged in a business or profession.[13] The explanation given by the adherents of ability is a tenacious refusal to concede unpleasant facts.

A few questions may linger on. But they are not serious once we grasp the ideology of barriers and deterrents as it applies to capital gains. Various doubters have wondered whether a 6-month holding period is a sensible way to distinguish investors, who deserve the dispensation, from speculators, who do not. If the purpose is to encourage the prosperous to invest in a new or growing business, they should also be encouraged to remain in the enterprise for a longer period. Is it wise to induce a quick sale rather than a sustained investment? Does a fleeting ownership of stock create a sufficient interest in the operation of the business? These questions are less searching than they may seem. In drawing the line at 6 months, Congress was not concerned with those who have already contributed new capital to a business. It was concerned rather with those who simply hold marketable securities or other assets without adding anything to any business. The lower rate after 6 months stimulates them to sell their securities and place the proceeds in an enterprise which needs new capital. Once they have provided the required funds, they have fully done their duty. What they later do with their stock is immaterial. The capital which they have supplied remains in the business, whether or not they hold on to their investment. In fact, a quick sale is the very essence of their function. The sooner they sell, the sooner they can supply capital to some other business in need of their aid. If we are to have new and growing businesses, they must remain free to contribute on short notice.

Some may ask whether this answer is adequate. If the purpose is as I have stated it, then the dispensation should be reserved only for those who actually convert their investments into new venture capital. Why should the dispensation be granted as well to investors who merely move from one marketable security to another without adding anything to the productive capital of the economy? Here, too, the questions reveal an unfortunate failure in understanding. If investors are to make the desired conversion to venture capital, they must have a going market in which they can promptly dispose of their prior investments. But, as the ideology of barriers and deterrents informs us, such markets will not be available if profits on the sale of securities are subjected to the progressive rates. They also serve who merely buy and sell pieces of paper in General Motors or Du Pont, for they stoutly maintain the required markets. Therefore, the dispensation is no less necessary for them—as long as they do not buy and sell too rapidly.

Now and then a stubborn doubter asks another question. Why should income from services be more heavily taxed than income from the sale of capital assets? Even if drones perform an important function, does it follow that they should be better treated than taxpayers who are more energetically engaged in earning their keep? Again the ideology provides the answer. The problem is a matter of economics, not ethics. One who invests will not move from one risk to another if he will be deprived of a substantial portion of his accretion in wealth. Unless he is otherwise threatened by a loss, he may as well continue with the same investments. But one who works is not similarly deterred by high taxes. It is always to his advantage to receive more income, though he may not keep as much as he would like.[14]

Someone may suggest that this explanation will not do, because it contradicts the ideology of barriers and deterrents. The ideology declares, through the dogma of declining effort, that if progressive taxes are too high, those who work and produce will also be deterred from contributing to the economy. Where, then, is the alleged difference in deterrence between income through capital gains and income through personal services? The easy answer is that it is not unusual for dogmas within the same ideology to be in a state of inconsistency. Since they are addressed to different problems, they are not always fully responsive to the demands of logic. Nevertheless we need not resort to such an answer here. If the matter is closely examined, the inconsistency soon disappears. The dogma of declining effort does not deny that there is an advantage in earning more income, though most of it is taken away. It simply asserts that if too much is taken, the advantage will not be considered worthy of the additional effort. In the case of capital gains the ideology goes one step further. It maintains that when the rates are high, there is not even the advantage of receiving more income. The taxpayer's risk of loss on a new investment exceeds his present profit, after taxes, on his old investment.

One other question may still be disturbing. Why do investors require a lower rate than businessmen in order to reveal their capacity to be enterprising and daring? Why should a sale of stock be treated more generously than a sale of groceries? A skeptic recently argued that if the dispensation for capital gains "spurs anybody into anything it spurs them into inactivity." The "benefits are available, in the main, only to those who invest and do nothing more to enhance the value of their investment."[15]

This is, indeed, a serious charge. It does not become less grave as it continues. Two individuals are compared. One buys a 20-acre tract "in the suburbs that looks like a good investment because of the anticipated future population growth." If he "holds it for a couple of years and does nothing whatever to improve it, he is assured of this special tax treatment on the gain he derives from this investment." The other buys a second 20-acre tract in the same area. In order to make it "attractive and available for residence purposes," he subdivides it and improves it. Unlike the gain of his inactive neighbor, his profits are taxed at the ordinary rates. For his pains in making "a useful and economic addition to the community," he has less after taxes than the one who does nothing. The criticism reaches still further. The theory of the dispensation for capital gains "ignores" the fact that the "commodity market is more hazardous than the stock market." Yet "millions are invested every day" in fluctuating inventories, though the resulting profits are taxed at the ordinary rates. Businessmen "are willing to take substantial chances" even when "the ensuing profits are to be taxed at the present corporate rate of 52 percent."[16]

While these strictures seem to be telling blows, they belabor an imaginary issue. The dispensation for capital gains was not devised for those who are creative and productive. Hence it is irrelevant to compare the tax burdens of active businessmen and inactive investors. Nor does the ideology of barriers and deterrents deny that businessmen take risks just as investors do. But it carefully adds that their risks are different. A businessman has no choice but to sell his goods if he is to remain in business. Continued sales at a profit are the core of his vocation. The function of an investor, however, is to supply capital where it is needed. If he is to perform his assignment adequately, he must feel free to shift his capital from one business to another. The special rate is necessary in order to make sure that he is not discouraged from responding to the call of duty. His lack of discouragement is known as mobility of capital.

Though a top rate of 25 per cent seems rather pleasant, the ideologists of barriers and deterrents are still dissatisfied. In their view the dispensation is much too niggardly; and, as usual, they contemplate disaster if Congress fails to be more generous. The present provisions, they say, critically retard economic growth, with "resulting ill effects on employment and wages." Vast sums are "locked in" or "frozen"—"immobilized by the present holding period and rate provisions of the capital gains tax law." Investors who would gladly offer venture capital to new and growing enterprises are deterred from doing so. And they are deterred because, first, they must wait as long as 6 months to obtain the special rate, and, second, the special rate is as high as 25 per cent. Even if many investors pay this onerous tax—as they apparently do—the situation is no better; for the tax "excessively erodes our reservoirs of capital wealth." A prompt solution is vital if we are to assure "ample equity funds for future capital investment and a stronger financial foundation for our country's continuing economic development." It would release billions of dollars for small business that are now reluctantly tied up in stocks of such corporations as Du Pont and General Motors. As a worried Congressman stated amid mixed metaphors, "we are killing the golden-egg geese, drying up the springs from which flow new money into the Federal Treasury."[17]

Fortunately, our economic condition is not as desperate as these observations suggest. As some ideologists of barriers and deterrents concede, the special rate of 25 per cent is beneficial as well as harmful. It "creates an incentive which motivates large numbers of investors in the upper income tax brackets to hold and even purchase common stock. They are interested in obtaining additional wealth subject to the lowest possible rate of tax." And so, despite a tax of 25 per cent, they are "providing a tremendous amount of capital for small business."[18] Where there are two sets of rates and one is much higher than the other, the well-to-do are induced to venture forth in quest of the other. They are impelled to engage in the kind of transactions which the ideology of barriers and deterrents seeks to foster.

The ideology, however, provides several answers for those who might be led astray by this confession. If a lesser tax on capital gains stimulates investments, a still smaller tax or no tax at all will be even more stimulating. Then there is the familiar argument that a tax on capital gains is akin to a levy on capital rather than income. Or, as the point is made by Congressman Wilson of Indiana, in "a real sense" the tax is a "confiscation of capital."[19] Evidently capital gains are a way of becoming wealthy without receiving any income. Charles Klem, of the New York Stock Exchange, has somewhat altered the argument. "In the eyes of many an investor," he states, "the capital gains tax is really a transfer tax which he is assessed for the privilege of shifting his investments."[20] This revised version invites a new problem which might well be avoided. If the capital gains tax is an unjust levy on investors for the privilege of shifting investments, then the ordinary income tax on employees may be regarded as an unjust levy for the privilege of working. Apparently economist Hayek has the most impressive answer of all. He carefully distinguishes between profits from business and income from services. The taxation of profits, he writes, "amounts in fact to a tax on the turnover of capital." For "from a social point of view, at least the larger part of profits" is not "income at all in the sense in which the average man thinks of income." It is rather "part of a constant process of redistribution of capital from the unsuccessful to the successful."[21] To put it simply, when investors realize profits, they are merely taking something out of the mouths of others. Only those who work should pay an income tax, because only they are successful enough to receive income.

Whatever the rationalizations may be, the ideal solution is obvious. The tax on capital gains should be completely repealed. A more modest proposal would eliminate the tax for those gains which are promptly reinvested in other capital assets. An investor would be able to move from one security to another without paying any tax as his wealth increased.[22] His freedom from tax would assure freedom of trade, and both freedoms would secure the future of those who would continue to pay. Other suggestions would settle for less—at least for the fleeting present. In 1950, for example, both tax committees tried hard to reduce the required holding period from 6 months to 3 months. They reasoned that 6 months is longer than necessary to distinguish investors from speculators. They also felt that a holding period as long as 6 months "has a disturbing effect on prices in the markets for capital assets." It compels investors to delay their sales in order to qualify for the special rate; and, as a result, the available supply of securities is too small to check rising prices. A shorter holding period would "reduce this tendency, thus contributing to the stabilization of the security markets." Yet the committees hesitated to be entirely logical. If a holding period induces investors to defer their disposition of securities, then we should have no holding period at all. But logic yields before another problem. If no holding period remains, how are we to distinguish between investors, who should be well treated, and speculators, who should not?[23] Finally, there are the perennial proposals which would reduce the special rate from 25 per cent to 20, 12½, or 10 per cent.

All these suggestions are accompanied by proper assurances. For example, a mere reduction to 12½ per cent will "put this country's economic house in order." As soon as the rate is cut, "some 400 individual investors" will "sell stocks having a current value of $32 million which cost the investors about $13 million, and pay a tax of over $2.25 million on the profit." The sales will "unfreeze vast amounts of capital and encourage reinvestment in new enterprises," and so provide "new jobs for the American people." Meanwhile the anxious 400 refuse to be helpful unless the rate of 25 per cent is first "reduced to a reasonable level."[24] Once again, if less is taken from those who have more, more will be given to those who have less.

However, others feel that the dispensation for capital gains is already much too generous. What is their response to the situation? Aside from a protest against the 6-month holding period, generally two answers are heard. The first is that some dispensation is necessary as long as the progressive rates are high and the tax on fluctuating income is not averaged. The suggested solution is to reduce the rates, average the tax over a number of years as if the income were the same from year to year, and treat capital gains like all other income.[25] The second answer is more restrained. The difference between the progressive rates and the special rate should be narrowed, and the holding period should be lengthened. In accordance with the ideology of ability, the argument is made that a dollar is a dollar, and that capital gains are like any other dollars. Nevertheless the unhappy critics are prepared to settle for less, because capital gains are realized in "special circumstances" which require "special treatment." Under the terms of one compromise the top progressive rate would be reduced to 65 per cent and the capital gain rate would be raised to 45 per cent.[26]

Neither solution is responsive to the issue. Each derives from the impression that the dispensation for capital gains is a sensitive reaction to high rates as applied to irregular incomes from sales of securities and other capital assets. But this view, as we have seen, is not faithful to the facts. The dispensation was initially bestowed at 12½ per cent when the top rate was 58 per cent on incomes over $200,000. Then in the Mellon era the dispensation continued at 12½ per cent though the top rate was only 25 per cent on incomes over $100,000. In short, there is no problem here of high rates. The dispensation is a means to an end prescribed by an ideology. If the dispensation is to be removed or reduced, the ideology must be effectively undermined as a system of belief. It is not enough to repeat what few are inclined to dispute—that capital gains represent ability to pay. The question is whether they should be differently treated for the sake of our economic welfare. On this question neither solution is helpful.

Meanwhile the dispensation works fairly well, for it relieves those whose state of contentment is vital. The special rate of 25 per cent is made available to individual taxpayers with incomes of about $20,000 or more. This select group receives about 55 per cent of all long-term gains. Even better, taxpayers with incomes of $100,000 or more receive 23 per cent of these gains, though they constitute only 4/100 of 1 per cent of all taxpayers.[27] As incomes increase, capital gains are an increasing share of total income. The dispensation is amply enjoyed by the intended beneficiaries.

In 1954 the ideology of barriers and deterrents produced a new dispensation for investors. It consists of the so-called exclusion and credit for dividends. The exclusion exempts an investor from tax on $50 of dividends. The credit further reduces his tax by 4 per cent of his remaining dividends. For the sake of simplicity, I put the exclusion aside and focus on the credit of 4 per cent.[28] The credit has been condemned as a flagrant departure from the principle of ability to pay. But when the ideology of barriers and deterrents bestows a dispensation, the mere invocation of ability to pay is not an adequate answer. For the ideology insists that the resulting benefits to everybody easily exceed the virtue of taxing the immediate beneficiaries according to ability.

The credit may be rightly regarded as a Republican achievement. Originally the Eisenhower Administration suggested a credit of 15 per cent. The proposal was then "watered down" to 10 per cent before the Republicans on the Ways and Means Committee "finally passed the thing out."[29] Eventually the credit was cut to 4 per cent due to political difficulties. Though it is much less than its advocates had hoped, the reasons conceived for its enactment have not diminished in interest. They nicely reveal the modes of thought which are peculiar to the ideology of barriers and deterrents.

Two rationalizations have been offered for the credit. We are first told that corporate earnings, in contrast to other kinds of income, are taxed twice. They are initially taxed as income to the corporation; and then, on distribution, they are again taxed as dividends to the stockholders. Dividends are doubly burdened in this fashion because, unlike wages or interest, they are not deductible by the corporation. At this point we come to the second ground, and the familiar vocabulary of barriers and deterrents takes over. We are informed that the "higher tax burden on distributed corporate earnings" has "contributed to the impairment of investment incentives." This deterioration, in turn, has led to an unfortunate sequence of events. Potential investors refuse to buy new issues of stock because the tax on dividends is too high; hence corporations in need of funds have not been sufficiently able "to raise equity capital"; and so they have had "to rely more heavily on borrowed money than is desirable either for the economy or for the firm." The dearth of investors "has been especially harmful to small business which cannot easily borrow funds and must rely on equity capital for growth and survival." The credit for dividends will remedy this undesirable condition. By reducing the tax on investors, it will make them more willing to furnish equity capital to the many anxious and harassed corporations.[30]

This verbal edifice rests on the premise that a stockholder pays two taxes on distributed corporate earnings—or, as the tax committees have pointedly stated, he is subjected to "the penalty of double taxation." He supposedly pays the corporate tax as well as his own tax, because the corporate tax reduces the dividends that he would otherwise receive. If a corporation earns $100 per share, it can only distribute $48—$100 less the corporate tax of $52. Then the stockholder must pay a second tax on the $48. Therefore, the argument concludes, in effect he bears both levies. On other occasions, however, the Republican ideologists of barriers and deterrents have reasoned very differently and no less confidently. They have maintained that the corporate tax reduces neither the amount earned by the corporation nor the amount distributed to the stockholder. Instead the tax is passed on to others through higher prices. It is the consumers who pay the tax, and the corporations are mere withholding agents for them. The tax does not diminish dividends any more than a general sales tax absorbed by customers. The late Representative Reed of New York, who sponsored the credit for dividends, customarily sustained this view with due vigor. One reason why prices are "inordinately high," he declared, is that "all products are increased in price in the exact proportion of taxation." A tax on the earnings of a corporation is a tax on "the people." Representative Martin of Massachusetts has been equally certain. "Any graduate economist can tell us," he assured his brethren, "that corporations compute profits after taxes, and not before, and their price scales are adjusted accordingly."[31]

I am not implying that these assertions are correct. The question of who bears the corporate tax is among the troublesome problems in taxation. Moreover, ideological observations are directed to a particular purpose. When the quoted statements were made, they were designed to forestall an unpleasant increase in the corporate tax. Hence it was politically desirable to indicate that the ideologists were not so much concerned with the lot of corporations as with the plight of "the people." As Justice Cardozo said, "New channels of thought cut themselves under the drive of a dilemma."[32] But no matter what the right view may be, an ideology which shuttles from one view to another may convey a meaningful message only to those who already believe. Or perhaps there is no view except as the need for one requires that something be said. A Congressional advocate of the credit has confessed, "The more I try to get . . . some economic facts in order to guide us in doing what we have to do in the tax field, the more I realize how grossly ignorant we are in this field."[33] However, when ideologists are doing their job, they are not so commendably humble.

Fortunately, I need not pursue this issue of double taxation any further. Representatives Mills and Curtis, of the Ways and Means Committee, have both emphasized that the adoption of the credit had nothing to do with any such problem. Congressman Curtis adds that if the credit is regarded as a "method of getting rid of double taxation"—even "triple, quadruple taxation"—he is "not interested."[34] Evidently all the talk of double taxation was for rhetorical effects. It helpfully suggested that certain taxpayers are victims of gross discrimination, and so the benefits conferred on them are only the alleviation of undeserved distress.

The one remaining basis for the credit is the economic rationalization. As we have seen, here, too, the reasoning is simple. Corporations depend too much on borrowed capital instead of equity capital; this situation has developed because individuals are unwilling to invest in new issues of stock; they decline to invest because dividends are too heavily taxed; the credit will reduce the undue burden and stimulate the potential investors to buy new issues. If I may again quote authoritative sources, the credit "was sold" to the Ways and Means Committee "for the purpose of accomplishing the economic result of increasing equity capital versus borrowed capital." The Committee became quite concerned because it was "told by economic observers, businessmen, and so forth, that the situation of equity capital was not healthy, and that something ought to be done to get a better balance in our corporations." In fact, "equity capital in our corporate structure was dangerously low." On the basis of "information" emanating from the Treasury and "other places," the Committee concluded that the credit "would tend in the direction of producing more equity capital, and thereby alleviate the necessity of as much debt financing in the overall structure."[35]

I conveniently pass over the argument that corporations are relying too much on borrowed money. Even if this view is correct, how can the credit remedy the situation? The credit, I gather, is bait thrown to reluctant investors. It is designed to tempt them into doing what is considered economically wise. If all goes well, it should induce them to furnish more equity capital to corporations in need of funds. This explanation, however, still leaves the question whether the bait is being offered to the proper fish. The credit presupposes that there has been an inadequate demand for new issues of stock. But, as a staunch defender of the credit has pointed out, the difficulty, if any, is due to a lack of supply, not a lack of demand. "The demand" for new issues "is there," says Representative Curtis. It is the corporations that prefer to borrow money rather than sell stock.[36] Their reasons for doing so are fairly well known. In the first place, interest rates have been low as compared with the earnings realized on borrowed capital. Secondly, a corporation can deduct interest, but it cannot deduct dividends. Thirdly, shareholders are also inclined to favor loans over a new issue of stock. The tax savings on the interest deduction increase the earnings of the corporation and the value of their shares. In addition, a new issue to new investors will dilute their equity in the business. And so the credit leaves us with an unresolved puzzle. If the evil to be corrected derives from the improvident conduct of corporations, how can a tax reduction offered to others induce the corporations to mend their ways—especially if their undesirable behavior gives them a lucrative deduction?

One puzzle leads on to another. The credit is supposed to persuade investors to provide equity capital. They are to be seduced by a lower tax on dividends. But those who are to be enticed are generally immune to temptation. As on other occasions, the ideology of barriers and deterrents is untroubled by the relevant facts. Most investors have little interest in new equities, regardless of taxes. Moreover, the small group that is favorably inclined toward them is attracted, not by a desire for dividends, but by a hope for capital gains taxable at 25 per cent. A lower tax on dividends, then, is essentially meaningless to these investors. The dispensation for capital gains has delivered them from any temptation that may be induced by the dispensation for dividends. I am merely saying what the adherents of the credit also recognize in their more dispassionate moments. As Congressman Curtis has stated, these investors have no use for dividends. They want a corporation to retain its earnings; for accumulated earnings enable them to sell their stock at a capital gain. And the special rate of 25 per cent is already inducing them to provide "a tremendous amount of capital for small businesses."[37]

Even Secretary of the Treasury Humphrey was aware of this difficulty, and he tried to resolve it. He tacitly conceded that the credit would not stimulate large stockholders to ask for more dividends. But, he painstakingly added, the credit will induce the small stockholders "to demand more dividends," and then "the high income fellow is just going to have to take it and pay his tax."[38] If we put all this Republican reasoning together, it tells us that the credit will encourage large investors to supply equity capital because it will force them to receive dividends that they do not want.

The explanation for the credit does not become less curious as we continue to contemplate it. The special treatment of capital gains is justified on the ground that sufficient equity capital cannot be obtained unless investors are stimulated to sell securities for a profit. But the special treatment of dividends is justified on the ground that sufficient equity capital cannot be obtained unless investors are stimulated to hold securities for dividends. Once again the easy answer is that it is not unusual for an ideology to be internally inconsistent. If it becomes too concerned with logic, it may not be as effective as it should be.

The ideology of barriers and deterrents is continuously confronted by a pressing problem. It must convince those with lesser incomes that they are being fairly treated. The usual solution is to say that large tax savings for the few will provide prosperity for the many, too. Yet at times the ideologists are uneasily aware that this rationalization alone will not do. Something more must be said if the many are to be pleased. The dividend credit, unhappily, induced this sense of discomfort. The advocates of the credit were charged with seeking a special reduction for the affluent. They were even accused of reversing the principle of ability to pay, and granting a tax advantage to unearned income over earned income.[39] Hence it was no longer enough to repeat the routine assurances of more jobs and a better standard of living. The advocates, however, were not discouraged, and soon devised the required reply. They vigorously explained that shares in American corporations are widely held; that stockholders in the lower brackets would fare much better than those in the upper brackets; and that the credit would encourage small taxpayers to become investors. This answer combined a resourceful use of statistics with a skilful mode of arithmetic.

The first argument is that America is a nation of stockholders and that the benefits of the credit accrue to many taxpayers throughout the country. Formidable figures are cited as proof that industry is broadly owned. As many as 12.5 million individuals have shares in our public corporations. Almost half of them have incomes between $5,000 and $10,000. The Eisenhower Administration gladly supplied further details along the same lines. In 1954 it pointed out that United States Steel had about 300,000 stockholders; that 56 per cent of them earned under $5,000 a year; and that more of them were in the bracket between $2,000 and $3,000 than in any other thousand dollar bracket.[40] Such figures suggest that the credit is grievously misunderstood. It was conceived for the benefit of rich and poor alike. Stockholders are not a class apart. They include skilled and unskilled laborers, as well as businessmen. As a persuaded Congressman told his brethren, "the little stockholder—the widow, the orphan, the retired, and the aged—wants relief from the double taxation of corporate earnings just as much as the rich."[41] But a different picture emerges if one other factor is added—the number of shares held as distinguished from the number of shareholders. Only about 1 family out of 10 owns stock in public corporations. And within the minority that owns stock, most of the shares are heavily concentrated at the upper levels of affluence. Less than 1 per cent of all families—those with a net worth beyond $250,000—holds about 70 per cent of the total value of the shares. More than 50 per cent of the shareholders own only 1 per cent of the stock. The families of wage earners hold 3/10 of 1 per cent. To summarize the omitted data another way, the number of individuals reporting dividends rises from 2 per cent in the lowest income groups to 90 per cent and over in the highest income groups.[42]

The ideologists themselves have left little more to be said. Four years before the credit was granted, they earnestly noted that "most stockholders hold only a few shares of stock" and "the great mass of stockholders receives only small amounts of dividends." Of course, when these words were written, the ideologists were concerned with something else. The Treasury had proposed the withholding of income taxes on dividends in order to prevent large-scale evasion. The ideologists, however, disapproved the suggestion because it would impose "real hardship on millions of honest American taxpayers." In an effort to sustain their sympathy they proceeded to emphasize the few shares that most stockholders own.[43] While this difference in approach is easily understood, the fact which so impressed them earlier still remains the same.

Professor Dan T. Smith is one of the warmer adherents of the dispensation for dividends. He has learned, with "some surprise," that the credit is criticized for giving unfair relief in the upper brackets. "As a matter of fact," he states, the credit "was adopted for the very reason that it would give the same dollar amount of relief on a given amount of dividends regardless of the individual's tax rate." To add to his chagrin, the credit was expressly designed to grant what he calls "greater proportionate relief to lower-bracket taxpayers."[44] Smith's astonishment is reflected by his arithmetic. Assume that two taxpayers have each received $100 of dividends. One is in the 20 per cent bracket and the other has reached the 91 per cent bracket. Their respective taxes on the $100 are $20 and $91. According to Smith, though their rates are quite dissimilar, each is entitled to "the same dollar amount of relief on a given amount of dividends"—4 per cent of $100, or $4. Again, according to Smith, greater proportionate relief is bestowed on taxpayers in the lower bracket. If a tax of $20 is reduced by $4, the saving is 20 per cent. But if a tax of $91 is reduced by $4, the saving is only 4.3 per cent. On the basis of such reasoning other adherents of the credit have readily agreed with Smith that the tax reduction "is greatest in the lowest bracket and declines progressively as the income level rises." "The larger the shareholder, proportionately smaller is the relief." Or, as Secretary Humphrey assured Congress, the credit "means much more to a little stockholder than to a big one."[45]

Despite Smith's careful calculations in their behalf, taxpayers in the upper brackets do their arithmetic differently. They measure their relief by the additional income made available to them—not by the formal reduction in rate. I return to the same example for another computation as they would make it. Again each taxpayer is entitled to deduct a credit of $4 from the tax that is otherwise due. Without the credit, the taxpayer in the 20 per cent bracket pays $20 and has $80 left; the taxpayer in the 91 per cent bracket pays $91 and has $9 left. With the credit, the first pays $16 and has $84 left; the second pays $87 and has $13 left. As a result of the credit, then, the disposable income of the first is increased by 5 per cent, and the disposable income of the second by almost 45 per cent.

By and large, I am only repeating what Smith himself has stressed on other occasions. Though at times he forgets what he has said, it may still be worth recalling. Smith has stated that it is pointless to appraise relative changes in burdens by simply looking at the changes in rates. The important question is how the revisions affect the income left after taxes. As an example he compares two tax increases at different levels of income—from 1½ to 4 per cent, and from 25 to 63 per cent. In each case the new rate is about 150 per cent more than the old rate. But in the first case, he notes, the taxpayer's income after taxes is reduced by merely 2½ per cent; while in the second case it is reduced by over 50 per cent. Hence Smith sharply disapproves the "inequity, and even absurdity, of looking only at relative increases in rates."[46] Of course, if it is unfair and foolish to look only at the rates when taxes are raised, it seems equally unfair and foolish to do so when taxes are reduced.[47] Yet we must realize that the ideologists of barriers and deterrents cannot be wholly consistent in such matters. Otherwise they would be unable to be surprised when they are criticized.

Smith's new mode of comparison overlooks something else which he and his fellow ideologists usually stress. They repeatedly reproach Congress for taxing dividend income twice—first to the corporation and then to its stockholders. If this complaint is correct, it is also true that small incomes suffer much more than large incomes. Again let us examine the lot of two stockholders—one in the 20 per cent bracket and the other in the 91 per cent bracket. Assume that each owns a share in the same corporation, which earns $100 per share. In the absence of a corporate tax each would receive $100. The first would then pay $20 and the second $91. Their incomes after taxes would be $80 and $9. But actually the corporation pays a tax of 52 per cent on each $100, leaving—the ideologists say—only $48 as a dividend. The first stockholder then pays 20 per cent of $48, or $9.60, and the second 91 per cent of $48, or $43.68. Their incomes after taxes are $38.40 instead of $80, and $4.32 instead of $9. Due to the corporate tax the total effective burden is 61.6 rather than 20 per cent in the bottom bracket, and 95.68 rather than 91 per cent in the top bracket. As these figures indicate, if dividends are taxed twice, then stockholders at the lower end of the scale are much more doubly taxed than stockholders at the upper end. For those in the bottom bracket the extra tax is 41.6 per cent; for those in the top bracket it is only 4.68 per cent. If a credit for dividends is at all proper, the credit should therefore be higher in the lower brackets. Instead, Congress has ordained the reverse. The larger the extra tax, the smaller the special relief. To return to my example, each stockholder is given a credit of $1.92—4 per cent of $48. As a result, the extra tax of the stockholder below is reduced from 41.6 to 39.68 per cent, while the extra tax of the stockholder above is reduced from 4.68 to 2.76 per cent. Or, differently stated, the credit eliminates 4.6 per cent of the "double tax" at the bottom and 41 per cent at the top. Those most burdened are least relieved.

The remaining argument for the credit is that it will encourage "millions of small investors to participate in the ownership of America." It gives "the little fellow" a "fairer chance to invest in good common stock," such as General Motors, General Electric, and Standard Oil of New Jersey. It gives "more and more Americans" an "incentive to see an expanding America."[48] But here, also, the explanation seems hastily contrived. The credit was not devised so that taxpayers, whether large or little, would buy "good" stocks in well-established corporations. Its stated purpose was to induce contributions of fresh capital to new and needy enterprises. Moreover, the ideologists who speak well of the credit usually contend that there is no reason to be concerned with the incentives of small taxpayers. They have neither the time to study investments in new ventures nor the money to assume the risks involved. As a defender of the credit has frankly stated, "the bulk of stock is held by the higher bracket income people," and so "they are the ones whose thinking we have to get into."[49]

All these difficulties may finally suggest that there has been much ado about very little. The dispensation for dividends was granted in order to coax the affluent into providing more capital to new and growing businesses. Why, then, should anyone fret over the treatment of the less prosperous? Obviously, the credit can hardly persuade them to invest, for they lack the required capital. Why, in fact, should they be given any credit at all if they have nothing to contribute? However, the ideologists of barriers and deterrents cannot be satisfied with such a simple approach. Like the adherents of ability, they also have a cross to bear. They, too, must indicate that they are duly dispassionate, since they are seeking special dispensations for certain groups. Hence they are obliged to talk of the number of shareholders in American corporations instead of the number of shares that are held. They must indulge in arithmetical comparisons that they would usually reject as absurd and deceptive. And they must stoutly insist that small stock-holders are better treated than the large. Indeed, they will even argue that the credit is one of the many benefits given to wage earners. It is all irrelevant but unavoidable. Somehow the greater benefits enjoyed in the upper brackets must conveniently disappear from view. And if the various explanations fail to persuade, one can always say that "the demagoguery on this complicated and difficult matter has badly hurt an intelligent understanding of it by the people and their representatives in Congress."[50] The going may be rough, but the job must be done.

Despite such earnest efforts the credit for dividends has not stimulated our affluent taxpayers to buy new issues of stock. Still, the credit is not a total loss. It bestows relief where relief was intended. Reported dividends total about $8.3 billion. Of this substantial sum, 60 per cent is received by those with incomes of $20,000 or more—or 1 per cent of all taxpayers. As much as 20 per cent is received by those with incomes of $100,000 or more—or 4/100 of 1 per cent of all taxpayers.[51]

While the credit has not induced a generous supply of new capital, this fact is not too important. We will continue to hear that the credit offers an "incentive for people to invest their money in American industry, so that more industries can be created and more jobs provided." If the credit is ineffective, it can always be argued that a larger credit will be more effective. And if the credit does nothing else but reduce the proper taxes, it is still worth keeping. For though it "is very small," the mere talk of repealing it "would be highly discouraging to the investor group in America." They would naturally "interpret that as a move to further penalize them in the years ahead." According to the ideology of barriers and deterrents, no greater wrong can be done than to be discouraging. A Senator managed to add a new thought in behalf of the credit. The repeal of the credit, he warned, "would result in taxing stockholders and giving the money to needy people, and that is an outrage."[52]

The ideology of barriers and deterrents has also produced further benefits that are quite rewarding. Here it seems enough to mention only two.

In 1942 Congress devised a special dispensation for taxpayers engaged in a trade or business. The dispensation was designed to stimulate them to help win the war. Specifically, it sought to induce them to sell their used plant and equipment to others who would then employ the facilities more effectively. In order to achieve this objective Congress provided different rules for property sold at a loss and property sold at a profit. If there is a loss, it is fully deductible against the ordinary income of the business. If there is a profit, it is merely taxable as a capital gain.

Tax experts who admire uniformity often criticize these rules on the ground that they are inconsistent. Gains and losses, they argue, should be treated alike. If the gains are considered capital gains, then the losses should be considered capital losses. If the losses are deemed ordinary losses, then the gains should be deemed ordinary income. The nature of the transaction is the same, regardless of what the particular result may be. This objection, however, misses the point of the distinction. The pursuit of victory required varying rules. The desired sales would have been seriously deterred if a loss had been treated as a capital loss. Aside from a minor exception, capital losses are deductible only against capital gains. Since businesses very often do not have such gains, the losses would not have provided any tax benefits. The desired sales would have been similarly discouraged if a gain had been treated as ordinary income. For the ordinary rates would then have taken away a good deal of the profit. The two rules may seem inconsistent, but actually they are not. In every case, whether it be a loss or a gain, the taxpayer consistently receives the better treatment.

I realize that hostilities have been over for some time, and there is no longer any need to stimulate sales "for the war effort." But even in times of peace businessmen have to be encouraged to do the right thing. If the economy is to keep going at a proper pace, they must be induced to sell their old property in order to acquire new property. Since a sale may result in a profit or a loss, the alleged inconsistency is still a virtue.

The other dispensation sustains another incentive. Corporate executives are often paid for their services through an option to buy stock in their employer. The option is an arrangement which enables them to obtain the stock at a bargain price after it has substantially appreciated. As the Supreme Court has held, the purchase of the stock at a cut rate is a financial or economic benefit conferred on the employee as compensation for his services. The compensation is the difference between the value of the stock received by him and the bargain price paid by him.[53] Income from services is usually taxable at rates ranging from 20 to 91 per cent. But what is appropriate for others is not necessarily suitable for executives. Under a special dispensation for stock options the compensation is taxable as a capital gain when the acquired shares are later sold at their appreciated value. In this way executives are given an incentive to be adequately interested in the success of their employers. Unless options were gently treated, enterprise would languish. In the emphatic words of two businessmen, "Salaries are a blunt and clumsy tool for motivating executives." Without options "executives might not find it worthwhile coming to work."[54]

This explanation does not please everybody. There are no signs, the critics say, that executives lose interest in their work if they pay the taxes that others are expected to bear. Nor are stock options the only means of supplying an incentive to executives who are sorely in need of it. An outright bonus in stock also stimulates incentive, and yet the value of the stock is taxable as compensation. In fact, all compensation, whether paid in cash or in kind, is an incentive to work. Otherwise it would not be paid. Moreover, few executives would deny that stock options are a mode of compensation. It is no secret that executives "desire and seek stock options as part of their own personal remuneration." Even a few ideologists of barriers and deterrents have conceded that options are compensatory devices. The late Congressman Knutson, who continuously worried over the decline of incentives, stated the matter very simply. The theory of the dispensation is that the executive's work "will be reflected" in the "increase in the value of the security." By "sharing in the resulting gains he is compensated for his additional efforts."[55]

Though all these observations may be correct, one fact seems indisputable. At the very least stock options enable executives to find more pleasure in their work. Let me illustrate the happiness that may be theirs. A president of a prosperous corporation was given an option to buy its shares at $33.75. Two years later he purchased 20,000 shares when the market price had doubled. The difference between his cost and the value of the acquired shares was $680,000. The eventual tax on this sum is 25 per cent, leaving a net of $510,000. Others who work without the incentive of stock options must earn about $4 million in order to retain the same amount after taxes.[56] Since the results may be quite agreeable, stock options are widely used. In 1957 three out of five companies listed on the leading stock exchanges resorted to options as a means of compensation.[57]

One of our prominent ideologists has described the treatment of stock options as "a relaxation of the high bracket rates to achieve a desired economic result." Another expert has put it differently. "Employee stock options," he writes, "offer a possible way of life to the corporate executive harassed by the high costs of a high standard of living and by ever increasing taxes."[58] "High costs," however, are not necessarily confined to those who would enjoy "a high standard of living." All in all, it seems much wiser to speak of the failing incentives of executives and the need to revive them.

Of course, such explanations will not overcome all doubts. Senator Douglas of Illinois is particularly dissatisfied. In his view the ideology of barriers and deterrents is guilty of a serious contradiction. It insists that "excise taxes on the poor cause them to work harder but income taxes on the well-to-do cause them to work less." But those who grasp the refinements of the ideology are unable to understand why the Senator is troubled. The answer is clear and to the point. When taxpayers become well-to-do, they cease to be industrious if they consider their taxes too high. The poor have little choice but to remain ambitious and ingenious.[59]

I have yet to consider one small item which others may find confusing. The ideologists of barriers and deterrents are also those who repeatedly proclaim that tax laws should be enacted for only one purpose—the collection of revenue. They should not be used for other social or non-fiscal purposes, such as "providing a direct incentive to production" or "supplying a positive stimulus to greater activity."[60] Yet the same ideologists are busily seeking tax dispensations that are specifically designed to induce more "production" and "greater activity." George Humphrey is a cogent example of this kind of behavior. As Secretary of the Treasury, Humphrey severely criticized "artificial stimulants" to production. The tax laws, he declared, should not serve as a means of "singling out particular taxpayers or particular facilities for more favorable treatment than others receive." They "should be used only to equitably raise revenue, not for other indirect purposes. It is dangerous to use the tax laws for social purposes, to favor one group of citizens over others, to exercise economic controls, or to indirectly subsidize any segment of our economy."[61] But as Secretary of the Treasury, Humphrey also sought and obtained the dividend credit and other special dispensations for particular taxpayers. And all were generously justified in the name of a social purpose—economic growth and universal prosperity.

While there may seem to be a discrepancy here, it is only in the eyes of the beholder. The various dispensations are not granted in order to provide incentives, though the usual vocabulary employed in their defense may convey that impression. The objective, rather, is to remove barriers and deterrents to incentives that are already there. Anyone who understands the ideology should easily see the difference.

CHAPTER 6

The Special Deduction for Imaginary Costs

Of all the dispensations produced by the ideology of barriers and deterrents, percentage depletion is the most remarkable achievement. It enables certain taxpayers to reduce their incomes by imaginary costs. Other taxpayers are not considered so deserving. They may only deduct what they spend.

The normal function of a depletion allowance seems too obvious to mention. Mineral properties and other natural resources are wasting assets. As production proceeds, the deposit is gradually exhausted. A depletion allowance permits the owner to recover his cost for the consumed portion of the property. It illustrates the familiar principle that in computing gain or loss, a business offsets the cost of its raw materials against its receipts. For many years, however, Congress has pursued a theory that those who profit from natural resources are a breed apart from all others. They are entitled to recoup much more than their cost. If they were merely treated like others, they would lose their desire to be productive and the nation would grievously suffer. Congress has met the menace of declining ambition by granting percentage depletion—an annual deduction measured by a portion of the annual income from the property. The amount of the deduction is not in the least related to the cost of the property.

Percentage depletion was initially devised for the benefit of taxpayers who derive income from oil and gas. Since 1926 they have enjoyed a recurrent deduction equal to 27½ per cent of the gross income from the well, but not exceeding 50 per cent of the taxable or net income.

The deduction continues as long as production continues, though they may have recovered their investment many times over. The larger the profit, the larger the deduction.

This dispensation would be quite impressive if it were merely a munificent substitute for a smaller allowance based on the true investment. However, the special taxpayers involved may deduct not only their imaginary costs, but also their actual costs of developing their wells. Moreover, these actual costs are immediately deductible as they are incurred in order to make sure that faltering incentives will not imperil the country. Other businessmen may not write off their capital outlays as current expenses. They must be satisfied with deferred allowances for depreciation. In short, there are three dispensations altogether—an immediate deduction for a capital investment; two deductions for one investment; and a continuing deduction for no investment. For every $5 million deducted by the oil and gas industry in 1946 as percentage depletion, another $4 million was deducted as development costs. For every $3 million deducted as percentage depletion in 1947, another $2 million was deducted as development costs.[1] Occasionally an ideologist will deny that deductions are generously duplicated. He will argue that the actual costs of development are deducted just once, because percentage depletion relates only to the expenditures incurred in the search for oil and not to those incurred in developing the well.[2] But the Supreme Court is not persuaded by such reasoning. It holds that percentage depletion represents the investment in the well together with the investment in the oil. And another court adds that the immediate deduction for development costs is a "special favor."[3]

The dispensations cooperate very nicely in behalf of affluent operators in oil and gas. Their development costs are fully deductible, and the resulting profits are only partially taxable. Percentage depletion may exempt as much as 50 per cent of the income produced by a well. In view of the high rates, the immediate deduction for development costs enables the Government to assume most of the risk. The later deduction for percentage depletion permits it to share much less of the income. For an individual in the top bracket, the expenses may be written off at 91 per cent while the income is taxable at 45.5 per cent. For a corporation the expenses may be written off at 52 per cent while the income is taxable at 26 per cent.

Tax dispensations have a faculty for expanding as they age. Percentage depletion is not among the exceptions. In an effort to be fair Congress has extended this dispensation to almost everything that qualifies as a natural resource. If oil and gas merit percentage depletion, so do sand and gravel, brick clay and monumental stone, and clam shells and oyster shells. Certainly, Congress cannot be criticized for being remiss in its solicitude. Aside from oil and gas, five groups of natural deposits are granted percentage depletion. The rates are not as high as 27½ per cent, but there is still good reason to rejoice. They range from 5 per cent to 23 per cent of gross income. The statute generously enumerates about 85 natural deposits, and winds up with a sweeping residuary clause for "all other minerals." Yet even Congress realizes that a line has to be drawn somewhere, and so it has carefully excluded "soil, sod, dirt, turf, water, or mosses," as well as "minerals from sea water, the air, or similar inexhaustible resources."

Obviously percentage depletion is very helpful to those whose incentives would decline without a deduction for imaginary costs. The total depletion deductions each year are 10 times as much as the actual investment in the depleted resources. The annual revenue loss due to percentage depletion is about $1.5 billion, and oil and gas account for 75 per cent of the loss. Since oil and gas enjoy the largest deduction at 27½ per cent, Senator Douglas has observed, "In the royal family of depletion allowances, oil and gas, like Abou Ben Adhem, lead all the rest."[4] However, the rate does not reveal everything. In the years 1946–1949 percentage depletion was 19 times as much as actual cost for oil and gas, but 200 times as much for sulfur.

Yet we need not go beyond oil and gas to see how useful percentage depletion is—especially when combined with the further deduction for development costs. In 1954 the average effective tax rate for all corporations was 48.1 per cent. But for 24 large oil companies it was 22.6 per cent. Various corporations specializing in crude oil production fared even better. For Humble Oil & Refining Co. the effective rate was 16.3 per cent; for Tidewater Associated Oil Co., 9.2 per cent. Amerada Petroleum Corporation has refrained from listing its tax as a separate item in its annual reports to stockholders. The tax has been too small to notice.[5]

Individuals do fairly well also. Over the five years 1943–1947 ten oil and gas operators received an aggregate taxable income of $52.6

million, computed under the rules that apply to other businessmen. Their income from further sources was $9.3 million, making a total of $61.9 million. On this formidable sum they paid an average effective rate of only 22.5 per cent. For one of the ten the effective rate was only 3/5 of 1 per cent. His total income over the five years was $14.3 million, while his total taxes were but $80,000. The results for another taxpayer were rewarding, too. Over the same period he was able to develop properties yielding nearly $5 million in one year on which no tax was paid. In escaping tax on his oil income, he also escaped tax on most of his other income. His total taxes for the period were less than $100,000, but his income from sources other than oil averaged about $1 million a year.[6] While the incentives of all these taxpayers were being amply maintained, the lowest rate for ordinary non-depleted taxpayers ranged between 19 and 23 per cent.

The Supreme Court has said that percentage depletion is an "arbitrary" allowance. It "bears little relationship to the capital investment," and is even available "though no money was actually invested." Senator Lausche of Ohio has been less restrained. "It is a fraud, it is a swindle, and it ought to be stopped." However, the ideologists who are well versed in oil have provided the required answers. Percentage depletion, they say, is not "an advantage amounting to a tax favor." It "does not give special treatment to the oil industry and is completely justified."[7] It expresses a sensitive wisdom which is beyond reproach. In order to understand this wisdom we must first turn back a few pages of history.

Originally depletion for oil and gas was computed in the usual way. The deduction was based on the cost of the output. In 1919 a significant change occurred. Congress decided that the country was imperiled by a dearth of oil. If it was to be adequately defended, more oil had to be found. A special dispensation known as discovery depletion was devised, so that venturesome individuals would go forth and alleviate the shortage. "The prospector" for oil, the Finance Committee stated, "expends many years and much money in fruitless search." A larger allowance for depletion would "stimulate prospecting and exploration." It would induce more prospectors to seek out the precious liquid. Congress, therefore, declared that if a taxpayer discovered a well, his deduction for each barrel of oil would be based, not on his investment in the well, but on the value of his discovery. Since this dispensation was designed to encourage the "wildcatter" or "pioneer," it was only given to those who made an actual discovery.[8]

Congress soon concluded that it had been too generous. A deduction based on discovery value could be large enough to offset all the earnings from some other business wholly unrelated to oil. Hence in 1921 the annual allowance was limited to the net income from the discovered property. Even a prospector for oil was not entitled to be overly rewarded. But the deduction was still too liberal. Three years later it was further limited to 50 per cent of the net income from the well.[9]

In 1926 percentage depletion replaced discovery depletion. The stated reason for the change was the administrative difficulty of valuing each well that was found. Percentage depletion was allegedly adopted in the interest of simplicity and certainty. As a Senator emphasized, it was a mere "simplification, getting rid of this everlasting accounting."[10] Since the new deduction was a fixed portion of annual income, it was readily computed. The rate of 27½ per cent was chosen as a fair equivalent of the deduction enjoyed under discovery depletion. And the allowance was similarly limited to 50 per cent of the net income from the property. A dissatisfied Senator offered a different solution. He suggested that the valuation difficulties would promptly disappear if depletion were based on the driller's actual investment.[11] Of course, this remedy was much too disagreeable, for investors in oil would then be treated like other investors who take risks. But the shift to percentage depletion raises additional questions which are not so easily dismissed.

Discovery depletion was conceived for the wildcatters of the industry—those who are eventually successful despite overwhelming odds. If I may quote from the many Congressional eulogies devoted to wildcatters, the avowed object of discovery depletion was "to give an advantage or subsidy to a man who goes into a new and undeveloped territory and 'wildcats,' gambling with fate, and spends a lot of money," as distinguished from "adjoining landowners who do no development work until others have demonstrated that theirs are oil-bearing lands." The wildcatter or pioneer who discovered an oil field served "society and himself." He was entitled to "some concession" in view of "the nature of his industry and the character of his risk."[12] In response to such sentiments discovery depletion was guardedly granted only to the prospector who made a discovery. Percentage depletion, however, is freely given to anyone who has an interest in oil. There is no longer any need to gamble with fate in the heroic fashion of a wildcatter. His peculiar "industry" and "risk" have been cast aside in the effort to assure "simplicity" and "certainty."

The special dispensation for wildcatters was originally justified on the ground that there was a serious lack of oil. If their taxes were reduced, they would find more oil. But by the early thirties even the tax committees conceded a state of overproduction. Despite a second world war and larger automobiles, the situation has not deteriorated. Our ample supply of oil is confirmed by the firmest adherents of percentage depletion. As Senator Long of Louisiana has stated, "We have enough oil" to meet our "requirements for the next 100 years." And now that shale has become a practical source of oil, "there is enough potential fuel in the known shale reserves to last this Nation 1,000 years." The country is in no "danger of running out of oil."[13]

A few basic facts emerge. Initially the deduction for imaginary costs was sustained by two related reasons. The nation was in dire need of oil, and a dispensation was necessary for those who discovered new fields. Now the nation is well stocked with oil, and the dispensation is given to those who do not discover anything. Though the emergency is over, the dispensation lingers on and is less exclusively enjoyed. However, the adherents of percentage depletion have not been discouraged. If the facts can change, so can the arguments. The revised rationalizations have fully conformed to the high standard of performance imposed by percentage depletion. Here, indeed, we see the ideology of barriers and deterrents at its best.

If an argument is repeated often enough, it soon becomes a respectable doctrine. Several arguments for percentage depletion have been echoed with the required regularity. These persistent observations may be identified as the doctrine of remarkable risk, the doctrine of depleted capital, the doctrine of replenished capital, the doctrine of capital gains, and the doctrine of national security. Many cooks do not necessarily spoil the broth. If one explanation fails to persuade, another may do better. There are ready replies for all occasions.[14]

The doctrine of remarkable risk declares, with due emphasis, that the oil industry is unique. It is beset by inordinate perils and hazards. It is "nothing more or less than a calculus of chances or of risks." Since the quest for oil is a dangerous enterprise, sufficient capital cannot be attracted unless there is hope of reward. The producers of oil "must be able to make enough profit to offset the risk that they will not find any oil at all." Percentage depletion is the indispensable solution to this problem. It makes the business more inviting by reducing the tax on the profits. A lesser tax provides a greater incentive to go on amid the hovering threats of disaster.[15]

The answer is often made that the risks of the oil business are exaggerated. From 1925 to 1954 the industry had the lowest percentage of failures. Dean Griswold, of the Harvard Law School, has suggested that the risks of the large oil companies are akin to the risks assumed by the New York Life Insurance Company. Besides, it is said, the substantial integrated companies have no choice but to drill for oil if they are to remain in business.[16] But the ideologists who dwell on the perils of oil are untroubled by any such doubts. The reply is already prepared and is always the same. It consists of compassionate references to the plight of "the independent wildcatter." Of every 9 wells that he drills, 8 are dry holes. No other venturer struggles against odds so grim. Though he may deduct his losses as others do, a deduction does him no good unless he has income against which to offset it. Something more is essential if he is to remain a rugged pioneer despite so many discouraging failures. He must be assured that "if he does find oil in the ninth well, he will be allowed to keep a fair profit, enough to keep him searching for more oil." Percentage depletion offers the necessary assurance; it "helps the roughnecks, it helps the drillers, it helps the tool pushers." "To deny this liberal depletion to the wildcatter and the pioneer simply destroys that historic figure in our economic development and enthrones the Rockefellers and the Mellons."[17]

This constant concern for the luckless wildcatter affords the advantage of ignoring others in the industry. It is well known that individuals in high brackets engage in oil ventures. Unlike the wildcatter with meager resources, they have large incomes against which to charge off their losses at the expense of the Treasury. They enjoy the privilege of being in a risky business without much risk. It is also known that for the industry as a whole the successful wells exceed the failures. Three out of 5 wells are producers. The dramatic talk of 8 dry holes applies only to the wildcatters who are boldly exploring unproven fields. Moreover, the large companies effectively spread their risks by drilling many wells. All the sorrow expressed for the wildcatters has the further virtue of overlooking certain disagreeable data. The fact is that corporations account for about 90 per cent of the depletion allowances; and of this lion's share, two-thirds goes to corporations with assets over $100 million. The proportion of tax-free income generally increases with the size of the corporation. As usual, when the needs of the "little man" are invoked, most of the benefits go elsewhere. The deduction is of small value to the small prospector in whose name it is granted and defended. Nor does the marginal operator derive much help from it. The deduction for imaginary costs is a percentage of the income produced by the property. Since his income is modest, he usually does better by deducting his actual costs.[18]

Those who supposedly need percentage depletion the most enjoy it the least. Hence suggestions have been made that the dispensation for the large operators should be reduced. But here, too, the doctrine of remarkable risk has a ready answer. I turn to Senator Long for an excellent summary of its content. The Senator refers us to "Grandma Jones, who holds 6 shares" in Standard Oil or a similar corporation. "Why should not the old lady," he pointedly asks, "who happened to own 6 shares of stock in a substantial company, receive the same tax treatment as the independent who might be worth $1 million?" This arresting question leads on to the conclusion that "small stockholders" in the large companies should be as favorably treated as "the independent producer of oil and gas." Any attempt to reduce their percentage depletion necessarily discriminates against "the vast majority of stockholders," who "are not wealthy."[19] It is difficult to improve upon this answer, for every large company has small stockholders like Grandma Jones. So in the end Grandma Jones is also a wildcatter and roughneck whose risks require a dispensation.

Even if elderly ladies are entitled to be well treated, on what ground should the passive owner of an oil royalty be given percentage depletion? What perils has he overcome in the quest for oil? To what extent has he been gambling with fate like a tenacious wildcatter? At this point the doctrine of remarkable risk has nothing more to say, and conveniently retires from the scene. Another doctrine emerges to provide the answers—the doctrine of depleted capital. Why talk of risks when it is easier to talk of other things?

The doctrine of depleted capital tells us that one who finds oil creates new capital. As the oil is removed, the capital is depleted. The amount deducted as percentage depletion from the proceeds of sale represents the recovery of that capital. If percentage depletion were repealed, the return of capital would be wrongly taxed as the receipt of income. "Percentage depletion merely places the oil industry, in so far as the taxing of capital is concerned, on an equal footing with other industries which do not create new capital through discovery of hidden resources."[20]

This explanation simply assumes that the capital in a well is the value of the discovered oil. While the thought is clear enough, the adherents of ability are apparently unable to follow it. They still indulge in the old-fashioned notion that the capital of a business consists of the actual investment in the enterprise. They cannot understand why receipts in excess of costs are a recovery of capital. Though their confusion may seem strange, it would be unfair to hold them entirely responsible. When the oil companies report their earnings to their stockholders, the profits are computed on the basis of actual costs, not imaginary costs.[21] The adherents of ability naturally wonder how income becomes a recovery of capital when it is reported to the Treasury. Again, if percentage depletion reflects a mere return of capital, why must it be repeatedly justified in terms of the special risks in the oil industry? Surely no one claims that a recovery of capital is taxable as income if a business is relatively safe rather than speculative. If percentage depletion truly represents a return of capital, all the repeated emphasis on risk should be unnecessary. But since the ideologists of depletion protest so much, the adherents of ability are prone to be suspicious.

We need not explore the questions raised by the doctrine of depleted capital. Though the doctrine may seem troublesome, it still has an important job to do. Not everyone is easily convinced that the oil industry is as risky as it is supposed to be. The doctrine is designed to reassure those who may have misgivings. It carefully informs them that risk is irrelevant, because in any event percentage depletion is only a normal allowance for the capital consumed in the production of income. Therefore, even the drone who collects royalties without incurring any risk also deserves percentage depletion. For he, too, has a known capital value in the oil as soon as production is established, and is equally entitled to the recovery of that value before his income is taxed.[22]

Despite its simplicity and clarity the doctrine of depleted capital does not convert everybody. For those who are unpersuaded a third doctrine has been devised—the doctrine of replenished capital.

This doctrine also identifies percentage depletion with capital, but the emphasis is different. Now the deduction for imaginary costs is rationalized as a way of obtaining new capital instead of restoring old capital. In order to stay in business, the doctrine runs, the producer must develop new sources of supply. Percentage depletion gives him the capital to do so. The "enormous risk capital" required for new operations is "regenerated out of the depletion allowance on the oil that is found and produced." Percentage depletion only enables the oil man to replace his capital for further explorations. "This is exactly what is done with the owner of the steel mill who is allowed depreciation on his plant investment." The doctrine then adds that the proof of the pudding is in the eating. Over the years the depletion deductions have been almost equal to the actual costs of finding oil. Unless the deductions continue, the industry will be unable to carry on with the hope of adding new reserves. A mere reduction in percentage depletion "would bring exploratory operations in this country to a standstill."[23]

An ideologist of depletion has declared, "To me this analysis is simplicity itself and I cannot see how its validity can be questioned."[24] Unfortunately a simple doctrine is not always as clear to others as to its adherents. No matter how hard they try to see the light, the revelation may escape them. Here, however, the doctrine itself must share some of the blame. Its alleged simplicity consists of the need for new capital and the comparison to the producer of steel. Yet it is precisely these items in the doctrine that trouble the disbelievers. If businessmen in oil need capital for further operations, so do all other businessmen. If percentage depletion is an apt method of regenerating capital, it seems just as appropriate for everybody else. The doubts are not resolved by emphasizing that the owner of a steel mill is allowed depreciation on his plant investment. The depreciation to which he is entitled is based on the actual cost of his facilities. Even though he must later replace them at a much higher price, the capital regenerated through deductions for depreciation cannot exceed his prior investment. The producer of oil, on the other hand, may deduct much more than his investment in the removed oil; and if the excess is then reinvested in new wells, he promptly deducts most of it once more as a current expense. Through percentage depletion he enjoys the rare privilege of expanding with tax-free profits. Producers of steel would be surprised to learn that they have been receiving exactly the same benefit all along.

Evidently a few problems still remain. And so the ideologists have gone to work and devised another answer—the doctrine of capital gains.

The doctrine of capital gains also attempts to be simple. As soon as oil is discovered, the doctrine states, it can be sold at a price equal to its estimated value in the ground. On such a sale the difference between the price received and the lesser cost of finding the oil would be taxable as a capital gain. Instead of selling his property, the doctrine continues, the producer retains and operates it as his own. Therefore, as he sells the oil piecemeal, he "realizes two distinct kinds of income: namely, a capital gain on the sale of an asset which has been held for a long period of time and a short-term income on the operation of a producing property. The capital gain is measured by the difference between his investment in establishing the production and the price at which he could sell the oil in place and turn it over to someone else who would then make the current profit on the operation of the producing property." Whenever a producer sells oil, then, a substantial part of his income is really a capital gain. As a capital gain, it is entitled to the special rate of 25 per cent which applies to other capital gains. Percentage depletion is essentially a convenient means of providing similar treatment through a special deduction instead of a special rate. In effect, the profit is separated into its two economic components, and one part is taxed as capital gain and the other as ordinary income.[25]

Dean Griswold does not concur in this reasoning, but he considers it the best argument developed for percentage depletion.[26] I prefer to describe the reasoning as highly imaginative. It illustrates once again how new excuses are resourcefully devised for old dispensations. Percentage depletion did not originate as a special method of taxing capital gains in the oil industry. Nor did it purport to segregate and tax, as a capital gain, the difference between the cost of finding oil and the value of the oil when found. As carefully conceived by its authors, percentage depletion is much better. It represents a complete exemption for that difference. In fact, the ideologists of depletion have long asserted, through the doctrine of depleted capital, that the difference between the value of the oil and the investment in the oil is capital which cannot be taxed as income. In noting these discrepancies I have no desire to deplore the inconsistencies in which the ideologists have indulged. I am more impressed by something else. In their attempt to identify percentage depletion with capital gains, even they at last concede that the proceeds of oil are fully income to the extent that the proceeds exceed the actual costs of obtaining the oil.

If this is so, then why should a considerable part of the income from a well be regarded as a capital gain? Businessmen who produce and sell other commodities cannot report their operating profits as capital gains. Why is the recurrent sale of oil different? The answer given is that if the producer sold all the oil in place in one transaction, his profit would be a capital gain taxable at the special rate. He should not be treated worse because he removes the oil himself and sells it gradually. But this response takes too much for granted. It assumes that one who is regularly engaged in finding and selling deposits of oil may report his profits as capital gains. However, he is no more entitled to pay the special rate than one who is in the business of buying and selling parcels of real estate. The same answer is often followed by the further thought that percentage depletion is in the public interest because it encourages small producers to retain and operate their properties. Without percentage depletion they would rather sell their holdings to the large companies, and our oil resources would soon be concentrated in a few hands. By allowing percentage depletion Congress serves the cause of free enterprise. While this fear of monopoly is commendable, there are more thorough ways of maintaining competition. Deductions for imaginary costs are not the only available solution. In any event, Congress seems unaware of the policy which is now attributed to it. For Congress has bestowed still another dispensation that is expressly designed to stimulate the sale of wells. If a taxpayer discovers and sells an oil property, the surtax on his profit cannot exceed 30 per cent of the price. This special rate was granted in order to induce him to sell his discovery. In short, one dispensation is supposed to discourage sales and the other is supposed to encourage them.[27]

If all other arguments fail, there is always the refuge of patriotism. We now reach the doctrine of national security.

This doctrine is an endless series of generalities concerned with our survival. A few quotations are enough to convey whatever has been said. We are pointedly reminded that of all the essentials of national defense, none "is as important for the waging of a war today as petroleum." "Both in peace and in war the country must have and is very dependent upon oil and gas." The "national safety would be jeopardized if we failed to maintain adequate reserves of petroleum" and "producing capacity." "We cannot depend upon foreign oil for our security." From this analysis the doctrine infers that the country cannot get along without percentage depletion. "Our very freedom is involved." Senator Dirksen of Illinois has stated this conclusion with admirable clarity. The oil companies must have percentage depletion in order to contribute adequately to our defense. That "is worth infinitely more than a question of whether the oil companies get a few million dollars more or a few million less." "There must be exploration. There must be incentive. Over and above everything else, there must be healthy, vital companies well directed, to take care of the needs of this country and of those with whom we are associated in the free world." By preserving percentage depletion we "manifest our devotion to the country."[28]

As I understand these moving words, if the oil industry were deprived of percentage depletion, it would not have the necessary incentives to make money and protect us. Petroleum and patriotism go hand in hand with percentage depletion. We cannot have security unless the industry has its dispensation. There are interesting implications here, but I pass on to other aspects of the doctrine.

The doctrine maintains that the industry must be stimulated to find more oil for the sake of our safety. Yet at the same time the adherents of percentage depletion assure us that we already have abundant reserves. Even if we were entirely cut off from foreign oil during a war, "the productive capacity of all the wells in America" would cover "our requirements for fuel." Those who lack a similar devotion to percentage depletion are unable to reconcile both positions. Senator Proxmire of Wisconsin is among the puzzled. Since there is already so much oil, he says, it seems "ridiculous" to "provide incentives for the more rapid exploration and development of the oil we have." If domestic production is accelerated, foreign oil has to be excluded; and meanwhile we "use up" our own "precious resource." Hence in the end we will be left "in a far less powerful position" to cope with a "catastrophe." The doctrine of national security is fully prepared for such unfriendly reactions. The problem, it states, is not one of sufficient oil but of sufficient wells. If new wells are not drilled, we will "not be able to provide the domestic requirements in the event of a national emergency."

Though the answer is lucid, Senator Proxmire is still perplexed. If we intend to preserve our military strength, he resumes, we cannot do so by encouraging the needless exploitation of our oil resources. Again the doctrine has a prompt reply. "Suppose we have to fight for survival in a national emergency. Then the steel we have could not be put in the oil wells, because the steel would be needed for tanks, for ships, for planes, for guns, and for all the various requirements of a war economy." We would have the oil, but we would lack the steel. If the oil is to be useful, we must "have the wells at the time the fighting starts." The danger is not one of "running out of oil," but of "not being able to produce the oil when it is needed."[29]

Very likely Senator Proxmire will continue to be puzzled by the deduction for imaginary costs. Originally the argument was that we do not have enough oil. Now the argument is that some day we may not have enough steel. Percentage depletion is therefore necessary in order to stimulate the producers of oil to buy the required steel while they can still get it.

We have not yet exhausted the doctrine of national security. The doctrine asserts that percentage depletion is essential to our safety because it encourages the industry to provide adequate reserves within the United States. In the absence of the dispensation we would be in serious straits. The country would be precariously dependent on foreign oil if war suddenly came. Only percentage depletion can assure us a sufficient supply of domestic oil. However, the deduction for imaginary costs knows no national boundaries. It applies to income from foreign oil as well as income from domestic oil. No parochial distinctions are drawn between wells in Saudi Arabia and wells in Texas. Yet if percentage depletion is patriotically designed to provide enough oil at home, why should it also help to develop more oil abroad—the very oil that is disparaged by the doctrine of national security? And if the purpose is to stimulate foreign production, then why are oil imports severely restricted? Is it rational to grant a special dispensation for oil that we refuse to use?[30]

Those who think that the doctrine of national security is embarrassed by such questions are sadly mistaken. Again the answer is simple. If we wish to be safe and sound, we must also induce the development of foreign oil. For "large reserves in the hands of friendly nations are very vital to our national security." Percentage depletion has the further merit of encouraging American capital to venture abroad.[31] The doctrine takes care of all contingencies. Percentage depletion is necessary at home because foreign oil may not be available; and percentage depletion is necessary abroad so that foreign oil will be available. The whole package is very nicely tied together.

I have summarized the five doctrines that are regularly invoked for percentage depletion in the oil industry. But a dispensation which is so rewarding inevitably inspires other elucidations. While these have not yet acquired the status and dignity of a doctrine, some of them are worth noting. There is enough variety to please everyone who wishes to be persuaded. We are told, for example, that if percentage depletion were repealed, the credit structure of Oklahoma would be undermined. The "whole banking system" there "is geared to oil." The deduction provides "the extra security" that the banks need when "they make the loans for the drilling of wells." What is true in Oklahoma is also true elsewhere. Or we are told that without percentage depletion we would have far less automobiles, and "the million miles" of roads paved since 1926 "would still be ankle-deep with dust in summer, knee-deep with mud in winter." Again, percentage depletion must be preserved "for the laborers in the oil fields." Many of them "are going to lose their jobs if the depletion allowance is drastically reduced." Percentage depletion, it seems, also helps to solve the farm problem. It stimulates drilling on the lands of farmers, who in turn receive royalties from producing wells. "Many a farmer has kept the wolf away from his door by reason of the 27½ per cent depletion allowance." Another explanation is more thorough. The true beneficiary of percentage depletion is not the industry, but the consumer. The industry simply "passes along to the consumer any so-called benefits it receives from the tax laws." And so it is the consumer who would suffer if the deduction disappeared. The benefits that may accrue to the operators are only illusory. Then there is the argument that refers us to the test of time. If a dispensation has survived for many years, it deserves to continue for many more. To quote an instructive analogy, "We no longer inquire into the workability of an internal combustion engine before we decide to buy an automobile any more than we investigate the theory of aerodynamics before we board a commercial airplane. So with the percentage depletion law." Finally, anyone who is still dissatisfied can derive comfort from Senator Dirksen. As he plainly puts the case, percentage depletion has enabled the oil companies to give "their best to their country." To repeal percentage depletion is to be ungrateful for what they have done.[32]

It is often said that percentage depletion is a subsidy to the oil industry. At times the ideologists of percentage depletion seem to agree, for they continually insist that the industry cannot get along without the benefits of the deduction. The risks would be too great and the profits too small. A "free-market price," they contend, is not a "sufficient incentive to develop our natural resources." There have even been overt confessions that the deduction for imaginary costs is a subsidy.[33] However, such intimations and admissions may be easily explained away as language loosely used. Over the years the ideologists have perceptively distinguished between percentage depletion and a subsidy. The difference seems to be that oil men are ingrained individualists who are unalterably opposed to subsidies. Percentage depletion is only something "in addition to the normal stimulus of profit." As the same thought has been differently expressed, whatever incentive the deduction may create is merely a happy coincidence.[34]

The dispensation for oil was initially justified in terms of its unique risks and peculiar importance. But now percentage depletion is bestowed on other minerals as well, regardless of their relative hazards and significance. If oil is beyond compare, why are other resources entitled to comparable treatment? "What is the danger of getting dry holes in connection with sand and gravel or clam shells and oyster shells?" Even an adherent of percentage depletion for oil may be troubled by such questions. Like Senator Monroney of Oklahoma, he may point out that "there is not much risk in going after coal or bauxite or monumental stones or sand or gravel."[35] But the Congressmen who insist on percentage depletion for oil are eminently wise in approving its extension to other resources. A vote for clam shells means more votes for oil. In taxation, too, much is to be said for hanging together lest someone be hanged separately.

While each mineral has its own interesting rationalizations, I will merely refer briefly to coal. In 1932 the coal industry obtained percentage depletion at the rate of 5 per cent. The approval of the dispensation followed the familiar observations on the poor state of the industry. As a Senator stated, "no industry" was "more desperately situated" and in "worse condition."[36] Twenty years later the rate became 10 per cent. Two reasons were given for the increase. First, the lower rate of 5 per cent was "of little practical value." Second, the industry was "peculiarly in need of more favorable tax treatment because of the inroads which alternative sources of energy, particularly oil and gas, have made on the potential markets of coal."[37]

This explanation has been criticized as an inexcusable display of inconsistency. On the one hand, percentage depletion is granted in order to stimulate the growth of the oil industry. On the other hand, percentage depletion is granted in order to alleviate the resulting distress of the coal industry. "If percentage depletion has any function in our tax structure, should it be used to encourage development of one group and 'bail out' another at the same time?"[38] Those who ask such questions are too bemused by small details. Even percentage depletion for oil does not rest on any one theory. There are many theories, and they are not always consistent with themselves or each other. An effective ideology must have room for more than one rationalization. Indeed, the argument for coal is especially cogent as arguments go. It rests on the new view of ability to pay, which was originally devised for elderly taxpayers and then applied to owners of coal royalties. As extended here, the new view states that taxpayers who derive income from coal mining should pay less tax because they cannot earn more income due to adverse competitive conditions. The active producers of coal are surely entitled to as much sympathy as the passive receivers of royalties.

If consistency is nevertheless the ultimate test, that standard is fully satisfied on the level that counts. In the case of coal, as of oil, percentage depletion is a means of enabling the industry to operate for our welfare. And in both cases the dispensation achieves the desired result by allowing a deduction for imaginary costs. Of course, variations in emphasis should be expected, for each extractive industry has its own problems. Yet despite the differences, the arguments have managed to be remarkably similar. Those who cavil at minor inconsistencies are not sufficiently impressed by this achievement.

Let us glance at the rationalizations for coal. It is too much to argue, in the fashion of the oil industry, that we are imperiled by a critical dearth of coal and that new mines must be found. The country has enough coal for at least another 2,400 years. But one can always talk of national security and the anxiety of the industry to do its part through reduced taxes. The argument flows with assurance. Coal is extremely important to our defense. "In war or peace the national economic strength is based largely on the production of steel and electrical energy." And coal is essential to the production of both. In the years to come coal will be even more important as "the basis of a synthetic oil and gas industry" to replace "our vanishing reserves of natural gas and oil." Eventually the country will "rely upon coal as its primary energy source." Though there is enough coal to do the required job, unfortunately the industry does not have the necessary capital. "Unlike most other industries," it "has no adequate source of profits from which to obtain such capital. Because there is available to the Nation no other source of energy capable of supplying the Nation's long-term needs, this threat to the coal industry's productive capacity is a threat to the Nation's well-being." This overwhelming problem can only be solved by an adequate allowance for depletion. Otherwise "the United States will soon join the ranks of the have-nots insofar as energy is concerned. If that happens, we will not be able to maintain our position of world leadership; we will not be able to maintain our standard of living; and we will be unable to defend ourselves."[39]

The eloquence is familiar. Certainly the rhetorical effects compare very favorably with those produced by the ideologists of oil. If oil is important, coal is more important. As usual, Congress is threatened with disaster untold unless the deduction for imaginary costs is granted in a proper amount. Only percentage depletion seems to stand between us and the Soviet Union. Here and there an incongruity may appear. The ideologists of oil argue that we have oil enough for 1,000 years. Percentage depletion is necessary so that the producers of oil will drill the required wells. The ideologists of coal argue that our supply of oil is vanishing. Percentage depletion is necessary so that the producers of coal will provide other sources of energy. But if we think hard, the discrepancy soon becomes too trivial to notice. Oil needs wells; wells need steel; and steel needs coal. Hence coal as well as oil must be endowed with percentage depletion.

But what of sand and gravel, and clam shells and oyster shells? Why should a deduction for imaginary costs be allowed for such items and many others? Senator Douglas has given us the answer. "If we start the defense argument, every industry comes in under the tent."[40] Military strength depends on economic strength; and economic strength depends on mineral industries with adequate inventories. There is no room for any exceptions. Aside from its fears for our security, Congress is also guided by the ideal of equality before the law. As percentage depletion is extended to one mineral, it must later be extended to another which competes with it or has "just as good a claim for such treatment." Otherwise Congress will be guilty of discrimination. If percentage depletion is given "to those who scoop sand off the seashore," it must also be given "to those who strip hillsides of gravel."[41] This process of distributing dispensations fairly and justly is known as equity—a subject which I am about to reach. If I may borrow from the late Congressman Jenkins of Ohio, "the depletion business has been pretty well handled." Everything is "supposed to work out fairly and properly" for everybody.[42]

The ideologists of ability are sorely distressed by the spread of percentage depletion. They are particularly aggrieved because this misfortune has occurred while taxpayers without mineral resources are being heavily burdened. But as I have already said, if percentage depletion is involved, there is always a ready answer. The higher the tax rates, the greater the need for relief. And so in 1951, when Congress imposed income taxes exceeding those of World War II, it also expanded percentage depletion. Though further revenue was immediately required, an annual loss of $76 million was cheerfully approved.[43] If we are to be prosperous and secure, we must have sound mineral industries that are properly inspired to serve us.

CHAPTER 7

The Wondrous Ways of Equity

I come at last to the third ideology—the ideology of equity. We are now in the presence of a hallowed principle to which adherents of all faiths regularly repair and plead due devotion. It is not improper for an adherent of ability to criticize the ideology of barriers and deterrents. Nor is it unseemly for a disciple of barriers and deterrents to belittle the ideology of ability. But to speak ill of equity is akin to an admission of inadequate patriotism.

Many words have been written in praise of equity. Since everyone commends it, we should not expect its meaning to be precise. It is a model of ambiguity, like truth, justice, and due process of law, which more metaphysical minds than mine have long sought to define. In a reported dialogue of many years ago a Roman official inquired, "What is truth?" He failed to wait for an answer, and none is recorded. Unfortunately, I cannot exercise the same privilege of merely asking a question and then departing.

Equity, in the realm of taxes, is commonly summarized in an engaging generality: Those who are similarly situated should be similarly taxed. The apparent theme of this attractive platitude is equality before the law. "Let all Americans pay taxes on the basis of equality."[1] At this point the bromide becomes uninformative, and the devotees are left to their own devices. As I need hardly add, the desire for equity does not inspire the same thoughts in all who labor over its content. To Aristotle, as to John C. Calhoun, the notion of equality was easily reconciled with the institution of slavery.

Let us consider so basic an issue as the relative equities of an income tax and a sales tax. Those who prefer an income tax will say that equity consists of similar burdens on similar incomes, after due allowance for appropriate deductions. Those who prefer a sales tax will reply, "there is nothing fairer than a system in which the more you spend the more you pay."[2] Both groups have a laudable interest in equality of treatment, but there the agreement rapidly ends. In one case the criterion of equality is the income that is realized. In the other case it is the income that is spent. Though the same concrete data are contemplated, the results are dissimilar. The conclusions vary because each abstracts a different part of the whole and treats it as controlling. The facts that are selected as relevant depend on the standard of relevance that is applied. However, the choice that is made has little to do with the abstract definition of equity.

This is not to say that the platitude is a useless collection of words. Otherwise we would fall into the error which Henry Simons failed to avoid. While Simons was an enthusiast of equity, he was unable to grasp its true significance. The burdens of taxation, he wrote, "should bear similarly upon persons whom we regard as in substantially similar circumstances, and differently where circumstances differ. This may seem like waste of words; but the point is important." Again and again Simons returned to this precept of equality. He condemned tax statutes "which discriminated grossly and arbitrarily between and among persons of substantially similar circumstances." Yet he also concluded, "The criterion of equity, by itself, leads only to a vague and elusive ideal, not to a sound and workable income tax."[3] What Simons strangely overlooked is that the homilies on equity serve as an ideology. They cannot be more than vague noises. An ideology must speak in majestic tones, but it should shun any effort to be too instructive. Its power to persuade hinges largely on its failure to enlighten. As Oscar Wilde remarked, nothing produces such pleasing effects as a good platitude.

Undoubtedly, those who regularly echo the generalities on equity take a different view. They assume that the utterances are informative. I quote three typical declarations on the nature of equity. One states that "individuals in like economic circumstances should be treated alike." The second states that "two persons whose relevant circumstances are the same should pay the same tax." The third states, "Equity is achieved when persons and businesses in a similar economic position are taxed the same."[4] Here are observations which few would dispute. But at no point are we told how to determine which circumstances or positions are "relevant," and whether "relevant" circumstances or positions are "like," "similar," or "the same." The generalities are available for almost any result that may be desired. One can argue that equal amounts of earned income and capital gains should bear like taxes because they represent like abilities to pay. Or one can argue that the burdens should be different because the "relevant circumstances" are different. Hence both the adherents of ability and the adherents of barriers and deterrents are dedicated to the cause of equity. Each school, in its own way, firmly disapproves of discrimination.

The adherents of ability embrace a view of equity which necessarily derives from their ideology. Theirs is not to reason why, as only one view can usually do. For the purposes of equity, they say, the relevant circumstances to be compared are the dollars of income that are realized. Persons are in like circumstances if they have like dollars of income. Since they are similarly situated, they should be similarly taxed. Such matters as the origin of the income or the risks of obtaining it are irrelevant. The essence of similarity is equivalence in dollars. In the words of Randolph Paul, equity is the "even treatment of persons with equal incomes," regardless of the source of the incomes.[5] This arithmetical view of equity has penetrated into documents printed at Government expense. A study published under the auspices of the Joint Economic Committee states, with overtones of approval, that this "basic principle of equity" commands "widespread agreement." A report by the same committee declares: "The basic goal should be that those with substantially the same incomes should pay substantially the same taxes."[6]

Under this notion of equity no distinction should be made between one kind of income and another. Income from services should not be taxed more heavily than income from dividends. Compensation through stock options should not be treated more pleasantly than compensation paid in cash. Capital gains are not entitled to a special rate, for it discriminates against persons in comparable economic circumstances. Yet even the adherents of ability should be troubled souls as they contemplate the virtues of simple arithmetic. Though they insist that persons with the same dollar income should be equally taxed, they may also approve the different burdens borne by the married and the single. Or they may grudgingly concede that capital gains should be more leniently treated than earned income. Again, if one taxpayer spends $2,000 in support of his mother while another with the same income donates $2,000 to some college, they will readily agree that the first should pay a larger tax than the second. Evidently the arithmetical view of equity is appropriate until one prefers to do without it. Then the same dollars are no longer the same circumstances.

The ideologists of barriers and deterrents are more discerning. The noble theme of equality, they say, cannot be reduced to mere arithmetic. Dollars may be relevant, but they are hardly conclusive. Persons may be differently situated though their incomes are the same. In an effort to do equity Congress has long provided special rules for distinct groups and activities. One general rule cannot be fairly applied to all alike. As a result, the adherents of barriers and deterrents can also speak well of equity without disturbing any dispensations that they approve. For an example of this settled procedure, I turn again to Roswell Magill and his colleagues of the Special Tax Study Committee. Its views on equity are as informative as its meditations on barriers and deterrents.

"Since the tax load now falls so heavily upon all classes of citizens," the Committee stated, "it is important that like incomes bear like burdens. No kind of income, nor any class of taxpayer, should be discriminated against or, by the same token, should any class of taxpayer enjoy special advantages." "Since income taxes will have to be heavy, we must use great care to see that they are spread as fairly as possible over the income producers in our population." The "purpose" of the Committee "in all cases" was "to eliminate manifest inequities." In response to this worthy aspiration the Committee then proposed about 50 revisions of the income, estate and gift tax laws. Amid this imposing total merely one group of taxpayers was exposed as paying too little tax when compared with others receiving "like incomes." After meticulously studying our tax system in a "nonpartisan, objective spirit," the Committee found that only certain aliens were avoiding a fair share of the burden. Otherwise "no kind of income, nor any class of taxpayer" was bearing less tax than it should. Or to restate the Committee's conclusion, such dispensations as percentage depletion and the special rate for capital gains were not considered "special advantages" or "manifest inequities." In fact, the Committee proposed additional dispensations because Congress had not provided enough. As the Committee thoughtfully noted lest it be misunderstood, "The interests of the Treasury have been constantly in our minds, and, in our opinion, they are adequately protected."[7]

Adherents of ability to pay are repeatedly astonished by such rationalizations. "Oh Equity," they say, "what things are done in thy name!" They are disagreeably surprised because they invariably overlook the same thing—that the conclusions derived depend on the criteria that are applied. As Magill and his colleagues recognized, equity requires that "like incomes bear like burdens." But they were no less persuaded that income from oil and gas is different from other income. Therefore, percentage depletion is fully in accord with equity, and cannot be regarded as a "special advantage." The report prepared under the guidance of Magill significantly indicates that equity consists of two basic propositions rather than one. If taxpayers in similar circumstances should be similarly treated, then taxpayers in different circumstances should be differently treated. While this additional information does not remove all the obscurities, it still helps us to understand that those who desire special exceptions are also devoted to equity.

A current quarrel over tax policy illuminates this devotion. The issue is whether income from business carried on abroad should bear a lower tax than income from business done at home. Naturally the adherents of ability to pay and the adherents of barriers and deterrents divide on this question. Each group invokes the sanction of equity, just as nations at war are simultaneously assured of the Lord's blessing. The adherents of ability argue, "The basic principle of fairness underlying the Federal income tax is that the amount of tax should be determined by the economic status or ability to pay of the taxpayer and not by the industry or the geographical location of the business activity." This principle requires "equal taxation of income," no matter where the income is earned.[8] The ideologists of barriers and deterrents assert that foreign income should be more lightly taxed because it is earned in more difficult circumstances. Of course, while all this goes on, the usual assertions are heard that lower taxes will eliminate barriers and deterrents. As one ideologist puts it, businessmen have "a spirit of adventure," and lower taxes will stimulate them to venture abroad. He compares the plight of discouraged businessmen to the predicament of Columbus, who was also discouraged from going overseas. A second ideologist adds a note of patriotism. Lower taxes on income earned abroad will increase the economic strength of the free world. If we are to remain free, the least we can do is reduce the taxes of certain taxpayers. Another ideologist promises that eventually all taxes will be reduced. If more American capital ventures abroad, it will create more "jobs and industries" there. These benefits, in turn, "will relieve the tax burden" of our "farmers and workers and other producers," who now have to support foreign economies.[9] In so far as equity is concerned, the crux of the dispute is clear. To the school of ability, the geographical source of the income is irrelevant. To the school of barriers and deterrents, it is decisive. Here, again, what one sees depends on how one looks at things as well as the things one looks at.

Other issues of the moment also contribute to the same wisdom. Few things are so dear to a Congressman as a stated concern for the problems of small business. Many words are spent each year on the financial difficulties that harass little companies in a competitive economy. If not very much is done for them, still a good deal is said. According to the observations that are commonly heard, small corporations are suffering from a chronic lack of capital. Unlike the large public corporations, they are unable to accumulate sufficient capital from within or to attract it from without. The ideology of barriers and deterrents prescribes the usual kind of solution. If small corporations and their investors were more leniently taxed, the necessary funds would soon be available. The specific suggestions have varied, but they all reflect the same understanding of equity. Small corporations and large corporations are differently situated, and so they should be differently taxed. To treat them alike "is to court economic disaster."[10]

But if someone tries to reduce the percentage depletion of the large companies, then the difference between large and small disappears. The same Congressmen suddenly see things that are otherwise unnoticed. We are promptly informed that large and small are similarly situated and should be similarly treated. We should not be led astray by mere size.[11] As I have already said, it would be inconsiderate to embarrass the ideologists by accusing them of contradictions. Their job is to be effective, not consistent. Though they appreciate the trials of the small producers, they also know that the large operators enjoy the bulk of percentage depletion. If this situation is to continue, large companies cannot be distinguished from small ones.

Why are all producers of oil in like circumstances, whether they be large or small? For those who fail to understand, Grandma Jones again provides the answer. She appears in the debate between Senator Proxmire and Senator Long which I noted in the last chapter.[12] Senator Proxmire offered an amendment which would have reduced the percentage depletion of producers with gross incomes over $1 million. Senator Long charged that the proposal was plainly inequitable. It would penalize Grandma Jones, who had inherited a mere 6 shares in a large oil corporation. "She would be denied the benefit of the 27½ per cent depletion allowance," while "an independent producer" worth $1 million would fully enjoy the benefit, "even though he was in better shape than Grandma Jones." Senator Proxmire observed that if his colleague's argument was correct, Congress should bestow a special tax exemption on all large corporations whose stockholders include a widow or an orphan. Otherwise Congress would be "hurting the poor orphan or widow" in requiring such corporations "to pay the same taxes as every other company." Senator Long answered, "I have been fairly consistent in my efforts to favor Grandma Jones. My efforts to provide welfare increase and adequate social security payments should show that my heart is in it." Though the Senator's interest in social security is commendable, its immediate relevance was rather obscure. Evidently the Senator himself came to the same conclusion, for he quickly returned to his prior concern for Grandma Jones as a widowed stockholder. The question of equity, he indicated, is not whether large and small oil companies are similarly situated, but whether the "vast majority" of small stockholders in the large companies should be mistreated. Surely, he reasoned, the small stockholders deserve "the same tax treatment" as the "substantial" independent producers with assets of $1 million.

The sympathetic allusions to Grandma Jones should clarify the nature of equity in taxation. If the objective is a special dispensation for small private corporations, the argument is that they should not be treated like the large public corporations. To tax them similarly is to discriminate against the little entrepreneurs. But if the objective is a special dispensation for the public companies, then the argument is that they should be treated like the private companies. To tax them differently is to discriminate against the little stockholders in the public companies. In the first case one speaks of humble corporations beset by overwhelming odds; in the other, of humble stockholders bereft of husbands. And if the tears for the widows fail to flow, one can always suggest that the preservation of percentage depletion is somehow related to social security. Even those who are not convinced should be impressed. The ideologists are performing admirably in difficult circumstances. I believe it was Goethe who said that an artist truly reveals his capacities when he works within exacting limitations. That is why lawyers are highly regarded when they win hard cases, though they may make bad law.

The ideology of equity, then, is sensitively concerned with both differences and resemblances. Just as those who are similarly situated should not be differently taxed, those who are differently situated should not be similarly taxed. Hence the ideology is always available to sanctify a special dispensation if an excuse is required. Indeed, the ideology applies even when the dispensation is carefully contrived for only one taxpayer.

Perhaps the most celebrated example is the statute which the Senate Finance Committee thoughtfully devised for Louis B. Mayer, of Hollywood. Though the story has often been told, it is worth retelling again. Mr. Mayer was about to retire from his eminent position as a contributor to American culture. He had faithfully served his employer for about 20 years; on retirement he was entitled to share in the future profits of his employer for about 5 years or until his death; and his contract of employment had so provided for about 12 years. Instead of assuming the risk of future operations, Mr. Mayer desired to depart with one large lump-sum payment. However, if he took the payment, relatively little would remain after taxes. The Finance Committee was informed of his acute problem, and proved to be a friend in need. It declared that an employee who was so unfortunately situated was in a peculiarly distressing situation. He was caught between the bleak prospect of an "unduly harsh" tax and the unpleasant alternative of leaving "his retirement income dependent upon the operation of the business."[13] In the light of its compassionate appraisal, the Committee graciously wrote a special statute for Mr. Mayer. The statute, like the Committee, refrained from mentioning him by name. It simply stated:

> Amounts received from the assignment or release by an employee, after more than twenty years' employment, of all his rights to receive, after termination of his employment and for a period of not less than 5

years (or for a period ending with his death), a percentage of future profits or receipts of his employer shall be considered an amount received from the sale or exchange of a capital asset held for more than six months, if such rights were included in the terms of the employment of such employee for not less than twelve years, and if the total of the amounts received for such assignment or release are received in one taxable year and after the termination of such employment.

In less elegant prose, Mr. Mayer's tax on his compensation was reduced from 91 per cent to 25 per cent. He reportedly saved about $2 million.[14] The statute which produced this beneficial result is known as the Mayer amendment, but the Finance Committee entitled it "Taxability to Employee of Termination Payments." Apparently the Committee wisely realized that others might also qualify for the same treatment under the same terms, and it refused to discriminate against them. As we have seen, equity requires that those who are similarly situated should be similarly taxed. The Committee's refined sense of equity was soon justified. In 1954 the Ways and Means Committee eliminated the statute in the process of re-writing the Internal Revenue Code. But the Finance Committee diligently restored it for the benefit of other executives who had already made similar arrangements. They, too, were entitled to pay only 25 per cent. It would be unfair to treat them less kindly than Mr. Mayer.[15]

Other taxpayers have also sought and obtained statutes skilfully tailored to their special needs. While the results are not always so profitable, they are still helpful. The deduction for dependents offers an instructive example. Various relatives qualify as dependents for income tax purposes, though they reside away from the taxpayer. The recognized categories embrace ancestors and descendants, brothers and sisters, uncles and aunts, nephews and nieces, sons-in-law and daughters-in-law, fathers-in-law and mothers-in-law, brothers-in-law and sisters-in-law. On the other hand, cousins are not included. However, a certain taxpayer had a certain cousin, and he so advised an appropriate legislator. The result was a special exception. Therefore, even a cousin is now an eligible dependent if he meets two requirements. He must first reside with the taxpayer, and then enter an institution because of a physical or mental disability. No other cousin will do.

In 1956 Congress came to the aid of Leo Sanders, of Oklahoma. Mr. Sanders was in the construction business. In 1943 he completed a project for the Government at an aircraft plant. As the work proceeded, there were costly changes in specifications, and Mr. Sanders filed claims for additional compensation. After considerable negotiations the claims were finally settled in June, 1949, for about $1 million. Mr. Sanders tried to have this amount taxed as a capital gain, but the courts held that it was ordinary income subject to the progressive rates. The tax due was about $700,000.[16] Mr. Sanders was not disheartened. It never hurts to try again—and sometimes it pays. He consulted a member of the Finance Committee, and a dispensation was soon obtained through a special statute entitled "Certain Claims Against United States." The statute provides that if an amount is "received by a taxpayer from the United States with respect to a claim against the United States," and the claim arises "under a contract for the construction of installations or facilities for any branch of the armed services of the United States," the resulting tax "shall not exceed" 33 per cent of the amount received—if the claim remained "unpaid for over 5 years from the date" it "first accrued," and if the claim was paid in 1949.

Mr. Sanders did not fare as well as Mr. Mayer. His tax was reduced to 33 per cent, not 25 per cent. But as an offset against such discrimination, he received very fast service in more critical circumstances. He did not finally lose in the courts until February, 1956, and by June, 1956, he already had his dispensation. Nor does everyone have the privilege of paying 33 per cent on an income of $1 million. Clearly, Mr. Sanders was regarded as a unique taxpayer whose relevant circumstances were wholly unlike all others. Those who granted his dispensation even served notice that it was not a precedent for any similar dispensations.[17] Equity must be handled with care and perception. If Congress were too generous, its judgment might be questioned. Only a special taxpayer should be given a special statute.

In early 1958 Congress added another to its many dispensations for isolated taxpayers. Charles E. Merrill, a partner in a well-known brokerage firm, died on October 6, 1956. He willed an interest in the firm to a charitable trust as a limited partner. Under the law which generally applies, the trust's share of the profits was taxable as income derived from a business. Both tax committees were soon persuaded that the rule which applies to others should not apply to the trust created by Mr. Merrill. Sympathy and understanding produced the desired dispensation. Congress approved an amendment which exempts the business income received by a trust as a limited partner, if the trust was created by the will of an individual who died after August 16, 1954—the date of enactment of the present Internal Revenue Code—and before January 1, 1957. No other decedent will do.[18]

The four examples which I have given, as well as the many which must be omitted, illustrate a common theme. A taxpayer concludes that a general rule is unduly burdensome. Impressed by his difficulty, he applies for relief on the ground that the relevant circumstances are dissimilar to those within the general rule. He invokes the principle of equity that taxpayers who are differently situated should be differently treated. In time those endowed with legislative authority are also convinced that equity calls for an exception, and the required dispensation is granted. The adherents of ability to pay condemn such dispensations as unwholesome departures from general rules. "Let us safeguard the uniformity of our taxes," they declare amid chagrin and distress, "lest this system become undermined and collapse."[19] This intense yearning for uniformity is scarcely a complete answer. All law proceeds on the basis of distinctions. For the purposes of equity the significant question is whether the distinction reflects a difference in circumstances which justifies a difference in treatment. The mere fact that relatively few are treated as a class apart is not necessarily proof that the distinction was wrongly conceived.

Certainly, if Congress isolates a small group and treats them less favorably than others, no one is disturbed because only few are involved. A recent amendment indicates this lack of concern. An exemption is allowed for a dependent who is not a relative if he has his principal place of abode in the taxpayer's home, and is a member of the taxpayer's household. Recently, however, Congress denied an exemption for a dependent with whom one regularly dwells in sin. We may safely assume that such deductions are not often claimed. Yet the adherents of ability to pay are untroubled, though only few are selected for special treatment. I am not suggesting that these adherents should be upset. They may well feel, as the Treasury does, that one who lives in sin should not be rewarded by a reduction in tax. The fact remains that the size of the group is deemed immaterial in appraising the merits of what Congress has wrought. But if numbers are unimportant when the burden is increased, why are they important when the burden is decreased? Surely equity is not a mechanical matter of counting heads. Aristotle wrote that the very essence of equity is an appropriate exception for particular cases. It is a deliberate deviation from a general rule in order to fit what he called "special circumstances" or "peculiar conditions."

Still, in final analysis the adherents of ability are not unreasonably troubled. If Mr. Mayer was entitled to pay only 25 per cent, why are others less deserving if their earnings are unusually bunched in a particular year? If a charitable trust need not pay a tax on its share of earnings as a limited partner, why must the creator of the trust die after August 16, 1954, and before January 1, 1957? If a cousin may qualify as a dependent, why must he first retire to an institution for a physical or mental disability? If a large recovery on a claim is taxable at only 33 per cent, why must the claim be against the Government; why must it derive from the construction of facilities for the armed forces; why must it be unpaid over 5 years; and why must it be paid in 1949? These are cogent questions. They remain searching when we sadly realize that a special statute for a special taxpayer reflects a special influence which most of us are unable to exert. As a well-informed legislator has stated, "it is pretty difficult" to obtain "one of these special provisions in the Ways and Means Committee."[20] Many try but few are chosen. The ears of a Congressman are not equally receptive to all who complain. Even if he were more generously inclined, he would have to ration the relief at his disposal. Since he cannot satisfy everybody, he pleases those whose influence is more compelling. The voice of the people does not speak with uniform authority.

I have said that equity is concerned with differences as well as similarities, and that a convenient way to a dispensation is to dwell upon alleged differences. But there is more than one route to salvation. A lower tax may also be obtained by emphasizing similarities with others who are already paying less. Even dispensations should be equitably granted; and so one dispensation leads on to another.

Income splitting is among the familiar illustrations. In view of my prior appraisal, little more need be said here.[21] Until 1948 there was a marked discrimination within the upper brackets. Married couples in the community property states paid substantially less than those in the common law states. In 1947 the Special Tax Study Committee described the distinction as "perhaps the most important inequity now in need of correction."[22] A year later this vexing problem was happily resolved. Those who were aggrieved became entitled to pay equally less. So equity was done, for equity is the even application of the tax laws.

The retirement credit is another example of how taxpayers are equalized. For many years various pensions, such as social security and railroad retirement benefits, have been tax-exempt. In 1948 the Republicans went one step further. They granted a special exemption of $600 to all taxpayers over 65, whether retired or active, prosperous or poor. The Finance Committee lauded this new dispensation as a significant advance in its persistent quest for equity. The exemption of certain retirement incomes had produced a demand for a similar exemption of other kinds, especially pensions of former school teachers and other government employees. The proper answer, the Committee reasoned, was a uniform exemption for all elderly taxpayers rather than further exemptions for particular types of income. However, the Committee modestly conceded that the new dispensation was not enough. Some better solution had to be found for the discrimination among the retired, and it promised to go into the matter with the next general revenue bill.[23]

As these reflections on equity indicate, the Committee was indisposed toward specific exemptions for particular pensions. Yet the Committee's performance may seem less impressive than its words. Everyone over 65 was given a special deduction, while those receiving certain pensions still had their special exemptions. The discrimination in their favor continued, and they paid even less tax than before. But the ways of equity are not always as simple and direct as we would like them to be. If the old dispensations remained, it is also true that a new one had been given. And unlike the old ones, it was equally kind to all taxpayers who had reached the required age.

The next general bill came along in 1950, but again the Committee failed to remove the discrimination that disturbed it. Senator Ives of New York, however, saw no reason for further delay. Why, he asked, should pensions paid to retired government workers be taxed if other retirement benefits are exempt? Since equity is the privilege of paying as little as somebody else, he proposed that the former should be given a similar exemption. Senator George, as Chairman of the Finance Committee, was unable to agree. The proposal, he said, would give a special exemption to elderly taxpayers who received a government pension. The exemption would be as large as $1,800. As these taxpayers already had personal exemptions of $1,200, the amendment would increase their tax-free income to $3,000. It was unjust to relieve pensioners of the government to that extent, unless "ordinary" citizens received the same exemption. In view of Senator George's doubts, Senator Ives' proposal failed.[24]

The debate between the two Senators points up a difficulty that often besets those who go forth in search of equity. In accordance with the usual procedure they will argue that a dispensation should be granted to certain taxpayers because other "like" taxpayers are already paying less. But their adversaries will just as easily argue that the dispensation should be denied because other "like" taxpayers will still continue to pay more. Hence what was elementary justice to Senator Ives was a special exemption to Senator George. The same debate also helps us to understand the subtleties of equity. Though Senator George resolutely opposed a special exemption for retired government workers, a year later he sponsored the special dispensation for Louis B. Mayer. At first blush the Senator's views on equity may appear incongruous. Why did he stand firm in one case and yield in the other? Yet there is no reason to be puzzled. Senator George resisted the proposed dispensation for government employees because he did not wish to discriminate against other workers. The amendment for Mr. Mayer, however, did not create any such acute problem of discrimination. Very few employees can claim that they are in a similar economic position. And unless they are, they are not entitled to be similarly treated. To this I should add one more thought in behalf of Senator George. The dispensation requested for retired government employees was clearly a special exemption. As much as $1,800 a year would have been completely tax-free. On the other hand, while the dispensation granted to Mr. Mayer was a special exception, it was not a special exemption. He still had to pay a tax of 25 per cent. The ways of our statesmen are not always as mysterious as they seem.

Senator George's problem of discrimination was soon solved in the accepted manner. The exemption already conferred on certain pensions and annuities was extended to other incomes received by elderly taxpayers in retirement. When a similar exemption is given to all who are similarly situated, it can no longer be called "special." This new venture in equity is the retirement credit—a dispensation which I previously examined among the ruins of ability to pay.[25] Since the tax reduction devised for the retired is an effort to be fair and impartial, it applies not only to pensions and annuities, but also to interest, rents and dividends. Congress refused to discriminate against individuals who provide independently for their old age. The elderly taxpayer who ruggedly relies on his own savings should not fare worse than one who draws a pension.[26]

There are critics who quarrel with this conclusion. The prior exemption for social security and railroad retirement benefits was essentially an exception for elderly individuals with small incomes. Why, they ask, should a similar dispensation be given to elderly taxpayers with large incomes from real estate or securities? Equity presupposes that only those who are similarly situated should be similarly treated. Why, then, is an abundant income considered akin to a meager one? Even Secretary of the Treasury Humphrey felt that the relief "should be limited to those who live principally on small pensions or other small incomes and not extended to those receiving relatively large pensions or other large income."[27] While the questions are well-intentioned, they reveal a basic misunderstanding of equity. Two taxpayers may have something in common though their incomes are quite different. Both, for example, may be married or single. Both may be executives or investors. Income is not the sole criterion of similarity. Equity is sufficiently done if two taxpayers are treated alike in the light of any resemblance that may be detected. It is immaterial that others are more impressed by the difference between their two incomes. The views of Congress are not so narrow and rigid. It declines to hold that only similar incomes make similar taxpayers.

When properly appraised the special allowance for retirement income easily passes as a respectable essay in equity. The necessary ingredients are clearly there. The dispensation is given to taxpayers who are over 65 and in retirement. They are all similarly situated because they are all elderly people who earn little or nothing by working. Therefore, they should be similarly treated. Those who are sustained by large incomes from investments may not need the tax reduction, but they are still similarly situated.

One further item should be clarified before we leave the elderly. These taxpayers now have two dispensations where before they had one: the extra exemption of $600 and the retirement credit. Each is equitable in a different way. The exemption of $600 asserts that all taxpayers over 65 are similarly situated. The allowance for retirement income adds that all taxpayers who are over 65 and retired are similarly situated. If many of the elderly now enjoy two dispensations instead of one, it is only because they are twice blessed with the required similarity.

I have been exploring an important principle of equity—that one dispensation justifies another. All who are similarly situated are equally entitled to pay less. The ideology of barriers and deterrents is a fruitful source for the application of this principle. If special exceptions are made for our general welfare, they should also be fairly distributed. Wise economics and impeccable equity go hand in hand.

At one time certain taxpayers in the timber industry were treated better than others. If a taxpayer sold his standing timber outright, his profit might be taxable as a capital gain. But if he cut the timber himself, or allowed others to do so and shared in the proceeds, his profit was taxable as ordinary income. In the early forties Congress concluded that this distinction discriminated among comparable businessmen.[28] Since special dispensations should be fairly distributed, they were all given the privilege of paying less. On this occasion Congress was particularly responsive to the call for equity. Taxpayers were retroactively relieved from 1913 on. Congress is not always so thoroughly considerate, but then again not everybody sells timber. In 1954 Congress added a further touch of equity. It provided that those who sell evergreen trees are entitled to the special rate of 25 per cent if the trees are sold for ornamental purposes and are over 6 years old when severed from the roots. Evidently taxpayers who sell younger evergreen trees are not yet similarly situated.

A new dispensation for inventors also illustrates how the removal of barriers and deterrents makes way for more equity. Until 7 years ago there was a basic, if elusive, distinction between the professional inventor who was in the business of selling his patents and the amateur inventor who made a sale now and then. The profit of the first was taxable as ordinary income; the profit of the second as capital gain. Those who were afflicted with a professional status earnestly pleaded that all inventors are similarly situated and that the lower rate should be available without discrimination. In 1954 Congress finally heeded the call for equity, and all inventors became entitled to like treatment. The tax committees had become aware that the distinction between one inventor and another was "arbitrary" and hence inexcusable. In order to remove any doubts that others might entertain, the committees also invoked the ideology of barriers and deterrents. Taxpayers who are not inventors were informed that the prior treatment "tends to discourage scientific work." The "genius of the independent American inventor" was thwarted and repressed. The "more liberal" treatment would "stimulate production and employment" because it would "provide a larger incentive to all inventors to contribute to the welfare of the nation."[29] Before 1954, it seems, many inventors were reluctant to be inventive because of the taxes they would pay. In asking them to pay less, we inspire them to return to work in our behalf.

Since equity includes the equal distribution of dispensations, the quest for equity is necessarily a search without end. As a prior dispensation is extended, a new discrimination is created; and the demand for equity is inevitably soon heard once more. All this is as it should be, if dispensations are to be impartially granted. Family income and discouraged inventors are again instructive examples.

Once income splitting is made available, it is hard to stop. As Senator Millikin of Colorado correctly anticipated, "Usually when you start off on a course of this kind, you are then called upon for relief in many directions by analogy."[30] The analogies were soon supplied. While single people do not enjoy the felicities of marriage, they may still claim that their financial problems are comparable. After a few years the Ways and Means Committee decided that there is much to be said for this attitude. Taxpayers without spouses, it found, are somewhat akin to married couples if they have to maintain a home for the benefit of others. As a case in point, the Committee referred to a head of a household who shares his income with a child. The "hardship" is "particularly severe," the Committee stated, "for a widow or widower with children to raise." The survivor of the marriage is not only "denied the spouse's aid in raising the children," but also pays the price of "heavier" taxes. Though the comparison with married couples was disturbing, the Committee detected a difference as well as a similarity. A head of a household, it added, does not share his income with children or others to the same extent as husband and wife do. Therefore, he should have only half the benefits of income splitting. The Finance

Committee agreed that a head of a household was in need of help, but felt that a fourth of the benefits was enough. The Ways and Means Committee finally prevailed, and heads of households were relieved through a special table of rates.[31]

In an effort to be equitable the committees had developed a new theory for the occasion. According to this later explanation, married couples are entitled to splitting because they share their income. Since they share, they are taxed "substantially as if they were two single individuals each with half of the total income of the couple."[32] From this it follows that a head of a household also merits some splitting because he shares his income with offspring or other dependents. Of course, the happy device of splitting was not born of any such close analysis of domestic economics. It was conveniently conceived as the only feasible means of equalizing husbands in the higher brackets. There was no need to indulge in any refined rationalizations. Indeed, if husband and wife "share" their income in a joint domestic enterprise, their community of interest suggests that they should be taxed as one rather than "two single individuals." On the other hand, if splitting is based on "sharing," then family income should be apportioned among all members of the household, children as well as spouses. Why should a couple without children receive as much benefit from splitting as a couple with children? If husband and wife are childless, the income should be split between two taxpayers. If they have three children, the income should be split among five.

I am saying that the tax committees simply improvised a revised explanation for income splitting. While such imaginative changes in theory may seem unfortunate departures from fact, they are hardly novel. It is not unusual to alter the reason initially supplied for a tax dispensation if others are later to be similarly blessed. If old reasons will not do, new reasons must be offered. The tax committees are not entirely free in the matter. Constituents who are aggrieved are like clients. They are primarily interested in results, not reasons. They are convinced that their ability to pay is no greater than the capacity of others who are paying less. And they expect a reason to be found for affording them the same privilege.

A single taxpayer who maintains a home for himself and others may appropriately ask why his lot should be much worse because he lacks a wife. Since he will fail to find an adequate answer, he will finally argue that his tax should be the same because his ability to pay is the same. The committees could not overtly approve this sort of argument, for splitting is not easily justified in terms of ability. Given this difficulty, the committees did rather well. Splitting was retroactively rationalized as a tax adjustment designed to reflect the sharing of income at home. This new excuse is a distinct improvement. It nicely takes care of both the married and the unmarried who support a household.

However, a problem still remains. If the tax essence of a household is the sharing of income within the residing group, why should the unmarried have only half the benefits of splitting? Here the committees did not do so well. They could only reply that less is shared with a child than with a wife. But "sharing" in this context is merely a way of saying that a wife is more expensive than a child. Even if this be admitted, it is not a complete answer. When there is no wife to be supported, the children may require larger outlays because of her absence. In any event, the added cost of supporting a wife suggests, at best, that the personal exemption for a wife should be higher than the exemption for a child—not that the benefits of splitting should be substantially different. It is not surprising that Congress soon returned to the distinction between the married and the unmarried.

By 1954 the Ways and Means Committee was very troubled because full income splitting was denied to "widows and widowers with small children who prior to the death of their spouses had this tax advantage." The Committee was also concerned in behalf of those who support their parents in a separate home instead of their own. In such cases the taxpayer's expenses may easily exceed the cost of sharing the same residence. The only proper solution was to extend full splitting to the unmarried who maintain a household. Half a loaf was no longer enough. The Democrats on the Committee, who were in the minority, did not quarrel with this reasoning. But, as defenders of "the average taxpayer," they felt obliged to observe that the proposal would help "relatively few individuals," whom they described as "exceptional, rather than average." They particularly noted that individuals with incomes under $5,000 would not profit from the change. Naturally they failed to indicate that the same criticism applies to splitting for husband and wife.[33] Here the devotion to "the average taxpayer" died away.

The Finance Committee, too, rejected the proposal. It was unable to agree because the amendment "did not treat all income groups equally," and would primarily benefit "the middle—and upper—income groups." The Committee fortified its disapproval by stating that its action would save $50 million of revenue. As a member of the Committee summarized its views, "nearly all" of this amount would go "into the pockets of the wealthy. This was indeed a rich man's relief provision."[34] Again we have an explanation that is curiously incomplete. If full splitting is an unworthy device for the middle and upper income groups, why is it more desirable when the benefits are bestowed on the married in the same groups? And if the effect on the revenue is relevant, the income splitting of the married costs $4 billion a year. Another $50 million seems a small price to pay for more equity. Senator Capehart of Indiana was perplexed for a different reason. "Why," he asked, should "a widow with a house full of children" be denied "as much tax relief as she was able to have" while her husband was alive and "she had the benefit of the income he was earning?" He accused his colleagues of trying "to penalize a poor widow whose husband died and left her with half a dozen children." Since the Senator was outraged by such behavior, he added, "shame on you for playing politics with the widows of America."[35]

The committees composed their differences through a special exception. Under this limited compromise a widow or widower who maintains a household with one or more dependent children has the benefits of full splitting for two years after the spouse's death. The apparent purpose of the exception is to help the survivor through a difficult period of transition. Without such a dispensation the taxes of the survivor might be too suddenly increased through the loss of a spouse. For widows and widowers of longer duration, as well as other heads of households, the quest for equity must still continue. The ways of equity are wondrous, but they are also thorny.

I return to inventors. As matters now stand, inventors and authors are differently treated. The profit on the sale of a patent is taxable as a capital gain, while the profit on the sale of a book is taxable as ordinary income. Formerly, however, authors and inventors were similarly treated. In both cases the efforts of the professional produced ordinary income, and the efforts of the amateur a capital gain. Hence the imaginative novice who penned *Forever Amber* and the successful general who wrote *Crusade in Europe* paid only the special rate to which most creative spirits are not entitled for their mental exertions. In 1950 the Ways and Means Committee decided that the dispensation enjoyed by amateur authors and inventors was a "loophole." It proposed that all income from writing and inventing should be taxed as ordinary income, regardless of professional or amateur status. But the Finance Committee refused to regard authors and inventors as birds of a feather. Though it agreed that the dispensation for amateur authors was a loophole, it insisted that "the occasional inventor" should be left undisturbed. The more refined views of the Finance Committee prevailed.[36]

Before 1950, then, authors and inventors were not different in kind. The critical distinction was between professionals and amateurs. In 1950 the categories were altered. Professional authors and inventors, together with amateur authors, became similarly situated. Amateur inventors were differently situated. Then, as we have seen, in 1954 the categories were again revised. Now amateur authors are as poorly treated as professional authors, and professional inventors are as well treated as amateur inventors. The vital distinction is not between professionals and amateurs, but between authors and inventors. But the story does not necessarily end here. Authors may now plausibly assert, in the customary language of equity, that they, also, are entitled to the capital gain rate. As a Treasury authority stated while inventors were securing their dispensation, "it is just a question of how far we want to go in extending capital-gains treatment."[37] But authors fail to realize that in our commodity-minded culture those who write a successful book are not viewed in the same light as those who make a lucrative gadget. As a result, the custodians of equity cannot be as deeply disturbed by the grievances of authors. Moreover, if authors are entitled to the same dispensation, how is Congress to distinguish the plight of others, such as composers and painters, lawyers and doctors, who also presumably add to the welfare of the nation? Even Congress must stop somewhere before we have too much equity.

Yet despite such difficulties, the ideology of equity confers a special advantage which even the ideology of barriers and deterrents cannot provide. When a dispensation is desired in the name of equity, the request need not be justified on the basis of alleged merit. It is enough that the dispensation is already enjoyed by someone else who can be considered similarly situated. Nor is it material that the dispensation was originally granted for some unrelated purpose. Equity is not concerned with such details. The sole question is whether those who are aggrieved have the required resemblance.

Since Congress is very discerning, resemblances are readily found. As I noted earlier,[38] in 1942 Congress bestowed a special dispensation in order to stimulate businessmen to sell their machinery and other fixed assets. If the sale is at a loss, it is fully deductible against ordinary income. If the sale is at a profit, it is merely taxable as a capital gain. Profits and losses are differently treated because otherwise businessmen will not replace their facilities as promptly as they should. They will delay as long as they can, and our economic growth will be stunted. Taxpayers who raise and sell livestock soon asked for the same treatment if the livestock are held for breeding or dairy purposes before they are sold. The request was easily rationalized. Animals held for such purposes, the argument proceeded, are similar to the facilities of other enterprises. They are business properties producing meat or dairy products. Therefore, if the animals are later sold at a profit, their owners are equally entitled to have the profit taxed as a capital gain. Congress found this analysis irresistible and equity triumphed anew.

The argument, of course, has little to do with the reason for the dispensation. Livestock are regularly sold in the ordinary course of business as they are replaced by others. Their owners will no more refrain from selling them than a grocer will refuse to do business unless Congress gives him a special rate. But all this is irrelevant. It is enough that an investment in a cow or a pig is considered akin to an investment in a machine. As an example, assume that a farmer has a herd of hogs. Each year he selects certain young to be bred. After each sow has one litter, she is turned out to be conditioned for slaughter. The profits on the sale of the pigs unbred are taxable as ordinary income. But the profits on the sale of the pigs bred once are taxable as capital gains. They have been held as business properties producing other pigs. The fact that all the pigs are equally destined to be sold and eaten is unimportant.

If profits from the sale of livestock qualify as capital gains, then why not the profits from the sale of poultry? Here, indeed, is a serious question. The Finance Committee tried to resolve it by extending the same dispensation to turkeys as distinguished from chickens. The difference seems to be that turkeys have a longer breeding career, and so they "take on the aspect of a capital investment, not meat."[39] Yet as one who has no preferences in the matter, I must confess that the case for chickens is as good as the case for turkeys. In the first place, the dispensation for livestock applies "regardless of age." Secondly, a bred chicken and a bred turkey are similarly situated. Each has feathers and two legs.

Someone may fretfully ask, What do turkeys and chickens have to do with the problem of inducing reluctant businessmen to replace their old facilities? The difficulty with this impatient question is that it seeks an irrelevant answer. For the purposes of equity the issue here is not whether a dispensation is sensible, but whether those who would like to have it are sufficiently akin to those who already enjoy it. And the required similarity may be present though the resemblance is not in the least related to the reason for the dispensation.

I turn to another example which should dissolve any lingering doubts. In 1958 Congress granted two special deductions for the aid and comfort of small business. If an individual invests in a corporation with an equity capital of $1 million or less, a loss on the investment, unlike other losses in stock, is fully deductible against his ordinary income. This allowance is supposed to stimulate affluent taxpayers to contribute needed capital to small corporations. If the investor is married, the deduction may not exceed $50,000. But if he is single, it is limited to $25,000. Under the other dispensation a business may immediately write off 20 per cent of the cost of newly acquired equipment with a life of at least 6 years. This allowance is supposed to induce small enterprises to replace or expand their facilities. Here, also, the married and the single are differently treated. If the business is owned by a husband, the deduction is available on $20,000 of equipment. But if the business is owned by a bachelor, it is limited to $10,000 of equipment.

Very likely those who are unfamiliar with the ways of equity will be puzzled by these distinctions. If the purpose is to help small business, why should a businessman who is single be less stimulated than one who is married? Why should a wife matter any more than the number of cousins he may have? Again the answer is clear. In each case there is no connection at all between the deduction that is granted and the distinction that is drawn. Nevertheless the distinction must be made if equity is to be done. The diverse treatment of the married and the single simply extends the equity of income splitting into new areas of fiscal wisdom. In a community property state husband and wife are considered co-owners and co-investors of the property accumulated by him, and so each is entitled to separate allowances for losses and depreciation. Therefore, the special deductions of the two will be twice as large as the deductions of a single individual. By the same token, the special deductions of a husband in a common law state must also be twice as large. Otherwise married couples will not be similarly treated even though they are similarly situated. If the single suffer by comparison, they are only the incidental victims of equity. For some reason, however, Congress has overlooked heads of households and surviving spouses who also enjoy some of the benefits of income splitting. As I have indicated,[40] a head of a household is placed midway between a married man and a single man. Hence his special deduction should be $37,500 for losses and 20 per cent of $15,000 for depreciation. A widow, of course, should have twice the deductions of a single taxpayer for two years after her husband's death. These suggestions may seem strange but they are surely equitable.

I believe that I have sufficiently outlined the ways of equity. Though many more illustrations could be given, they would only burden my appraisal with too much detail. Equity in taxation consists largely of two principles. The first principle is that equity is a special dispensation for those who are differently situated. As Magill has summarized Congress' application of this principle, certain transactions "deserve lower rates or no taxes at all."[41] We are now better able to understand why the Special Tax Study Committee was fully devoted to the cause of equity. The second principle is that equity is the privilege of paying as little tax as somebody else. Someone is always paying less; hence it is always possible to ask for equity. For the purposes of this principle the merit of the desired relief is wholly irrelevant. The test is whether similar relief is already enjoyed by others.[42] Since equity is the fair distribution of dispensations, Congress is busily emulating the Dodo. Like Congress, the Dodo tried hard to be fair and impartial. After watching a curious race he dispassionately declared, "Everybody has won and all must have prizes."

And so we may be sure that the quest for equity will continue unabated. But as Edmond Cahn has wisely written, "those only are equal whom the law has elected to equalize."[43]

CHAPTER 8

What Is a Loophole?

An income tax is commonly conceived as a progressive levy imposed on all income. This simple view corresponds with the usual notions of taxation in accordance with ability to pay. Actually, of course, all sorts of distinctions are made in terms of who receives the income or the source from which it derives. And the distinctions have little to do with ability to pay as generally understood. In effect, our income tax is many taxes—and often no tax at all.

The distinctions among individuals are variously contrived. But essentially there are three devices: income splitting, incorporation, and special allowances. Income splitting creates large disparities between a married person and a single person; between a single person who is head of a household and a single person who is not; between a widow or widower for two years and a surviving spouse who is longer bereaved. These diversities serve the estimable cause of equity among taxpayers. Another basic distinction is drawn between those who do business as individuals and those who operate as corporations. The top rate for corporations is 52 per cent—which is only one-third up the ladder of rates prescribed for individuals. Corporations, then, are a sturdy refuge from the discomforts of progression. Income over $36,000 may be accumulated subject to a rate of 52 per cent instead of 53 to 91 per cent.[1] While John Marshall declared that corporations are "invisible" and "intangible," the tax benefits which they provide are easily perceived and readily felt. However, not everyone can freely resort to the sanctuary of a corporation—especially professionals and

142

employees. Taxpayers who are less fortunate must look to other dispensations that are available. The special allowances are known as deductions, exclusions, and credits. They sensitively distinguish between those who are over 65 and those who are under 65; between those who are over 72 and those who are over 65 and under 72; between those who are blind and those who are differently disabled; between those who are over 65 and disabled and those who are under 65 and disabled, or over 65 and not disabled; between those who are widows and those who are orphans.

The differences by source are also revealing. To begin with, certain gains are entirely exempt. Among them are life insurance, gifts, interest on state and local bonds, and compensation earned abroad. Other incomes are more delicately treated. For death benefits paid by employers there is an exemption of $5,000. For wages paid during illness there is an exemption of $100 a week. For income from natural resources there is percentage depletion. For dividends there are an exclusion and a credit. For profit on the sale of a capital asset there is a special rate of 25 per cent. A capital asset is defined so as to exclude property used in the conduct of a business, or property held for sale to customers in the ordinary course of a business. The purpose of this thoughtful distinction is to segregate the profit realized in operating a business from the profit realized in disposing of an investment. Only the latter is considered a true capital gain.

Yet only the pedantic would insist that merely capital gains should be taxed as capital gains. After all, a definition is but a means to an end. Though Congress has methodically defined the difference between business profits and investment profits, surely Congress may ignore the definition and the difference in response to a higher wisdom. Since the special rate is so helpful where help is deemed urgent, Congress has graciously extended it further. In some cases there need not be a capital asset; in other cases there need not be a sale; and in still other cases there need not even be a gain from property. So far the results have been quite fruitful. The special rate is generously bestowed on business profits from the sale of several kinds of property. These include operating assets, such as facilities and equipment, as well as patents, timber, and certain livestock. It is immaterial that the profits are realized in the regular course of business. The special rate is also benevolently bestowed on royalties received under leases of coal and timber properties. Finally, the burdens of hard-pressed executives have not been forgotten. They, too, are well treated if they are discreetly compensated in certain ways—through options to buy stock at a bargain price or lump sum distributions under pension and profit sharing plans. A top rate of 25 per cent is no longer a dispensation reserved for capital gains. It is a felicitous way of relieving particular incomes, whether they be earned or unearned.

I have not tried to be thorough in summarizing these distinctions. Nor have I allowed for the statutes that are carefully drafted for specific taxpayers with the required influence. Yet for present purposes the picture is clear enough. By and large, the only taxpayers who are expected to bear the progressive rates are employees, professionals, and others who work for a living. However, a number of those who work are also variously relieved through income splitting, incorporation, and other dispensations. All in all, the alleged pain on the upper levels of income is far less acute than it is supposed to be. The rates bark more than they bite. Married couples with incomes over $100,000 pay, as a group, an average effective rate of only 28 per cent. The arithmetical results are even more impressive if we compare married couples at different levels. The average effective rate rises from 23 per cent on incomes between $25,000 and $50,000, to 30 per cent on incomes between $150,000 and $200,000. It then declines until it reaches 24 per cent on incomes over $1 million. In other words, it is about the same at $25,000 as at $1 million. Or, to take another look at our alleged progression, the average effective rate at $1 million is only about twice as much as at $10,000, though one income is 100 times as large as the other.[2] According to the table of progressive rates, the effective rate should be 26 per cent at $10,000; 40 per cent at $25,000; 78 per cent at $200,000; and 88 per cent at $1 million. Of course, an average effective rate for a particular bracket presupposes that a number of those within the bracket are paying more. But it also indicates that others are paying even less.

In view of this situation a disconcerting question emerges. Should we proceed to infer that the Internal Revenue Code is replete with loopholes? The mere question is inevitably distressing, for it suggests that Congress may be busily engaged in improper activities. However, Senator Goldwater of Arizona has implied that there is no need to regard Congress like Caesar's wife. The "whole tax structure," he says, is "filled with loopholes." Senator Douglas goes further. He asserts that the "loopholes" have become "truck holes." Chairman Mills, of the Ways and Means Committee, describes our tax system as "a house of horrors" furnished with "loopholes." These harsh words are accompanied by the further thought that the tax laws are "a mess and a gyp," and that various taxpayers are coddled as "pets" while others are treated as "patsies."[3] Such charges are undoubtedly severe and disturbing. Yet they are not too meaningful except as we first resolve a more basic problem. What is a loophole? I am well aware that loopholes are repeatedly disapproved with persuasive vehemence. But we should not assume that what is roundly condemned is always clearly perceived. It is usually easier to deplore sin than to explain its content.

In an effort to find an answer I start with a familiar source of instruction. The dictionary defines a loophole as "a hole or aperture that gives a passage or the means of escape; often used figuratively, and especially of an underhand or unfair method of escape or evasion."[4] A tax loophole, then, is an unfair means of escape from a burden that others are obliged to bear. Since this appraisal has distinct moral overtones, it is often supposed, in deference to Congress, that the members of that body would not deliberately devise any loopholes. In the light of this reverential attitude loopholes are narrowly conceived as unintended openings which clever lawyers skilfully uncover in behalf of their clients. They are a failure to tax through inadvertence rather than design. Much as I admire the ingenuity of my hard-working brethren, there is no reason why the notion of a loophole should be so closely confined. It only leads to needless complications. Roswell Magill illustrates the difficulties that are gratuitously introduced. On the one hand, he emphasizes that "Congress has been eager to plug loopholes." This statement seems to say that Congress would never knowingly construct a loophole. But on the other hand, he also indicates that loopholes may be intentionally created or tolerated. Such incongruities are avoided if a loophole is simply regarded as any unfair deliverance from a tax, whether it be due to oversight or design. As Representative Mills has noted, loopholes may be "accidental" or "put into the laws deliberately."[5]

Though I have made some progress, I have not gotten very far. At this point, apparently, a loophole is an unfair privilege of paying less tax than others are required to pay. But this understanding of the term necessarily implies that the privilege may be fair rather than unfair. How, then, are we to determine whether it is one or the other? While this question seems troublesome, answers have been given with remarkable ease. Senator Humphrey of Minnesota is among those who fail to see any problem. Loopholes, he writes, are "provisions which give special tax treatment to particular groups."[6] If I may rephrase his definition, the "special treatment" of "particular groups" is necessarily unfair.

On analysis, such revelations are uninformative. Recipients of income are not a homogeneous mass of indistinguishables. Hence the tax laws have always classified them into different groups that are differently treated. Corporations are distinguished from partnerships; insurance companies from other enterprises; and husbands from bachelors. Each "particular group" has its own "special treatment." At the very outset, in 1913, Congress granted special exemptions to business leagues, chambers of commerce, agricultural organizations, and labor unions. These few examples are merely isolated instances of innumerable special treatments. But there is no need to compile a fuller inventory, interesting as it might be. The crux of the matter is that we cannot do without categories. Any intelligent scheme of thought must classify the phenomena with which it deals. To understand is to classify, and to classify is to create particular groups. Therefore, it is essentially meaningless to censure the special treatment of particular groups. Even the sternest adherents of ability to pay divide taxpayers into particular groups that are diversely treated. Otherwise they would not insist that an income of $100,000 should be more heavily taxed than an income of $5,000. Yet they would be the last to speak kindly of loopholes.

Evidently, I have again made little headway. A loophole is necessarily a special treatment for a particular group. But not every special treatment for a particular group is necessarily a loophole. I think I will do better if I change my approach. Instead of seeking a comprehensive definition let us consider a specific case.

A number of years ago the motion picture industry developed a method of tax avoidance known as the "collapsible corporation." Like most ventures in avoidance the procedure was quite simple. A corporation was organized to produce a picture. When the picture was completed, the corporation was promptly liquidated or collapsed. The film was distributed to the stockholders, who reported the difference between the cost of their stock and the value of the film as a capital gain. The stockholders then released the picture and amortized its value against the income that it earned. No further tax was due unless the income eventually exceeded that value. As a result, the parties concerned were twice blessed. The corporate tax on the income was entirely eliminated, and the income was converted into capital gain. At the request of the Treasury, Congress concluded that collapsible corporations were a loophole and enacted a special statute which penalizes their use. Now let us assume that Congress had responded differently. Suppose Congress had reasoned, in the language of barriers and deterrents, that motion pictures are peculiarly vital to the American way of life, and that the industry cannot sufficiently prosper unless producers are permitted to have collapsible corporations. Then such legal entities would no longer be disparaged as a loophole. The industry would be given a special statute permitting their use, and the privilege of paying less tax would be justified in the fashion of other dispensations. If I may borrow the language of President Eisenhower, who liked to speak of barriers and deterrents, we would be told that the special treatment should "restore normal incentives for sustained production and economic growth," and "permit traditional American initiative and production genius to push on to ever higher standards of living and employment."[7]

In short, whether a dispensation is a loophole depends on the guiding concept of right and wrong. As on other occasions, one man's meat is another man's poison. Professor Surrey has looked with marked favor on income splitting. But Senators Douglas and Humphrey disapprove it as an "indefensible" loophole.[8] As we have seen, the profits of inventors are now taxable as capital gains. In 1950 the Ways and Means Committee regarded this dispensation as a loophole. Four years later it had changed its mind.[9] To Congress the dispensation for stock options is an indispensable incentive to discouraged executives. To Dean Griswold it is just another "handout" to "a special few taxpayers."[10] The oil industry continually explains that percentage depletion merely places it on "an equal footing with other industries." Those who disagree insist that the deduction is "the biggest of all tax loopholes"—"a tremendous tax-free bonanza"—"an unconscionable giveaway."[11] The ideologists of barriers and deterrents maintain that the credit for dividends is essential to the preservation of private enterprise. Those who disagree describe the credit as a loophole—as well as a "barbarous" and "monstrous" provision which is "arrant class legislation."[12] The Special Tax Study Committee of 1947 appraised its proposals as estimable efforts "to eliminate manifest inequities." The lonely dissenter called them "bigger and better loopholes."[13] So it is throughout the realm of tax policy.

Jerry Cruncher has probably said all that can be said here. Jerry is an enterprising "odd-job man" who appears in *A Tale of Two Cities*. He supplements his income by removing bodies from their graves. Mrs. Cruncher is deeply distressed over this occupation, and calls it a "dreadful business." But Jerry takes a different view of his activities, and prefers to be known as "a Resurrection-Man."

Now let us admire the wisdom of Jerry by glancing at a few other examples. Colleges and churches are generally exempt from the obligation to pay income taxes. But this rule of immunity is qualified by a nice distinction between the two. If a college goes into some unrelated business, like the manufacture of spaghetti, the resulting profits are taxable. If a church goes into business, its profits are tax-free. Why, then, should colleges be treated less favorably than churches? The answer is that a failure to tax colleges would be an unseemly loophole, while the refusal to tax churches is only a due regard for the free exercise of religion. Congress gravely fears that unless colleges are taxed, they will unfairly escape the burdens borne by their competitors. Under the sovereign principle of equity competitors should be similarly taxed, even if some of them are also engaged in improving the mind. To exempt some while taxing others is to sanction a loophole. However, all this concern for fair competition rapidly recedes if faith and worship are involved. The exemption conferred for our spiritual needs also embraces the worldly pursuit of profit.[14] Anyone who meditates on the distinction made by Congress should soon recognize the point made by Jerry.

Since 1926 individuals residing abroad have been excused from paying taxes on compensation earned abroad. This exemption has been justified as a way of "increasing our foreign trade." It encourages "our citizens" to go elsewhere and sell "our merchandise." Many would refuse to venture forth in our behalf if they were treated like those who stay at home. In recent years a new reason has been found. The exemption is essential to peace as well as to trade. It induces "men with technical knowledge to go abroad" and improve the lot of retarded nations whose friendship we seek. In helping them we help ourselves.[15] Yet not everyone has appreciated the virtues of the exemption. From time to time attempts have been made to repeal it as an "unjust discrimination."[16] Here, again, I cannot improve on Jerry Cruncher's insight. If the exemption is simply appraised as a benefit unfairly bestowed on a select group, it is a loophole. But if the exemption is more elaborately viewed as a measure designed to keep us prosperous and free, it deserves another name which suitably describes its worthy purpose.

For those who may still be troubled by doubts, I turn to another subject—life insurance. Usually the proceeds received after the death of the insured are exempt from income tax. For many years this exemption was accompanied by a related refinement. If the beneficiary received the proceeds in a lump sum and placed them in a savings account or in bonds, the interest was taxable as interest normally is. If the proceeds, instead, were left with the insurance company under an agreement to pay interest to the beneficiary, the interest was also taxable. But if the company paid the proceeds in deferred installments which included intervening interest, the interest was not taxable. In 1950 the Treasury informed the Ways and Means Committee that this further exemption was a loophole and asked that it be closed. A majority of the Committee, composed of Democrats, agreed. The exemption, they stated, was "an unjustifiable discrimination." Interest was variously treated, depending on how the proceeds were paid.[17]

The Republican minority, however, failed to perceive the loophole. To them the alleged discrimination was a "wise social policy of discouraging lump sum settlements in favor of installment payments." Beneficiaries who receive lump sums—the argument ran—often waste the proceeds in foolish investments. The exemption of the interest protected them from their own improvidence. It gave them an incentive to take the proceeds piecemeal over an extended period. The need for a "wise social policy" was fortified by observations on the plight of widows and orphans. Congressman Reed of New York was especially disturbed and solicitous. He declared "without fear of successful contradiction" that the repeal of the exemption would provide "a racket for the confidence men and the swindlers." It would "force lump-sum payments," and so "aid a racketeering group of gougers in exploiting the insurance benefits bequeathed to the widows and orphans of the Nation." For "there are vultures who prey upon the widows and orphans where benefits from insurance policies are paid to them in a lump sum." These "racketeers" would "hail" the newly imposed tax "as manna from Heaven."[18]

Four years passed, and the Republicans became the majority. Responsibility brought restraint. Now it was no longer enough to speak of "swindlers," "racketeers," and "gougers" who feed on indiscreet widows and helpless orphans. The Republicans suddenly discovered that the exemption was a loophole because installment payments "include interest earned after the death of the insured." As Congressman Reed now indignantly stated, the exemption was "a tax avoidance" by "wealthy individuals." They buy "extremely large policies for the sole purpose of enabling their beneficiaries to obtain tax-free interest which may amount to thousands of dollars annually." But the Republicans were still worried about widows who are unable to handle money prudently. They finally resolved their dilemma by taxing the interest, subject to a special exception. Interest paid to a surviving spouse is still exempt to the extent of $1,000 a year. This exception was made in order "to encourage" widows to take their proceeds in installments "so as not to waste the principal"—though the exception also applies to widowers who are presumably more sophisticated in monetary matters. On the other hand, the interest payable to surviving children is fully taxable. As the Finance Committee judiciously explained, children need not be as well treated as a widow. If they are under 21, "their interest in the principal is protected by guardianship laws." And if they are over 21, "there appears to be no reason to encourage them to leave the proceeds in any particular form."[19]

These varying views on life insurance indicate why loopholes elude definition. In 1950 the Republicans argued that the exemption of interest received through installment payments served a worthy purpose. It stimulated our widows and orphans to protect themselves from hovering "vultures." By 1954 the melody had changed. The same exemption became a loophole, except for a limited allowance which supposedly prevents widows from going financially astray. A spokesman proudly announced that the exemption was one of the "more important" loopholes closed by the Republicans.[20] What was once a desirable exception was now a glaring loophole. While the ability to change one's mind is an admirable quality, this expression of self-appreciation leaves more questions than it answers. Was the newly found loophole truly closed if widows, and even widowers, continue to enjoy a special dispensation? Why is an exemption for orphans a loophole if an exemption for widows is not? Those who seek answers should consult Jerry Cruncher.

My next example is a proposal designed to alleviate the burdens of businessmen and professionals who are self-employed and prosperous. At present executives and other employees in the upper brackets enjoy a special dispensation. They may have their taxes reduced through exempt pension and profit-sharing plans. Under these plans an employer provides retirement benefits for his employees by making contributions to a trust in their behalf or purchasing annuities for them. The amounts paid out by the employer might otherwise have been paid directly to them. No taxes are due on the benefits until they become available to the employees. These arrangements offer three distinct advantages. First, interim earnings on the employer's contributions may accumulate tax-free. Second, when the employee receives his benefits after retirement, he is usually in a lower bracket. Third, if he takes his benefits in one lump sum, they are taxable as a capital gain. In short, income which would be taxable immediately at high rates is, instead, taxable later at lower rates. The burdens are both deferred and reduced.

The self-employed do not have a similar dispensation. Whatever is put aside for their declining days must be accumulated out of currently taxed income. This unpleasant distinction has distressed the American Bar Association and others who speak authoritatively for the self-employed. And so, in accordance with an honored principle of equity, the argument is made that one dispensation justifies another. The self-employed are also entitled to reduce their burdens by saving untaxed income. The proposal commonly made is that they be given an annual deduction for amounts set aside in a retirement fund. These amounts would be taxable later as they were received. Naturally, the usual observations on equity are rehearsed in the approved manner. We are told that "two classes of our citizens" are now taxed in "drastically different" ways. It is "unreasonable that self-employed persons should be precluded by law from obtaining equivalent tax treatment" for their "retirement savings." Professionals who are self-employed should be given "the same opportunity as the professional man on the payroll of another." The suggested remedy "will correct a discrimination" that "was never intended." It will provide "equality of tax treatment."[21]

As on other occasions, the request for equity is reinforced by the ideology of barriers and deterrents. The present discrimination, we are warned, is inducing "the graduates from our law schools, engineering schools, and other schools to go to work for the large companies, rather than to strike out for themselves." The proposed dispensation will restore their initiative. It will give them an incentive "to fare forth on their own." Nor are the professionals the only ones whose sagging spirits will be revived. The dispensation will also give "hope, help, relief, and encouragement to the small, independent businessman"— the butcher, the baker, the grocer, the druggist, the carpenter "and many others." These are "the entrepreneurs, the modern prototypes of the yankee trader with his bundle of wares and the western pioneer with his dream of the future." Yet the benefits promised by the ideology of barriers and deterrents hardly end here. If the courage of our entrepreneurs will be enhanced, so will the "American principle of thrift and saving." More savings will bring more investment. In fact, the desired dispensation involves our very "form of Government" and "way of life," for these depend on "new plants" that provide "new jobs." Or, if these exhortations are not enough, we are told that the self-employed must be relieved "if they are to maintain a standard of living comparable to that to which they are accustomed." Congressman Wainright of New York even adds a religious note to the animated discussion. "The American Republic," he declares, "was founded on the thesis that God helps those who help themselves." The principle of the desired tax reduction "is just that." Those who wish to reduce their taxes will be given the option to do so by saving instead of spending. The choice will be entirely theirs.[22] Of course, it is always easier to help oneself if Congress offers a little assistance.

The arguments resort to the customary platitudes of equity and barriers and deterrents. Any deviation from the usual clichés might be viewed with suspicion. My immediate problem, however, is not whether the dispensation should be granted, but whether it would qualify as a loophole. Those who disapprove the dispensation contend that it will simply provide a special reduction for a "special group" of prosperous taxpayers. Most of the "prototypes" of "the western pioneer" have little to gain. Their earnings are too low to be set aside or to provide any substantial tax savings. About 80 per cent of the total relief will inure to the self-employed with incomes over $10,000. As Secretary of the Treasury Humphrey felt obliged to say despite his sympathetic concern, the benefits "will accrue largely to people in the middle and upper income tax brackets." Moreover, the self-employed are not the only victims of alleged discrimination. Two-thirds of all employees in private industry are not covered by any exempt pension plans. Their small savings must be accumulated out of tax-paid income. And many who are covered receive only nominal benefits. The dispensation, then, will merely add still another discrimination—between the self-employed who will profit, and the employed and self-employed who cannot profit.[23] These criticisms clearly suggest that the proposed dispensation is a loophole, even if the harsh word is graciously avoided.

But those who approve the dispensation will wisely speak of other things. They will describe the self-employed as "decent, honest," and "hard-working." They will recall that our country "was built by individuals who had the initiative to go forth and carve their own way"—or, in Senator Bricker's phrase, the "courage to face the battle." And they will remind us that the self-employed are the "self-reliant," possessed of "fortitude and foresight." As we "honor them for their valor," so should we relieve them of their burden. The allusions to the virtues of the self-employed seem to imply that they should be even better treated than the employed. They who take special risks deserve a special reward. If it be said that the dispensation will only help a "special group," the answer is that there are 7 million self-employed, and that a group so large is not "special." If it be said that the dispensation will deprive the Treasury of needed revenue, the answer is, "It will be a sad day for America when discrimination is tolerated on the ground that its elimination would be expensive." And if this answer is inadequate, then the lost revenue can be recouped from others. At any rate, a statute which improves the lot of the virtuous can scarcely be called a loophole.[24]

Though I am quite satisfied with the insight of Jerry Cruncher, others are less impressed. It leaves matters too untidy for them. It fails to offer any impartial criteria for determining whether a dispensation is a loophole. Scholars who are hot for certainties cannot rest content with such a precarious situation. They must have answers if they are to be happy, and the answers must derive from some uniform standard which is objectively applied. Besides, the term "loophole" has become too charged with emotional overtones for the staid world of tax scholarship. A learned discussion requires a restrained vocabulary. And so the scholars have turned to other words that are supposedly less partial and hence more informative.

There are enough words to please everybody who wishes to appear impersonal and detached. Instead of loopholes the enlightened now speak of "erosions" of the tax base. Or they refer to special treatments and special provisions, special deductions and special exclusions, special exceptions and special accommodations, differentials and preferentials, discrepancies and discriminations, openings and leakages, tax shelters and tax havens, tax favors and tax advantages, tax mitigations and tax concessions. All these words, as well as others now in fashion, disclose a marked capacity for devising polite synonyms. They produce an air of impartial judgment. To call percentage depletion a loophole is to indulge in a personal prejudice. To call it an erosion is to make an objective appraisal.

Although the current vocabulary is considered less emotional, it seems to provoke the same quarrels. Arguments over loopholes have merely shifted to other words. Professor Dan T. Smith illustrates the lack of progress. Income splitting, he writes, "is sometimes referred to as an unjustified differential or leakage in the tax base. This, of course, is incorrect in a literal sense because it does not reduce the total tax base at all."[25] The income is simply taxed at a lower rate available to certain taxpayers. In Smith's view, not every dispensation is a leakage or a differential. The answer turns on the precise procedure that is followed. If income is removed from the tax base through a deduction, as in the case of percentage depletion, the answer may be yes. But if income is left in the base and taxed at a special rate, as in the case of capital gains, then the answer is no. Therefore, it seems, the dispensations conferred on Mr. Mayer and Mr. Sanders were neither differentials nor leakages. Their income was fully taxed. They were only given a special rate.[26] It would be interesting to pursue the meticulous distinction suggested by Smith, but I doubt that the results would justify the effort.

What is more instructive is that the new terminology does not reveal a new wisdom. While the label on the bottle may change, the contents remain the same.

Let us examine some critical comments by Professors William Cary and Stanley Surrey. Both are devoted to ability to pay, and both are fond of the new vocabulary. Cary is alarmed by the steady growth of "special legislation." There is, he states, "an accelerating tendency away from uniformity and toward preferential treatment." Congress "has responded to pressures for the benefit of specific individuals, industries, and income groups." He then emphasizes that tax laws are unfair if they are not uniform. Surrey is equally disturbed amid similar words. It is largely agreed, he observes, that Congress "has adopted provisions favoring special groups or special individuals and that these provisions run counter to our notions of tax fairness. Moreover, the tendency of Congress to act this way seems to be increasing." In an effort to be dispassionate, he calls the statutes in question "special tax provisions"—a phrase which he terms "fairly neutral."[27]

As I noted earlier, indignant references to "special legislation" and "special provisions" are overly simple. There are few taxes more "special" than the estate tax. It reaches only one decedent out of a hundred. But I doubt whether Cary and Surrey would condemn it as "special legislation." Nor are they more illuminating when they dwell on the virtue of uniformity. The essence of progressive taxation is that taxpayers are not treated alike. Yet this lack of uniformity seems quite compatible with "our notions of tax fairness."

If we look closely, all we have here are some carefully chosen words that enable one to deprecate loopholes without resorting to this unseemly term. But the words that are used are no more neutral than the word they replace. I turn again to the new verbal fashions as they are displayed by Surrey. Tax statutes which grant "special treatment to certain groups or individuals," he explains, contravene "the criterion of equity or fairness. Stated simply, this criterion demands that the income-tax burden should as far as possible apply equally to persons with the same dollar income."[28] These sentences convey the impression that some self-evident truth has been objectively ascertained. The writer is merely reporting what is necessarily so—that the inherent essence of equity is the equal taxation of equal incomes. Actually, however, he is only saying in a genteel manner that a loophole is a failure to abide by equity as he prefers to define it. His view simply echoes the usual concept of equity approved by the adherents of ability to pay.

Surrey tries to introduce a note of impartiality by describing his understanding of equity as "our notions of tax fairness." Again he implies that he is recording some truth that is universally accepted. It is not only his view, but "our" view. While it is always pleasant to speak in the name of everybody, the collective pronoun seems rather inappropriate here. Congress has cogently indicated that "our" notions are not its notions. Time and again unequal taxes have been imposed on equal incomes. Congress refuses to believe that the same dollar income should be uniformly treated.[29] If Surrey is correct, we would have to infer that Congress has been repeatedly unjust. The better explanation is that there is more than one sense of justice. Even Surrey and Cary are not consistently faithful to their notion of equity. Though they are deeply troubled by special legislation for special groups, they are conspicuously silent on income splitting. Evidently when the married are distinguished from the single, equity does not demand that the income tax should "apply equally to persons with the same dollar income." It turns out, then, that equal incomes should be equally taxed unless they should be taxed unequally.

The phrase "special provision" is as informative as the word "loophole." If a provision for certain taxpayers is distasteful, it is called "special." If it is palatable, it is differently described. The colonists who refused to pay customs duties were patriots in America and smugglers in England.

Representative Curtis has also pondered at length on the nature of loopholes. He has tried to solve the problem by distinguishing between "preferentials" and "differentials." As he uses these terms, they seem to be precise words of art. A preferential is a tax benefit that "is not open to all individuals in our society." A differential is a tax benefit that is available to all without discrimination. In order to make sure that he is not misunderstood, Congressman Curtis has given two helpful examples. Percentage depletion is a differential rather than a preferential because "actually any individual can go into" the oil business and obtain the deduction. "Any investor can be in this field; any American." "There is no question of inequality" here, as all "citizens derive the same benefits if they go into this occupation." Similarly, the dispensation for capital gains is also a differential because everybody is free to invest in stocks or other assets. "Thrift is open to any individual."[30] Apparently, if only the affluent could embark on oil ventures or go into the stock market, these dispensations would be preferentials. On the same reasoning, I gather, the dispensation for stock options is another differential. Any American may become an executive and obtain an option. The distinction drawn by Mr. Curtis can be endlessly illustrated. Income splitting is a differential since anybody may acquire a husband or a wife. But if tall taxpayers were better treated than short ones, the disparity would be a preferential. Not all Americans can attain the required height.

The animating theme of Congressman Curtis' analysis is a rule of equality. Preferentials discriminate among taxpayers while differentials do not. As long as a dispensation is fairly bestowed on rich and poor alike, it is properly conceived. Some who would like to approve this principle are disturbed by the notion of equality on which it rests. Various dispensations that are given to any American are enjoyed by only certain Americans. However, it seems unnecessary to probe much further among the niceties of Mr. Curtis' distinction. He himself has regretfully conceded that "any differential can become a preferential," and that "many of our differentials" already have.[31] We would only be pursuing a distinction which leads nowhere.

My inquiry into loopholes confirms anew a familiar truth. Better answers require wiser questions. Ultimately dispensations for certain taxpayers are condemned, not because they conform to some definition of a loophole, but because they are considered undesirable for various reasons. That is why Surrey and Cary can refrain from criticizing income splitting, though it falls well within their stated understanding of a loophole. Or Senator Javits of New York can say that percentage depletion for oil is a loophole, and at the same time request "tax advantages" for private investments abroad.[32] We cannot learn very much by asking what is a loophole. The only meaningful questions are those which focus on the precise purposes and effects of a dispensation. Of course, the answers will vary, for they will reflect different standards of good and evil. But at least they will deal with the relevant issues.

At this point I have completed the circle. My initial question was whether Congress has been busily creating loopholes for select taxpayers. The time has come to provide an answer, but the answer must be exceedingly modest. The concept of a loophole derives from the criteria that are applied in appraising the efforts of Congress. To ideologists of ability the dispensation for capital gains is a loophole because incomes should be uniformly taxed, regardless of their source. To ideologists of barriers and deterrents it is not a loophole because it preserves our system of private enterprise. To ideologists of ability the dispensation for inventors discriminates in favor of a special group. To ideologists of barriers and deterrents it rightly encourages inventors to be ingenious in our behalf. Whenever Congress grants a dispensation, it has a reason for doing so. The benefits that accrue to certain taxpayers are merely the convenient means to a worthy end. And so everyone can safely abhor loopholes, just as everyone can freely applaud equity. By the same token, the members of Congress can constantly reassure themselves that they are rigidly opposed to all loopholes, and always anxious to close any that may be found.[33] No larger wisdom is discernible.

CHAPTER 9

The Pursuit of the Public Interest

When special dispensations are discussed, it is customary to end on a note of reasonable cheer. Even those who are deeply disturbed refuse to despair. All is not lost, they say. If Congress will merely mend its ways, dispensations will soon abate and taxes will be more fairly imposed. The required change in conduct is essentially simple. Congress need only devote itself to the "public interest" instead of "private interests."[1]

These tidings of hope reflect two premises. The first is that Congress grants dispensations because it fails to behave as it should. It is more attentive to the clamor of private interests than the demands of the public interest. The second is that private interests and the public interest may be readily distinguished. Congress should be able to perceive the difference without too much difficulty. To these propositions I would add a further thought. Neither premise is meaningful unless the concept of public interest provides a standard of right and wrong on which reasonable men commonly agree when they meditate on tax policy. Otherwise all we have here is a display of words that are soothing to the ear but uninformative to the mind. At this point my difficulties begin. For the phrase "public interest," like other pleasant generalities, means different things to different men.

The adherents of ability do not accept this flexible notion of the public interest. While the phrase seems replete with ambiguities, they have isolated at least one certainty. Dispensations, the adherents state, are not in the public interest because they afford special benefits to

159

certain groups. This position is continually reaffirmed as if it were too obvious to explain. As a result, we have little more than a series of rhetorical observations that are duly indignant within the habitual restraints of scholarship. The taxing process emerges as an unceasing struggle between good and evil. The "general taxpayer," the "general public," the "people" are on one side; "organized groups," "special groups," "pressure groups," on the other. In the same fashion "plain John Q. Taxpayer" is distinguished from "some particular group of taxpayers," and tax statutes in the "public interest" from "special tax provisions." As the adherents of ability would summarize the certainty to which they cling, taxation in the public interest is "objective" and "balanced" legislation "in a judicious manner," with close concern for "the integrity of the tax structure."[2]

When we ask ourselves what such words mean, we should be quite puzzled. The "public" or the "people" necessarily consist of individuals, and individuals fall into various groups. Not even the adherents of ability insist that all taxpayers should be similarly treated. If they are not to be treated alike, they must be treated as distinctive groups. Moreover, in a democratic society the "pressure" of "organized groups" is a normal and respectable source of legislation. Congressmen are not aloof philosophers who are expected to consult only their own collective wisdom. However, I need not dwell at length on the various words which I have quoted. In order to understand them we must look beyond them. The adherents of ability are speaking as ideologists, and their vocabulary is nicely designed to express their ideology in terms of the public interest. They speak for the "people" rather than for "groups." In this way their tenets are endowed with an appearance of impartiality—and appearances are important to them. According to their basic precepts, equal incomes should bear equal taxes, and larger incomes should bear higher taxes. The adherents of ability then assume that these precepts are "objective" and "balanced" criteria of the public interest. Hence deviations from the precepts through special dispensations are necessarily biased surrenders to private interests.

But why should we agree that only the adherents of ability are the genuine guardians of the public interest in taxation? The ideologists of barriers and deterrents are also dedicated to our well-being. Though they are constantly seeking special dispensations for specific groups, the dispensations are generously conceived. As one of them has eloquently emphasized, their concern for the public interest is large and spacious. It embraces no less than the welfare of "the country as a whole."[3] Why, then, should we suppose that the ideologists of barriers and deterrents are less mindful of the public interest? When the adherents of ability imply that they alone have a true grasp of the public interest, they take too much for granted. The public interest is not some manifest essence that transcends the realm of private interests. It is a changing product that is periodically distilled from the pressures of competing interests in response to the prevailing preferences of the moment. The ideologists of ability pursue certain ends while the ideologists of barriers and deterrents pursue others. In each case benefits are sought for distinct groups; and these benefits, in turn, are identified with the public interest. The ideologists of ability urge that the best of all possible worlds is one in which the more affluent bear the larger burdens. The ideologists of barriers and deterrents reply that private enterprise cannot function amid such discrimination. The larger burdens must be shifted to the less affluent for their very own benefit. By paying more they will profit more.

To offer the public interest as a solution is to offer no solution at all. The phrase is no more instructive than other abstractions that circulate in the world of politics or law. It enables men to disagree under cover of the same words. Nor do the adherents of ability add much by insisting that "the integrity of the tax structure" must be maintained. Here again they are conveniently assuming that only their view of the income tax expresses an "objective" and "balanced" ideal to which Congress should faithfully adhere. But a progressive income tax is not an essay in objectivity. Their assumption does not improve when we recall that even the adherents of ability fail to practice what they preach. They, also, approve special dispensations. Few are so devoted to a progressive income tax as Senators Douglas and Humphrey. Yet their devotion does not prevent them from proposing helpful exceptions for particular groups, such as farmers.[4] And so the ideologists of barriers and deterrents may rightfully say that the basic quarrel is not over "integrity," but the precise dispensations to be granted. The public interest is an empty vessel into which everyone pours his private preferences.

Let us turn to a statement by Congressman Mills, the Chairman of the Ways and Means Committee. Mr. Mills has long been troubled by the steady spread of dispensations or, as it is now generally put, the erosion of the tax base. Under his guidance the Committee recently held elaborate hearings on this matter. Before these hearings began, Mr. Mills announced that the Committee would make "an extensive inquiry" in the light of "the public interest under today's conditions." He then defined the public interest as including two basic objectives. One is an income tax which will impose equal burdens on equal incomes and heavier burdens on larger incomes. The other is an income tax which will promote economic growth and stability.[5] The result is a statement of public interest that is sufficiently obscure to please everybody. The first objective presupposes that special dispensations should be repealed in order to abide by the tenets of ability to pay. The second objective presupposes that dispensations may be granted in order to remove barriers and deterrents to our economic welfare. Hence we are carefully left with the familiar ambiguities. Indeed, the current observations on the public interest are scarcely different from the prior utterances of Andrew Mellon. Evidently the Secretary set a verbal style which is still the prevailing fashion. "A sound tax policy," he counselled his countrymen, "must lessen, so far as possible, the burden of taxation, on those least able to bear it; and it must also remove those influences which might retard the continued steady development of business and industry on which, in the last analysis, so much of our prosperity depends."[6] These words might easily have been written the other day. While the tax philosophies of Mr. Mills and the Secretary are quite distinguishable, the same generalities continue to appear in the name of the public interest. There is the usual suggestion that ability to pay is a guiding principle, and then the usual addition that exceptions are permissible for our economic welfare.

The same generalities are perennially repeated because they are vacant expressions. Everyone may freely put into them whatever he wishes to take out. That is why they are beyond dispute. For the same reason they are also very useful. Dispensations may be broadly condemned and then selectively approved without fear of engaging in any contradictions. Senator Wiley of Wisconsin, for instance, declares that taxes "should be as fair and equitable as possible." They should be "based primarily on ability to pay," and they should not discriminate "as between different groups." But at the same time the Senator also maintains that taxes should, "as a matter of principle," provide a "reasonable incentive to earn, to grow, to expand." Therefore, he warmly recommends such special dispensations as a credit for dividends and a reduced rate for income from foreign investments. Apparently dispensations which remove barriers and deterrents do not discriminate "between different groups." The public interest similarly enables Congressman Mills to distinguish between one dispensation and another. Our income tax, he charges, is "riddled with preferential benefits." The statutes are "full of special provisions through which a shrewd or lucky taxpayer can often escape paying anywhere near his full share." But having said all this, Congressman Mills indicates that it would not be "desirable to eliminate all the special provisions that we now permit."[7] Those who fail to pay their "full share" may also serve the public interest.

Though the adherents of ability regularly resort to a meaningless phrase, their message is nevertheless fairly clear. Let us continue with their appraisal of our current ills. Their basic point is that the income tax is not what it is supposed to be—a progressive levy that uniformly applies to all income, from whatever source derived. Instead Congress has devised a complex system of dispensations that variously absolve certain taxpayers from the burdens borne by others. For this condition there is only one solution. The dispensations should be drastically curtailed if not entirely eliminated. Actually, as we have seen, the adherents of ability do not reject all dispensations. But for the moment let us put this unpleasant fact aside and focus on the proposed remedy. How will Congress be persuaded to abandon its present mode of behavior?

The hopes of the adherents are generally sustained by three exhortations. There would be a marked change for the better, they plead, if our tax lawyers were more civic-minded, if the Treasury enjoyed more respect, and if Congress were more informed on tax issues. Congress would then be less prone to make special exceptions for special groups, and would legislate with a strong sense of uniformity.[8] The outlook which I have just summarized is impressive if one believes in the efficacy of prayer.

The tax bar is a strange excuse for great expectations. Admittedly, no other group is more familiar with the ramifications of our tax system both major and minor. And no other group is so sensitive to special exceptions, whether they are generously large or grudgingly small. A lawyer is not a competent tax adviser unless he is well acquainted with the highways and byways of avoidance. In the words of a hallowed cliché, his function at the very least is to minimize his clients' taxes "by means which the law permits." A client who pays more is unduly patriotic. Yet it is not enough to praise the intellectual attainments of the tax bar, however impressive they may be. Tax avoidance is a thriving business, and tax lawyers are an essential component of that business. They are the retained rationalizers that keep the business going. In the process of selling their skills, they soon become the mental captives of those they serve. Before long they either believe what they are paid to say or they hesitate to say what they believe. Dean Griswold has suggested that tax lawyers should "sell their services," not "their souls."[9] While there are singular attorneys who have eluded spiritual captivity, they are only the proverbial exceptions which prove the general rule. A Randolph Paul does not often appear on the scene.

Even the adherents of ability wonder at times whether the tax bar can lend them a helping hand. Most tax lawyers, they sadly admit, "are usually quite incapable" of appraising questions of policy with the required insight and breadth. Aside from their narrow vision, they labor within a tradition that severely inhibits their freedom of expression. "Lawyers as a profession are deeply conscious of a duty of loyalty to their clients." This profound sense of devotion necessarily deters them from asserting their views freely and honestly. They are constantly haunted by a pervasive anxiety. In stating their personal opinions as citizens they may violate their fiduciary responsibilities as lawyers. Still, hope stubbornly lingers on despite these recurring doubts. "After all," the adherents reason, "most members of our tax bar are really opposed to 'special privileges.'" Even when they are paid to "lobby directly for a special tax favor," they rarely "relish the task." "The difficulty is largely one of lack of experience, not lack of judgment or moral values." It is not impossible to educate tax lawyers to be objective rather than biased.[10]

This explanation may reassure the tax bar, but otherwise it seems inadequate. If most of our tax lawyers really dislike special privileges, then why are they quite incapable of thinking about them? I would assume that they reasonably understand what they readily disapprove. Nor is there any evidence that tax lawyers usually regard lobbying as a very distasteful activity. It may not be a simple labor of love, but the practice of law rarely is. Lawyers who lobby seem sufficiently happy at their work—especially if they are well paid. The adherents of ability are merely indulging in self-deception when they stress the problem of professional loyalty. No one is suggesting that a tax lawyer should take a position contrary to the interests of a particular client. What is involved here is a general state of mind that permeates the tax bar, whether or not some client is affected. Tax lawyers move in the orbit of the prosperous, and their attitudes faithfully reflect the views to which they are daily exposed. They may think for themselves, but only within premises supplied by others. The ability to absorb the notions of others is reinforced by two factors. There is the fear that if they say the wrong thing, prospective clients will take their problems elsewhere. There is also the fear that if they oppose special dispensations, they will displease the members of Congress who sponsor the dispensations. It seems poor business to antagonize those whose aid will be required on other occasions.

The picture scarcely changes when we turn to the professional societies in which lawyers spend their spare moments. Among these the American Bar Association is clearly the most vocal and effective. For present purposes it seems enough to appraise the potential virtues of that organization. I doubt whether much is to be gained by going further afield.

Each month the American Bar Association Journal reminds its readers that the Association is promoting the "public good." According to its periodic spokesmen, the Association is "free from self interest or the desire of personal gain." Its members are "guardians of the public good and trustees of the common weal." Since they are moved by "ideals," they are unaffected by "selfish reasons" or "the interests of any client." In tax matters the Association is usually served by a large body of experts known as the Section of Taxation. The Section is often praised for its aspirations and achievements. If I may quote some of the many eulogies, the Section is "unselfish and public spirited." It refuses to make recommendations in behalf of clients or "particular groups." It deals "with tax questions on the basis of public interest alone," and lets "the chips fall where they may." It is a "disinterested" group, unlike the "pressure" groups that selfishly ignore the welfare of "the country as a whole." It studiously refrains from "special pleading." Its "aims, purposes and objectives" have been wholly "altruistic." In view of these alleged virtues the Section is called "the people's tax attorney"—"a worthy successor" to Brandeis, who "was popularly known as the people's attorney, because of his selfless devotion to the cause of the public during his career as a lawyer in Boston."[11] Those who are less emotionally involved may find this a curious comparison. When Brandeis was appointed to the Supreme Court, seven former presidents of the Association pronounced him unfit to be a member because of his "reputation, character, and professional career."[12]

Occasionally the Tax Section is accused of being oblivious to the public interest. The charges are that it is preoccupied with the "narrow interests" of affluent taxpayers; that many lawyers have enlisted its aid in seeking special provisions for their clients; and that very often it has been "an ally of the special pressure groups." Along the same lines, the Section has even been regarded as a "business group" rather than a professional association, because its members are more concerned with the problems of their "clients or employers" than with their own.[13] While such words of reproof may seem serious, I prefer not to join the quarrel. I would only be absorbed into a fruitless debate over the meaning of "public interest." Since the Section is "unselfish" and "altruistic," I assume that it is as attached to the public interest as it purports to be. But I must still conclude that the adherents of ability are waiting in vain for the Section to help them. The Section's notion of the public interest prominently includes the effective advocacy of lucrative dispensations for groups in the upper brackets and a silent acquiescence in those obtained by others. Though the Section is undoubtedly devoted to the cause of equity, its usual concept of equity is that one dispensation justifies another.[14] If "the chips fall where they may," they also fall in a certain direction. We should not expect the direction to change.

The American Bar Association is engaged in other tax ventures besides those entrusted to the Section. In recent years the principal project of the Association has been a proposed amendment to the Constitution. The amendment has been carefully conceived. It would completely deprive Congress of the power to impose estate and gift taxes, and generally prohibit Congress from imposing an income tax above 25 per cent. The Association has determined that the economy moves from security to disaster as the rate of income tax passes beyond that limit. However, despite its fears for the economy, the Association is prepared to tolerate one exception. Under the terms of the amendment Congress would remain free to disregard the limit of 25 per cent as long as the spread between the highest rate and the lowest rate did not exceed 15 percentage points. Specifically, if Congress wished to impose a rate of 80 per cent on all taxable income over $1 million, it would also have to impose a rate of 65 per cent on the very first dollar of taxable income. The Association is bravely carrying on where Mellon left off—except that Mellon refrained from any attempt to rewrite the Constitution.[15]

The Association insists that its amendment must be approved because taxes "are destroying incentive and drying up the sources of capital." "The power to tax has become the power to enslave." If disaster is to be avoided, "the American lawyer" must "buckle on his shield and undertake to save his country in its headlong path toward a welfare state." An authoritative member of the Association adds that any opposition to the amendment "can be explained only by an adherence to the taxation philosophy of Karl Marx." Those who support progressive rates, "whether they realize it or not, are following the Marxian doctrine." The time has come to choose between "socialism" and "private enterprise and our constitutional form of government." Evidently even Calvin Coolidge was an unwitting Marxist, for he also approved progressive rates on "economic, social, and moral grounds."[16] Aside from its tireless efforts to alter the Constitution, the Association, like the Tax Section, is dedicated to the proposition that dispensations should be equitably granted. If executives, for example, are entitled to a tax reduction through pension plans, then professionals and other self-employed are equally entitled to a similar reduction.[17] Lawyers who are so deeply concerned over barriers, deterrents, and equity can hardly be too troubled by special dispensations. In short, the Association is a venerable organization from which very little should be expected.

In order to sustain their lingering faith in the tax bar, a few adherents of ability point with pride to the American Law Institute. The Institute, we are told, amply indicates that tax lawyers should not be written off as a complete loss. Its efforts in taxation, as in other legal areas, are guided by a formidable group of experts. Among them are many leading "craftsmen of the tax bar." The "research and discussion" of these "craftsmen" proceed in a "nonpartisan" atmosphere. They meditate on "a high level of objectivity," and the "concept of equity among taxpayers" is "constantly in the forefront" of their reflections.[18] In the light of these achievements the Institute is cited as cogent proof that tax lawyers can rise above their private preferences. Though I would like to agree, the evidence fails to persuade me. In fact, the Institute reinforces my less cheerful evaluation of the tax bar.

In appraising the labors of the Institute we must carefully distinguish between what it tries to do and what it declines to do. As its spokesmen have often emphasized, the Institute is solely concerned with improving the so-called "technical provisions" of the tax law. Its "objective" meditations do not extend to "broad" issues of policy—fiscal, economic, political, or social. These forbidden questions include such matters as income splitting, percentage depletion, the special rate for capital gains, the exemption for interest from state and local bonds, the credit for dividends, and the retirement credit for the elderly. Even the deduction for working wives is beyond the scope of the Institute.[19] Of course, all tax statutes, however "technical," are designed to execute some broad policy which is fiscal, economic, political, or social. Why, then, does the Institute conspicuously contrast "technical" questions and "broad" questions? The answer given is that "broad" questions provoke responses that "are almost emotional rather than analytical." If the members of the Institute became embroiled in such disturbing differences, their debates would be "neither tranquil nor contemplative." Worse still, the resulting "tempers and passions" would soon spread to "less combative issues," and the emotional experts would no longer be "objective." The more removed they are from "broad" questions, the better able they are to resolve "technical" problems.[20]

This explanation is less than complete. Actually the Institute handles many questions that are well within the realm of "broad" policy. It only avoids those which fail to evoke an "objective" spirit of togetherness. But those involve the very dispensations which the adherents of ability continuously deplore. On critical issues, then, the Institute is "nonpartisan" only in the sense that it is discreetly silent. If the Institute tried to speak, too many excited voices would be heard. It is not difficult to be nonpartisan if one studiously avoids partisan issues. The Institute has been praised for demonstrating that lawyers "can on most technical tax matters develop constructive proposals which balance fairly the interests of the 'Government' and the 'taxpayer'."[21] But the truly important questions in tax policy are not problems in balancing the interests of government and taxpayer. They are problems in distributing the burden among contending groups and interests. The Treasury may obtain the same revenue whether percentage depletion is granted or denied. The effect of the dispensation is that others pay more, not that the Treasury receives less.

Before we take leave of the tax bar, I pause for one further inquiry. Let us precariously assume that tax lawyers suddenly became as objective as the adherents of ability would like them to be. Would this remarkable transformation significantly change the situation? At the risk of offending my brethren, I am obliged to say no. The tax bar does not bring any special wisdom to the problem of dispensations. Neither the issues nor the solutions lie within its peculiar intellectual province. What unusual insight can the tax bar contribute to such matters as percentage depletion or the credit for dividends? On such questions, as well as others, the tax lawyers can hardly purport to speak as experts, for the questions involved are issues in economic and political policy. Dean Griswold has declared that if the tax lawyers will not "exert" their "talents" to resist special dispensations, "there will be few others who can."[22] Fortunately, the tax bar is not as important as he implies.

The Treasury has also inspired exaggerated hopes among those who are distressed by dispensations. At times they almost regard the Treasury as some Dispassionate Presence which is unsullied by the pressures of private interests. On the whole, they often state, only the Treasury "speaks for tax equity and tax fairness." If the Treasury "fails to respond, then tax fairness has no champion before the Congress." There is "virtually" no one else to defend "taxpayers in general" or "the taxpaying public as a whole" from "special provisions" for particular groups.[23] These words and phrases are akin to the mystical observations which I previously examined.[24] Here I must be content to say little more than I have already said. The precise views of the Treasury depend on those who happen to occupy its seats of authority. We should not be led astray because the platitudes remain the same from one administration to another.

Let us sample a few typical bromides of the Eisenhower Administration. The President solemnly announced: "Every real American is proud to carry his share of the burden." He "doesn't ask for favored protection or treatment." "We shall continue our efforts to assure that no one can avoid paying his fair share of the country's total high tax burden." "The Treasury Department will continue to review the operation of the tax laws and make recommendations for such additional changes as are needed to close loopholes." Secretary of the Treasury Humphrey and his aids issued similar statements. "All Americans ought to make the same contribution to their Government, in relation, of course, to what they can afford." No American wants "to pass his fair share of the load off to some other fellow." "Our program is based upon principle, rather than upon favoritism. It is a program aimed at helping you, each American individual." The Treasury is "firmly opposed to any tax legislation which gives any American an unfair advantage over another taxpayer." It "will always recommend prompt action" against "windfalls to any taxpayer." "Loopholes" are "always a matter of concern" because "we must maintain fairness and equality" in applying our tax laws. Tax reductions should be general, not selective. In the admonitory words of the Secretary, "Every time you give a special group relief, you are just putting that much burden on everybody else, and I think it is high time we quit burdening everybody else for special people and we should try to get everybody down all at one time."[25]

Yet throughout this diligent "review" and "concern," large dispensations for "special people" were quietly left unmentioned. Nor could the Eisenhower Treasury behave very differently, for its guiding spirits were devoted ideologists of barriers and deterrents. They were continuously worried that the income tax is impairing our economic system. In view of their abiding fears, they labored hard for still more dispensations, such as the credit for dividends. While the Treasury's "program" was undoubtedly based on "principle," the "principle" was especially designed for certain Americans. We may even say that the policy of the Eisenhower Treasury was essentially the same as the program of the Special Tax Study Committee headed by Magill. Here, again, as we note the Treasury's intense dislike of loopholes and windfalls, we should recall the insight of Jerry Cruncher. Those who look to the Treasury for salvation are thinking of another Treasury which would conform to their understanding of the public interest.[26]

The Treasury is by no means as free as it would like to be in identifying itself with certain groups. In the first place, the Treasury is politically obliged to reassure "each American individual" that it is "firmly opposed" to any "favored protection or treatment." Hence it cannot cooperate indiscriminately. It can only approve those dispensations which it deems more urgent and politically palatable. In addition, the Treasury is always concerned with the state of the budget. A failure to balance the budget is still a supreme fiscal sin—at least in a period of prosperity. The Treasury, therefore, must often say no though it would prefer to say yes. In the words of a common Treasury refrain, "As the budget is balanced, the tax burden can be eased." When the American Bar Association proposed its constitutional amendment in order to preserve private enterprise, even Secretary Humphrey had to disagree. Large tax reductions, he replied, "cannot be made now without seriously weakening our national defense or incurring large deficits."[27] The fact remains, however, that within the limitations of political necessity and fiscal responsibility, the Treasury enjoys an ample discretion to join forces with "special people" seeking special dispensations. The necessary platitudes are always available to justify any conclusion that it may reach. If the Treasury disapproves a proposed dispensation, it can speak ominously of unbalanced budgets or decry "special relief" for "special people." But if the Treasury approves, it can speak expressively of the need to encourage people to work and produce. Like Pooh-Bah, the Treasury easily performs diverse functions without undue embarrassment.

Inevitably we come at last to Congress, for the taxing process is a political process. As I earlier noted, the point has been made that dispensations would diminish if Congress were better informed. This attractive thought is combined with a specific suggestion. In order to educate itself sufficiently, Congress should equip its tax committees with additional staffs of experts. The experts, in turn, would diligently advise the committees of "any evidences of special favor," and the committees would then be less inclined to grant dispensations.[28] This request for more experts has a distinct ring of despair. The primary purpose of a Congressional expert is to justify what Congressmen otherwise desire or prefer. He illustrates Harold Laski's discerning dictum that experts should be on tap, not on top.

Needless to say, members of Congress are not as well versed in taxation as they should be. Of course, they are also inadequately informed on other matters which are entrusted to their care. It is no secret that votes are commonly cast without a firm grasp of the issues involved. In taxation, however, knowledge comes with unusual pain and suffering. The statutes are enveloped in a peculiar verbal fog of their own. The Internal Revenue Code, indeed, is a remarkable essay in sustained obscurity. It has all the earmarks of a conspiracy in restraint of understanding. The conspiracy never ends because amendments never cease. Year after year many minds combine anew against the grave danger of being understood. Tax law has reversed Dr. Butler's celebrated definition of an expert. A tax expert has become someone who knows less and less about more and more. Surely, the nimblest member of Congress can hardly hope to perceive in a day what the alleged experts are unable to understand over the years. Most members are soon lost and bewildered when they move beyond the rates and personal exemptions. As Representative Patman gently understated the ignorance of Congress, "the tax laws are passed with the Members not knowing exactly what they mean."[29]

Consider, for example, the enactment of the Internal Revenue Code, which the Republicans proudly produced in 1954. This unusual collection of words was designed, among other things, "to express" the tax laws "in a more understandable fashion." Yet, after meditating for a month and a half, the Democratic minority of the Ways and Means Committee declared, "We frankly admit that we do not fully understand or comprehend many of the changes proposed in the bill." Mr. Forand, of the Committee, complained that "not a man" in the House could "properly interpret the bill for the benefit of the members." Mr. Mills was less restrained, and described the bill as one "which no expert in the country now understands." Several Representatives confessed that "they had only the vaguest idea as to the content and the probable effect" of the bill. And one of the confused Congressmen simply stated, "We are in the dark indeed." When the bill reached the Senate, the illumination scarcely improved. If it be said that I have merely quoted disgruntled Democrats, the answer is that the Republicans were also admittedly uninformed. Since they were obliged to speak well of the bill, their confession was naturally more delicately phrased. It seems enough to quote Mr. Jenkins, a ranking Republican of the Ways and Means Committee. "The bill," he assured the House, "is entirely too complicated to be mastered in detail in the time that we have in which to study it." Hence he could do little more than say that the bill was "wonderfully prepared."[30]

A vote on a tax bill, then, is an act of faith. With few exceptions the members of Congress helplessly approve whatever the tax committees may choose to offer. They "must take the word" of the committees.[31] While the committees usually provide reports for each bill, the reports hardly qualify as guides for the perplexed. As a rule, they merely fortify the sense of organized confusion. If the members look for enlightenment during debate, they rarely learn much more. Complex tax bills are poorly discussed and hastily enacted. At times there is no discussion at all. The special dispensation for Mr. Merrill's trust passed through the House without the least comment. After the House approved the bill, its sponsor heartily commended it "because of my interest in charitable works and because I feel that a need exists to encourage those whom God has placed in the fortunate position of being able to give for the good of others."[32] While this interest in the good of others was obviously laudable, it did not remotely explain the contents of the bill. If a need exists to encourage those who are generous, we may still ask why only one taxpayer was sufficiently fortunate to be encouraged—particularly since he was already deceased and beyond encouragement. As no questions were heard, no answers were necessary.

The House, in fact, proceeds on the theory that individual members should generally abstain from thinking for themselves. This principle of parliamentary behavior is known as the "gag rule." The members are discreetly denied the right to offer any amendments or to vote on separate sections of a bill. They can only accept or reject the bill as a whole. Since their function is so limited, they have little incentive to be enlightened. In any event, too many questions cannot be asked because debate is carefully curtailed. The House, for example, was given 40 minutes to consider a complicated bill for the relief of so-called small business. The same time was allotted to a special dispensation for the self-employed. A complete revision of the Code in 1954 was entitled to only seven hours over two days. Very often the members of the House are even too helpless to use the short time that is available to them. In 1958 three hours were set aside for a comprehensive bill containing many important amendments. The bill was approved in half that time with practically no debate.[33] I am not unaware that the Ways and Means Committee is supposed to educate their less learned brethren of the House before votes are taken. But too often the explanations on the floor sound as if the halt were leading the blind.[34]

I agree that Congress, like all of us, would profit from more understanding. However, dispensations will not magically dissolve if Congress becomes better informed. For the problem here is not a case of good men gone astray for lack of sufficient knowledge. When the Finance Committee voted to relieve Mr. Mayer and Mr. Sanders, it knew well what it was doing. Representative Curtis has concisely isolated the crux of the problem. "We have pressures put on us." And, given the political framework within which Congress operates, each member will continue to respond to those pressures which impress him the most. As Senator Douglas has summarized the situation, virtually all members of Congress are "sincere," but the question is not one of "sincerity." It is "a question of forces which are operating in the community," and "this is in part an economic struggle between people with different economic interests." If I may make a timely comparison, a Senator from an oil state will not vote against percentage depletion any more than a Senator from a southern state will praise the Supreme Court for its views on segregation.[35] Those who would keep pressures out of taxes are suggesting that Congressmen should refrain from acting as Congressmen.

Though taxation is a political process, it does not follow that many significant differences divide our two major parties. Tax law provides an excellent example of bipartisanship in action. Where dispensations are involved, Democrats and Republicans are barely distinguishable. The Democrats, of course, continuously carry on as if there were a vital difference. In 1952 they declared that they would "adhere to the principle of ability to pay," that they had "vigorously attacked special tax privileges," and that they would persist in "continued efforts" to eliminate "remaining loopholes." In the same year President Truman let it be known that the Republicans were voting for "special favors." Four years later the Democrats asserted, "The immediate need is to correct the inequities in the tax structure which reflect the Republican determination to favor the few at the expense of the many." The same views are repeatedly heard in Congress. As the alleged distinction is commonly put, the "Democratic tax philosophy" is "to deal fairly with all the people." The Republicans are concerned with "the interest of the high-income groups," while the Democrats labor in behalf of "the average American who earns his living by the sweat of his brow."[36] This sort of rhetoric is admirably conceived, but it ignores the relevant facts. With few exceptions dispensations are beyond partisan politics. The Democrats are simply more adept in the use of such words as "equity" and "ability to pay." The Republicans seem unable to produce the same moral overtones.

I have examined several suggestions offered by the adherents of ability in order to cope with special dispensations. All are merely delusive efforts to remove taxes from politics. They are like the exhortations of Canute, as he sat on the shore and ordered the tides to recede. Recently the adherents of ability have developed a further thought which I find even more interesting.

According to the ideologists of barriers and deterrents, dispensations are granted because the rates are much too severe—especially in the upper brackets. The heart of the problem is high progression. Dispensations are only piecemeal attempts to alleviate excessive burdens. If the rates were lower, dispensations would be unnecessary and Congress would not have "these temptations" to relieve selected groups of taxpayers. "It is these excessive rates which are the villain of the income-tax problem."[37] In the measured words of a notable ideologist, "it seems unlikely and indeed, undesirable" that dispensations "should be discarded." As long as "the top rates remain as they are," most dispensations "are almost a necessary cushion against the impact of surtax rates which Congress knows are too high." Certain "methods and plans must be given lower rates or special treatment lest the high rates prevent them entirely."[38]

All this talk is very contagious. Even the adherents of ability have come to believe that dispensations are deliberately contrived as a means of escape from unduly high rates. Instead of reducing the rates, Congress supplies special exceptions for special groups. Senator Humphrey, for instance, says: "The story is always the same. Higher rates are imposed and at the same time loopholes are carefully framed which permit the wealthy to get out from under the higher taxes." Surrey's view is about the same. We "must conclude," he says, "that the average congressman does not believe in the present high rates of income tax, especially those applicable in the upper brackets. When he sees these rates applied in individual cases he thinks the rates are too high and therefore unfair." Otherwise how can one explain "the steady growth in special legislation relieving a particular taxpayer or group of taxpayers from these rates? True believers in these rates would long ago have torn down the tax shelters and resisted all pressures for special relief. Instead, the reverse is true."[39]

Such reflections proceed on the simple premise that substantial rates and special exceptions are intimately related as cause and effect. When the rates are very high, the exceptions soon multiply. From this premise the adherents of ability easily infer that if the rates in the upper brackets are considerably reduced, the walls of many "tax shelters" should come tumbling down. In the light of such reasoning, they bravely suggest that the top rate be pared from 91 per cent to about 65 per cent.[40]

The adherents of ability are again indulging in self-deception. Dispensations have little to do with immoderate rates. Of the many dispensations conferred by Congress, the most conspicuous are probably three. These three are the exemption of interest on state and local bonds, the special treatment of capital gains, and percentage depletion for oil and gas, and other natural resources. Unlike the exceptions for those who profit through capital gains and natural resources, the exemption for investors in state and local securities did not derive from the ideology of barriers and deterrents. It was granted under the assumed compulsion of the *Pollock* opinion, which had decreed that Congress may not tax the interest from such holdings.[41] However, the essential point is that none of the three exceptions came as a response to high rates. The exemption of interest on state and local bonds was originally bestowed in 1913, when the top rate was 7 per cent on net incomes over $500,000. The special treatment of capital gains was initially approved in 1921, when the top rate was 58 per cent on net incomes over $200,000. Percentage depletion was first allowed in 1926, when the top rate was 25 per cent on net incomes over $100,000.

The adherents of ability have failed to remember Humpty Dumpty's celebrated lecture in semantics. Words "can do a lot of work," he informed a confused Alice, if they are skilfully handled. When the ideologists of barriers and deterrents attribute special dispensations to high rates, the adherents of ability are too easily impressed. Naturally, if the top rate is 91 per cent, a reduction to 65 per cent is gladly welcomed. But once the reduction is made, then some lower rate becomes the highest peak to which Congress should aspire. The sights vary as the rates change. Already the National Association of Manufacturers would set the limit at 35 per cent, while the American Bar Association insists that 25 per cent is still better. Then, again, there is the ultimate objective of Andrew Mellon—a maximum rate of 10 per cent.[42] To the ideologists of barriers and deterrents the rates will always be too high. For in their considered view income taxes are inherently evil. As they tirelessly say day after day, the basic incentive for human effort and risk is the monetary gain to be obtained. An income tax necessarily impairs the required incentive because it reduces the gain that is realized. Hence as long as such a tax remains, businessmen are doomed to do less than their best. No matter what the rates are, we will continue to hear: "Taxes are eating at the foundation of our free-enterprise system; are stifling the incentive and ambition to produce; and are enslaving the American people by depriving them through excessive taxation of their right to spend their own money."[43]

Since the rates will always be too high, the pressures for special dispensations cannot be bought off through general reductions. When the top rate was only 25 per cent, the United States Chamber of Commerce proposed that capital gains be taxed at 5 or 6 per cent.[44] Moreover, dispensations will still retain their peculiar charm for Congressmen, for they have several inviting virtues. They enable certain taxpayers to be relieved without reducing the revenue received from others. They usually fail to attract public notice because they are conveniently described as "technical amendments." To paraphrase Representative Curtis, the benefits to certain taxpayers are merely coincidental.[45] Finally, instead of stating that it is reducing taxes, Congress can explain that it is eliminating inequities or stimulating incentives. If Congress had frankly summarized income splitting as a tax reduction in the upper brackets, it would have been hard put to justify the results. Perhaps many who derived no benefits would have become too inquisitive. Congress avoided the risk of such discomfort by dwelling on the inequity that it was wisely removing. There is more than one way to skin a cat.

Meanwhile we may safely assume that the demand for dispensations will not abate. Groups and interests are never at a loss to sustain what they seek. Even the nobility of eighteenth-century France were serenely certain that they contributed special benefits to society that called for a special immunity from taxes. They, also, had incentives that had to be preserved for the welfare of others. Hence the ideologists will continue to strike attitudes and utter their platitudes. The requests and rationalizations presented to Congress will remain as interesting as ever. Though inventors already have capital gains, they would also like to have percentage depletion. If oil and gas are important, so are inventors. Similarly, if coal royalties are taxed as capital gains, iron royalties are no less deserving. Those who advocate lower taxes on foreign income will urge that their proposal is "vital to" our "paramount interest in honorable peace." Others will blandly argue that dividends should be taxed at a flat and "relatively moderate rate" in order to foster the growth of our economy. Even an adherent of ability to pay can say that since investors now have a dividend credit, executives should be given "more incentives," too.[46] And we will continue to observe that though everyone is entitled to equity, some are entitled to more equity than others.

CHAPTER 10

A Restrained Conclusion

I have been dispassionately examining the ideologies of taxation—the modes of thought to which groups and interests resort in order to obtain tax laws to their liking. Each ideology has its own style of thought, and its own collection of platitudes. These are repeatedly echoed as if they were divinely inspired. My appraisal of the ideologies led on to a survey of our system of special dispensations. Under that system Congress periodically relieves certain taxpayers with the required influence from the progressive burdens that others must bear. I then considered a question which might trouble many who had come so far. How can special dispensations be removed from our income tax structure? Since the adherents of ability have studied this problem at length, I turned to the results of their deliberations. I soon found that their meditations are not too fruitful. The adherents are inclined to forget that our tax laws must reflect the pressures of competing interests and groups. The relevant question is not whether such pressures can be overcome, but which ones shall prevail.

The adherents of ability are apparently unable to reconcile themselves to this conclusion. They even attempt to persuade themselves, as well as others, that they are above the continuing struggle of diverse interests. Professor William Cary, for example, has tried to regard himself as an impartial spirit who is opposed to "preferential" treatments, "irrespective of what group is preferred." But then he also observes that "all provisions" in the Internal Revenue Code "basically are preferential in one way or another."[1] What troubles Cary is his recurring

179

awareness that the progressive rates are just as partial as the dispensations that he regularly deplores.

Cary's discomfort returns us to a more basic matter. The ideologists of taxation, like other mortals, are constantly attributing their own preferences to some higher disinterested wisdom. Yet, no matter how persuasive they may sound, their articles of faith are refined rationalizations in behalf of the groups and interests for which they speak. Though they look toward heaven, their creeds are rooted in the soil of competing economic pressures. Taxes not only raise revenue, but they also have other social effects. Each ideologist will appraise these other effects in terms of the precise advantages or disadvantages to his own particular groups and interests.

A given amount of revenue can be obtained from either a general sales tax or a progressive income tax. However, the burdens of the two are different. A general sales tax weighs more heavily on small incomes; a progressive income tax, on large incomes. Whether one prefers the first or the second will depend on how one evaluates their social consequences. Or, again, let us take the special dispensation for income from dividends. The spokesmen for those with large dividends will confidently regard the dispensation as essential for our economic growth and prosperity. The spokesmen for those with little or no dividends are equally sure that we will do better without the dispensation. In principle, then, the best taxes are those which are designed to produce the best effects—quite apart from the mere collection of revenue. By the same token, though, there are no ideal solutions in taxation that can pleasantly satisfy everybody. Each group or interest that seeks solutions will always have its own views on the most desirable effects, just as philosophers have disagreed on the nature of the true and the beautiful. All this may seem rather obvious, but in taxation, as in other areas of life, a good deal of time is spent in avoiding the obvious.

I am merely restating what the Penguins of Anatole France discovered many years ago on their famous island. The Elders assembled in order to levy "a just tax" for public expenses and the support of their abbey. The venerable Father Maël proposed that everyone contribute according to his means. "Therefore he who has a hundred oxen will give ten; he who has ten will give one." Then Morio, one of the affluent Penguins, rose to speak. "O Father Maël," he replied, "I think it right that each should contribute to the public expenses and to the support of the Church. For my part I am ready to give up all that I possess in the interest of my brother Penguins, and if it were necessary I would even cheerfully part with my shirt. All the elders of the people are ready, like me, to sacrifice their goods, and no one can doubt their absolute devotion to their country and their creed. We have, then, only to consider the public interest and to do what it requires." In the light of these earnest generalities Morio turned to the nature of the public interest. "Now, father, what it requires, what it demands, is not to ask much from those who possess much, for then the rich would be less rich and the poor still poorer. The poor live on the wealth of the rich and that is the reason why that wealth is sacred. Do not touch it, to do so would be an uncalled for evil. You will get no great profit by taking from the rich, for they are very few in number; on the contrary you will strip yourself of all your resources and plunge the country into misery. Whereas if you ask a little from each inhabitant without regard to his wealth, you will collect enough for the public necessities and you will have no need to enquire into each citizen's resources, a thing that would be regarded by all as a most vexatious measure. By taxing all equally and easily you will spare the poor, for you will leave them the wealth of the rich." Taxation according to wealth, Morio concluded, is a seductive illusion. "The signs of opulence are deceitful. What is certain is that everyone eats and drinks. Tax people according to what they consume. That would be wisdom and it would be justice." The Penguins also had their ideologies of taxation.

Our statesmen commonly suggest that tax policy represents the collective choice of the American people as expressed from time to time. An intelligent choice, however, presupposes an adequate understanding. Most voters are not even dimly aware of the nature of our income tax—especially its elaborate system of special dispensations.

Two reasons are usually assigned for this situation. The first is that taxes are unfortunately a dull subject, and hence it is impossible to arouse a sustained interest in them. Yet I doubt whether most people would be bored by percentage depletion or some other dispensation if it were sufficiently explained to them. A state of ignorance may easily engender a lack of interest. Anything that involves human beings and money cannot be dull.

The second reason given is that taxes are too difficult for the man in the street—or the man in the subway, as Jerome Frank called him.

Concededly, a good deal of tax law is exceedingly technical and abstruse. But no one claims that voters can be magically transformed into tax experts in several easy lessons. The question rather is whether they would grasp the basic essentials of tax policy if the issues were adequately presented to them. The real difficulty, I suspect, is that they might understand too well. If this second reason is tenable, then most Americans should not be concerned with the social problems of atomic energy, because nuclear physics is beyond their comprehension. In any event, where taxes are involved, our Congressmen and others of authority are noticeably reluctant to speak informatively for general consumption. The discourse, as a rule, is on a high level of platitude. If the public is unenlightened, the fault is not theirs.

In the 1960 Presidential campaign we were nicely shown how most of us are left in the dark. During their third television debate Senator Kennedy and Vice-President Nixon discussed percentage depletion. The Senator was asked whether he regarded the allowance for the oil industry as "inequitable." He replied that all depletion allowances "should be gone over in detail, to make sure that no one is getting a tax break; to make sure that no one is getting away from paying the taxes he ought to pay. That includes oil; it includes all kinds of minerals; it includes everything within the range of taxation. We want to be sure it's fair and equitable." If there are "any inequities in oil or any other commodity, then I would vote to close that loophole." The Vice-President responded differently. "I favor the present depletion allowance," he declared. "I favor it not because I want to make a lot of oil men rich, but because I want to make America rich." The depletion allowance is the "stimulation, the incentive for companies to go out and explore for oil, to develop it." If we are to have the economic growth "that we want," people must be encouraged to "discover more oil and minerals."[2]

On analysis the Senator simply stated that he was ill-disposed toward loopholes. Burdens should be "fair and equitable," and everyone should pay the taxes that "he ought to pay." The Vice-President was more precise, in the fashion of Senator Dirksen. What is good for the oil industry is good for the country. Percentage depletion is almost synonymous with our survival as a great nation.[3] But at no point did either speaker explain to his vast audience what percentage depletion is and how it operates. There are always reasons for such discreet omissions. Yet the fact remains that tax issues are rarely, if ever, instructively analyzed for the benefit of those who are supposed to vote intelligently.

As we approach the end I turn again for illumination to William D. Guthrie, of the *Pollock* case. A few years after that case was decided, he told a fellow lawyer that progressive taxation would "lead to the most arbitrary and confiscatory law." In the same despondent mood he advised a client of "the danger involved in graduated taxation in a democracy where the majority rules." The very "future of the Union" was at stake.[4] To Guthrie, as to others similarly concerned, progression was a standing invitation to mistreat those who are rich in dollars but poor in votes. He therefore maintained that the few can be protected from the many only if the many bear the same rates as the few. Various friends of progression, like the economist Seligman, have also alluded to the same menace. "There thus emerge," he wrote, "the social and political implications of a tax reaching only the few in a state controlled by the many." Some of the most fervent advocates of graduated rates have been sensitive to charges of undue unkindness to the affluent. When Congressman La Guardia proposed a tax increase in 1932, he carefully suggested a top rate of 49 per cent, instead of 50 per cent, on incomes over $2 million. He did not "want these citizens to go around moaning that Congress had taken just half of their income away from them."[5]

Seligman wrote in the early thirties, when the income tax was a special levy on a small minority. Evidently he did not expect that the tax would spread to the many as well as the few. The bottom rate for the many is now almost as high as the top rate for the few between 1925 and 1932.[6] Of course, the rates indicate that though the many are heavily taxed, the few may be even more heavily burdened. However, as all tax lawyers are happily aware, tax law consists of much more than a table of rates. When we look beyond the rates, the lesson which Carter derived from history is still informative. If the few understandably desire to be protected from the many, the many still need to be protected from the few.[7] The many have not been as grasping as Guthrie feared they would be. Over the years our income tax has become a "thing of shreds and patches." Our vaunted progression is largely a myth. Only people who work for their income are supposed to pay at the graduated rates—and a good number of them are also methodically excused from this unpleasant obligation.

What I have said should not be construed as a counsel of despair to those who cherish ability to pay and progressive rates. Dispensations are a system of special relief based on political influence. Though the pressures for dispensations will continue to be felt, Congress need not continue to yield. The answer is to elect Congressmen who do not feel that they have to yield. I realize that this answer is more easily stated than applied. Most taxpayers are not familiar with our system of dispensations, and neither political party is anxious to inform them. How, then, are the required members of Congress to be obtained? This is indeed a difficult question, but on such questions I can no longer purport to speak as an expert.

Notes

1. Groups, Interests, and Ideologies

1. See H. R. Rep. No. 871, Pt. 2, 78th Cong., 1st Sess. 3 (1943).
2. Pollock v. Farmers' Loan & Trust Co., 157 U.S. 429, 516 (1895).
3. Adams, *Ideals and Idealism in Taxation,* 18 Amer. Econ. Rev. 12 (1928).
4. See Compania de Tabacos v. Collector, 275 U.S. 87, 100 (1927); Frankfurter, Law and Politics 78 (1939). Cf. Mr. Justice Stone, in Carmichael v. Southern Coal Co., 301 U.S. 495, 521–523 (1937).
5. Holmes, Book Notices and Uncollected Letters and Papers 107–108 (Shriver ed. 1936).
6. 2 Holmes-Pollock Letters 137 (Howe ed. 1941). The "good little book" was Taxation: The People's Business (1924).
7. The Federalist No. 10. (Italics in original.)
8. See p. 125.

2. The Troubled Creed of Ability

1. The Federalist Nos. 12, 21.
2. In contrast, the income tax of the Civil War was progressive. Initially the exemption was $600; and the rates were 3 per cent on the first $10,000 and 5 per cent on any excess. Later the rates were raised to 5 per cent on the first $10,000, and to 10 per cent on any excess.
3. See Paul, Taxation in the United States 34, 36, 38 (1954).
4. Warren, *Chief Justice William Howard Taft,* 67 Yale L. J. 353, 360 (1958).
5. Pollock v. Farmers' Loan & Trust Co., 157 U.S. 429 (1895), *rehearing,* 158 U.S. 601 (1895).

6. 157 U.S. at 444, 498. Before the tax was imposed, apparently the same 2 per cent paid only 2 per cent of the taxes but received half the total income. *Id.* at 517.

7. *Id.* at 512.

8. *Id.* at 532–533.

9. *Id.* at 596.

10. *Id.* at 518, 532.

11. H. R. Rep. No. 5, 63d Cong., 1st Sess. 36, 37, 39 (1913). Cf. H. R. Rep. No. 922, 64th Cong., 1st Sess. 2–3 (1916); H. R. Rep. No. 1681, 74th Cong., 1st Sess. 1–2 (1935); *1 Hearings before the Committee on Ways and Means on Revenue Revision of 1951,* 82d Cong., 1st Sess. 3 (1951).

12. H. R. Rep. No. 922, 64th Cong., 1st Sess. 3 (1916). However, a consumption levy may bear more heavily on the upper levels of income. It is all a matter of what is taxed. Undoubtedly a tax confined to such items as yachts is less burdensome on the lower levels. But sales or other consumption taxes, as normally understood by those who desire them, are not so narrowly viewed.

13. *1 Hearings before the Committee on Ways and Means on Revenue Revision of 1941,* 77th Cong., 1st Sess. 4, 5 (1941).

14. H. R. Rep. No. 179, 68th Cong., 1st Sess. 5 (1924); Sen. Rep. No. 960, 70th Cong., 1st Sess. 7 (1928); H. R. Rep. No. 704, 73d Cong., 2d Sess. 5–6 (1934); Sen. Rep. No. 558, 73d Cong., 2d Sess. 8–9 (1934); H. R. Rep. No. 1681, 74th Cong., 1st Sess. 1–2 (1935); H. R. Rep. No. 1040, 77th Cong., 1st Sess. 19 (1941); 100 Cong. Rec. 9150, 9153–9154 (1954).

15. See Paul, *op. cit. supra* note 3, at 14. Cf. Blough, The Federal Taxing Process 400 (1952).

16. Blum and Kalven, The Uneasy Case for Progressive Taxation 64 (1952).

17. Compare the penetrating discussion in Goode, The Corporation Income Tax 34–37 (1951).

18. Blum and Kalven, *op. cit. supra* note 16, at 69.

19. In the *Pollock* case Mr. Justice Field argued that such a distinction was exceedingly improper. See 157 U.S. at 596.

20. Simons, Personal Income Taxation 18 (1938).

21. Smith, The Wealth of Nations 777 (Mod. Lib. ed.).

22. Hayek, *The Case Against Progressive Income Taxes,* 4 The Freeman 229 (1953).

23. Seligman, Progressive Taxation in Theory and Practice 72 (1894); 1 Mill, Principles of Political Economy 357 (1848 ed.).

24. 4 Cong. Globe 1876 (1864); 71 Cong. Globe 2783 (1866).

25. Smith, *op. cit. supra* note 21, at 794.

26. See, *e.g.*, NAM, A Tax Program For Economic Growth 6 (1955).
27. Smith, *op. cit. supra* note 21, at 792–794, 779 n. 8.
28. Simons, *op. cit. supra* note 20, at vi; Seligman, *op. cit. supra* note 23, at 195. See also *id.* at 51–52. Holmes' remarks are taken from Tyson & Brother v. Banton, 273 U.S. 418, 446 (1927).
29. Donald B. Woodward, in *Hearings before the Subcommittee on Tax Policy of the Joint Committee on the Economic Report,* 84th Cong., 1st Sess. 11 (1955).
30. Simons, Federal Tax Reform 144 (1950).

3. The Dissolution of an Ideal

1. Sen. Rep. No. 673, Pt. 3, 77th Cong., 1st Sess. 3 (1941).
2. For a brief survey of earlier notions of ability, see Buehler, *Ability to Pay,* 1 Tax L. Rev. 243, 245 (1946). The capacity to pay taxes has been measured by various indications of worldly substance. In medieval days ability was appraised in the light of such external criteria as the number of servants or clocks in a taxpayer's household. *Id.* at 246.
3. The Senate Finance Committee tried to fix an exemption of $500 for each minor child, but not exceeding two. It felt that allowances for children are "equitable as recognizing the added obligations on account of marriage and children and salutary as emphasizing the family as the unit in our social structure." Sen. Rep. No. 80, 63d Cong., 1st Sess. 25 (1913). There was no effort to indicate why those with more than two children should be taxed as if they had stopped at two. Where ability to pay was involved, even the Finance Committee did not regard children with unrestrained enthusiasm. Their "salutary" effect rapidly ended with more than one.
4. The exemptions periodically changed over the intervening 25 years. In 1917 the exemption for a married couple became $2,000; in 1921, $2,500 for net incomes up to $5,000 and $2,000 for net incomes over $5,000; in 1924, $2,500; in 1926, $3,500; and in 1932, $2,500. In 1917 the exemption for a single individual became $1,000; in 1926, $1,500; and in 1932, $1,000. An exemption for dependents was introduced in 1919 at $200 per dependent. It became $400 in 1921, and continued at that level through the twenties and thirties.
5. Again there were intervening changes. In 1940 the exemption for a married couple became $2,000; in 1941, $1,500; in 1942, $1,200; in 1944, $1,000; and in 1948, $1,200. In 1940 the exemption for a single person became $800; in 1941, $750; in 1942, $500; and in 1948, $600. In 1942 the exemption for a dependent became $350; in 1944, $500; and in 1948, $600.
6. Heller, *The Federal Income Tax and the Working Man,* a paper presented

on October 16, 1953, in Washington, D.C., at a conference called by the C.I.O. Economic Policy Committee.

7. See The Federal Revenue System: Facts and Problems 1959, Materials Assembled by the Committee Staff for the Joint Economic Committee, Joint Committee Print, 86th Cong., 1st Sess. 17 (1959). This estimate includes a relatively minor loss reflecting a similar increase in the special exemptions of the elderly and the blind.

8. 100 Cong. Rec. 3311 (1954). The late Senator Eugene Millikin of Colorado, on the other hand, thought that the present exemptions for children "are very high." *Id.* at 9270.

9. Those who are not ideologists of ability provide other arguments for keeping the exemptions as they are. Congressman Smith of Virginia fears that if exemptions are raised, many individuals will be dropped from the income tax rolls—"and when we do that, we are making second class citizens out of 7 million of our people who will never have any interest in the budgetary situation of their country, or care whether we spend a lot of money or whether we spend the proper amount." 100 Cong. Rec. 3419 (1954). Raymond Moley adds the further thought that larger exemptions will "create a society in which some support others. This involves a concept abhorrent to free men." 100 Cong. Rec. A2397 (1954). Evidently both are unaware that individuals who earn too little to pay income taxes may still pay sales and other consumption taxes.

10. See H. R. Rep. No. 180, 80th Cong, 1st Sess. 15, 41 (1947).

11. Surrey, *Federal Taxation of the Family—The Revenue Act of 1948,* 61 Harv. L. Rev. 1097, 1103 (1948). See also Surrey, *The Federal Income Tax Base for Individuals,* 58 Col. L. Rev. 815, 823–824 (1958); *The Congress and the Tax Lobbyist—How Special Tax Provisions Get Enacted,* 70 Harv. L. Rev. 1145, 1147, 1153, 1157 (1957).

12. H. R. Rep. No. 180, 80th Cong., 1st Sess. 15 (1947). See also Sen. Rep. No. 173, 80th Cong., 1st Sess. 3, 14 (1947); H. R. Rep. No. 1274, 80th Cong., 2d Sess. 20 (1948); Sen. Rep. No. 1013, 80th Cong., 2d Sess. 21 (1948).

13. These limitations relate to a taxpayer over 65 and under 72. If he is under 65 and receiving a government pension, the credit is reduced if his earnings exceed $900 for the year; and it is completely gone if his earnings come to $2,100. There are no such restrictions for a taxpayer over 72. He is free to earn as much as he can, without fear of losing the credit.

14. Surrey, *Federal Taxation of the Family—The Revenue Act of 1948,* 61 Harv. L. Rev. 1097, 1103 (1948).

15. See Surrey, *The Federal Income Tax Base for Individuals,* 58 Col. L. Rev. 815, 826 (1958).

16. See Surrey, *The Congress and the Tax Lobbyist—How Special Tax Provisions Get Enacted,* 70 Harv. L. Rev. 1145, 1147 (1957); Surrey, *supra* note 15, at 824, 830; Pechman, *Erosion of the Individual Income Tax,* 10 Nat. Tax J. 1, 6 (1957).

17. See Surrey, *supra* note 16, at 1153; Surrey, *supra* note 15, at 824–826. Cf. *id.* at 821–822, 825–826. The deduction for working wives and widowers covers only actual expenses and is confined to $600. If a working wife is married to a husband capable of self-support, the deduction is reduced to the extent that their joint adjusted gross income exceeds $4,500. Others have felt that the allowance is so meager "as to border on the ridiculous." See H. R. Rep. No. 1337, 83d Cong., 2d Sess. B9–B10 (1945).

18. Poe v. Seaborn, 282 U.S. 101 (1930).

19. According to Randolph Paul, in 1942 the Ways and Means Committee was ready to eliminate the income tax advantages in the community property states. But the members from those states wisely "arranged a deal" to vote for a higher corporate tax if those favoring the corporate increase voted against the community property proposal. Paul, *Taxation in the United States* 302 (1954).

20. Treasury Department Release, The Revenue Act of 1948 (April 14, 1948); Blough, The Federal Taxing Process 320–321 (1952).

21. In each case I am assuming that the husband is the sole source of the income. The amounts of $20,000, $50,000 and $100,000 are income after exemptions and other deductions.

22. For the rationalizations which I have just described, see Surrey, *Family Income and Federal Taxation,* 24 Taxes 980, 985–986 (1946); Surrey, *supra* note 14, at 1103. Walter Heller has mysteriously observed that "broad social considerations" motivate the allowance of income splitting. What these considerations are he fails to indicate. See 45 Amer. Econ. Rev. 441 (1955).

23. See Atlas, *Personal Exemptions,* in 1 Tax Revision Compendium on Broadening the Tax Base Submitted to the Committee on Ways and Means 525, 526, 529 (1959).

24. See Daniel M. Holland, in *Hearings before the Subcommittee on Tax Policy of the Joint Committee on the Economic Report,* 84th Cong., 1st Sess. 281 (1955); The Federal Revenue System: Facts and Problems 1959, *supra* note 7, at 17–18; Pechman, *Income Splitting,* in 1 Tax Revision Compendium, *supra* note 23, at 473, 474.

25. See Surrey, *supra* note 14, at 1103; and *supra* note 15, at 824.

26. Even Surrey concedes that the alleged increased expenses of marriage disappear as a rationalization on the higher levels of income. And eventually he also admits that income splitting discriminates against the single. However, he apparently derives solace from the thought that this discrimination is less serious than the prior discrimination among the married. See Surrey, *supra* note 22, at 985–987.

27. Sen. Rep. No. 1631, Pt. 2, 77th Cong., 2d Sess. 4 (1942); Sen. Rep. No. 1310, 84th Cong., 2d Sess. 9 (1956). See also Surrey, *Do Income Tax Exemptions Make Sense?* reprinted in 102 Cong. Rec. A3053 (1956); 105 Cong. Rec. 15590 (1959). But cf. Twentieth Century Fund, Facing the Tax Problem 294, 300, 456–457 (1937); and Buehler, *supra* note 2, at 252.

28. See Mellon, Taxation: The People's Business 54, 56 (1924).

29. H. R. Rep. No. 179, 68th Cong., 1st Sess. 5 (1924). See also Sen. Rep. No. 398, 68th Cong., 1st Sess. 7–8 (1924); H. R. Rep. No. 704, Pt. 1, 73d Cong., 2d Sess. 6 (1934); Sen. Rep. No. 558, 73d Cong., 2d Sess. 9 (1934); Mellon, *op. cit. supra* note 28, at 56–57.

30. A recent British study states: ". . . even when some allowance is made for some differences in needs, the bare figure of a man's income for a year remains no more than a rough measure of capacity to pay tax in respect of it. The higher the rates of income tax, the more important become the considerations that capacity to pay depends upon the nature of the source of the income as well as the income itself . . . ; and that, to put it generally, capacity to pay is affected by the quality of the income as well as its quantity." Royal Commission on the Taxation of Profits and Income, Second Report, Cmd. No. 9105, at 32 (1954).

31. See H. R. Rep. No. 586, 82d Cong., 1st Sess. 31 (1951); Sen. Rep. No. 781, 82d Cong., 1st Sess. 42 (1951).

32. If he pays himself more than the value of his services, the excess may be disallowed as a corporate deduction. Compensation is deductible only to the extent that it is "reasonable."

33. R.I.A. Tax Coordinator, Tax Planning Report, *Year-End Dividends and Distributions* 1 (Nov. 1958).

34. Hall, Taxation of Corporate Surplus Accumulations, Prepared for the Joint Committee on the Economic Report, 82d Cong., 2d Sess. 81, 135, 138, 185, 188, 191 (1952). See also Hall, *Small Business and the Nonintegrated Income-Tax Structure,* in Federal Tax Policy for Economic Growth and Stability, Joint Committee on the Economic Report, 84th Cong., 1st Sess. 682, 683–684, 689 (1955); Rudick, *Effect of the Corporate Income Tax on Management Policies,* in *id.* at 632, 639–641.

35. Gifts are subject to a gift tax. But the imposition of a gift tax does

not answer the question whether gifts should be taxed as income to the recipient. The income tax law of 1894 defined income as including "money and the value of all personal property acquired by gift or inheritance." See further Simons, Personal Income Taxation c. vi (1938).

36. See Simons, *op. cit. supra* note 35, at v, 5, 14, 17, 22 n.13, 31, 41, 138. See further Simons, Federal Tax Reform 144 (1950).

37. These computations include social security taxes. See Musgrave, *The Incidence of the Tax Structure and Its Effects on Consumption,* in Federal Tax Policy for Economic Growth and Stability, *supra* note 34, at 96, 98, 102; *Hearings before the Subcommittee on Tax Policy, supra* note 24, at 55–56.

38. See also Supplemental Views of Senator Douglas, in Sen. Rep. No. 1310, 84th Cong., 2d Sess. 12–13 (1956); 100 Cong. Rec. 9153–9154 (1954).

4. The Ideology of Barriers and Deterrents

1. 96 Cong. Rec. 9389 (1950). References to statements of the Special Tax Study Committee are taken from H. R. Doc. No. 523, 80th Cong., 2d Sess. 1, 5, 9 (1947).

2. Magill is repeatedly concerned with the fate of young men who are busily climbing ladders. For another example of his anxiety, see *Hearings before the Committee on Finance on H. R. 1,* 80th Cong., 1st Sess. 470 (1947).

3. For more recent observations along the same lines, see Dresser, *The Case for the Income Tax Amendment: A Reply to Dean Griswold,* 39 A.B.A.J. 25 (1953); Davidson, *Stimulation of Consumption or Investment Through Tax Policy,* and Schmidt, *Tax Policy for Growth and Stability,* in Federal Tax Policy for Economic Growth and Stability, Joint Committee on the Economic Report, 84th Cong., 1st Sess. 200, 235 (1955); Davidson, *Objectives and Guides for Tax Rate Reform,* in 1 Tax Revision Compendium on Broadening the Tax Base Submitted to the Committee on Ways and Means 139 (1959); Sen. Rep. No. 98, 86th Cong., 1st Sess. 32 (1959); 105 Cong. Rec. 16845–16846 (1959).

4. Smith, The Wealth of Nations 778 (Mod. Lib. ed.).

5. *Id.* at 814.

6. Pepper, Philadelphia Lawyer 281, 385 (1944). See also The Wall Street Journal, June 6, 1958, p. 6, col. 1.

7. Blakey, The Federal Income Tax 124 (1940).

8. See NAM, A Tax Program For Economic Growth 27 (1955); NAM, Facing the Issue of Income Tax Discrimination 7, 30 (rev. and expanded

ed. 1956); Davidson, *supra* note 3, at 206, 209. For the American Bar Association's views, see pp. 166–67.

9. H. R. Rep. No. 2333, 77th Cong., 2d Sess. 185, 187 (1942); H. R. Rep. No. 2319, 81st Cong., 2d Sess. 149 (1950). On the latter occasion Congressman Nicholson declared that when the corporate tax exceeds 33 per cent, "we become slaves of the state." 96 Cong. Rec. 9397 (1950).

10. Greenewalt, *Tax Squeeze Checks Progress,* Nation's Business 36 (April 1, 1958).

11. See Paul, Taxation in the United States 131–133 (1954). The gospel is set forth in Mellon's concise little book, Taxation: The People's Business (1924).

12. Mellon, *op. cit. supra* note 11, at 12, 14, 18, 78, 83, 93, 106–107, 136, 172–173, 181, 224.

13. *Id.* at 112, 116–120, 122–123. For further statements of the Mellon thesis, see Sen. Rep. No. 275, Pt. 1, 67th Gong., 1st Sess. 4 (1921); H. R. Rep. No. 179, 68th Gong., 1st Sess. 3–4 (1924); Sen. Rep. No. 398, 68th Cong., 1st Sess. 5 (1924); Sen. Rep. No. 52, 69th Cong., 1st Sess. 1–2 (1926).

14. H. R. Rep. No. 1, 69th Cong., 1st Sess. 5 (1926).

15. Compare, for example, the admonitions of Mellon, quoted at p. 62, with the utterances of the Special Tax Study Committee, quoted at p. 58. It would be hard to say which came first on a mere reading of the sentences.

16. NAM, Facing the Issue of Income Tax Discrimination 71 (rev. and expanded ed. 1956); Davidson, *supra* note 3, at 210. See also Sligh, *The Place of a National Sales Tax in Our Federal Tax System,* in Proc. Nat. Tax Ass'n 12 (1951).

17. H. R. Rep. No. 1337, 83d Cong., 2d Sess. B2 (1954). See further 100 Cong. Rec. 3530, 3538, 3540, 3542–3543, 3555, 3557–3558, 9294 (1954); Sen. Rep. No. 36, Pt. 2, 84th Cong., 1st Sess. 1 (1955).

18. Blakey, *op. cit. supra* note 7, at 190.

19. See H. R. Rep. No. 180, 80th Cong., 1st Sess. (1947); Sen. Rep. No. 173, 80th Cong., 1st Sess. (1947); H. R. Rep. No. 795, 80th Cong., 1st Sess. (1947); Sen. Rep. No. 468, 80th Cong., 1st Sess. (1947); H. R. Rep. No. 1274, 80th Cong., 2d Sess. (1948); Sen. Rep. No. 1013, 80th Cong., 2d Sess. (1948).

20. *Hearings before the Committee on Finance on H. R. 1,* 80th Cong., 1st Sess. 471 (1947).

21. Smith, *Taxation and Executives,* in Proc. Nat. Tax Ass'n 234, 235–236, 246, 267 (1951). Cf. Smith, Effects of Taxation on Corporate Financial Policy 2, 8–9 (1952). Still later Professor Smith wrote that taxation

"generally discourages effort, efficiency, and investment"; and that "the problem is to reduce this general discouragement." Smith, *The Philosophy of Tax Policy*, in Proc. Nat. Tax Ass'n 540, 544 (1953). By this time, however, he had joined the Treasury and become an official molder of tax policy in accordance with the creed of barriers and deterrents. His prior views, on the other hand, were based on the empirical findings contained in Sanders, Effects of Taxation on Executives (1951).

22. Sanders, *Op. cit. supra* note 21, at 12–14, 17, 20–22, 72. The younger executives who have never enjoyed low rates have escaped any need for adjustment.

23. Hall, Effects of Taxation: Executive Compensation and Retirement Plans 8, 138, 149, 254–256, 258 n. 6 (1951). See further Break, *Income Taxes and Incentives to Work: An Empirical Study*, 47 Amer. Econ. Rev. 529 (1957).

24. Greenewalt, *The Effect of High Tax Rates on Executive Incentive*, in Federal Tax Policy for Economic Growth and Stability, *supra* note 3, at 185, 188; *Hearings before the Subcommittee on Tax Policy of the Joint Committee on the Economic Report*, 84th Cong., 1st Sess. 141, 155–156 (1955). See also Elliott, Men at the Top 22–23 (1959).

25. Greenewalt, *supra* note 24, at 187–188, 191. For further expressions of the same fears, see *Hearings before the Subcommittee on Tax Policy*, *supra* note 24, at 137, 141–142; Greenewalt, *supra* note 10.

26. Professor Clarence P. Long, of Johns Hopkins University, in *Hearings before the Subcommittee on Tax Policy*, *supra* note 24, at 152–153. Cf. Galbraith, The Affluent Society 340 *et seq.* (1958).

27. Pechman and Mayer, *Mr. Colin Clark on the Limits of Taxation*, 34 Rev. of Econ. and Statistics 232, 240 n. 30 (1952).

28. Smith, *Taxation and Executives*, in Proc. Nat. Tax Ass'n 234, 236 (1951).

29. See *Hearings before the Subcommittee on Tax Policy*, *supra* note 24, at 150; Magill, *The Impact of Tax Leakages—A Postscript to Randolph Paul*, 12 Tax L. Rev. 1, 4 (1956); p. 72.

30. Magill, *supra* note 29, at 3–4.

31. Butters, Thompson and Bollinger, Effects of Taxation: Investments by Individuals 16, 18, 54–55, 59, 167, 243–244, 304, 314–315 (1953). As later footnotes indicate, I am heavily indebted to this study for a number of the paragraphs that follow. For short summaries of the study, see Butters, *Tax Influences on Investment Classes*, Proc. Nat. Tax Ass'n 260 (1951); *Effects of Taxation on the Investment Capacities and Policies of Individuals*, in Federal Tax Policy for Economic Growth and Stability, *supra* note 3, at 126; *Hearings before the Subcommittee on Tax Policy*, *supra* note 24, at 314.

32. Butters *et al., op. cit. supra* note 31, at 9, 34–36, 146.

33. *Id.* at 36–42, 50–51, 66, 178–179, 195, 229–230. See further c. VI.

34. *Id.* at 61, 243–244, 250–252, 276–277. Professor Butters and his associates add that tax-exempt securities have not materially affected the supply of funds available for equity investments. *Id.* at 287, 290, 296, 298.

35. H. R. Rep. No. 2319, 81st Cong., 2d Sess. 148 (1950). For a few other statements, see 103 Cong. Rec. 4720 (1957); Davidson, *supra* note 3, at 152; pp. 59, 68.

36. Berle, Power Without Property 32–36, 47 (1959). See also *id.* at 36–45.

37. See Butters *et al., op. cit. supra* note 31, at 2–8. "Only in the late 1920's—the heyday of financing by new stock issues and in the early 1930's when corporate retained earnings were negative and new stock issues were negligible—were more funds raised through new stock issues than through retained earnings. Even in these years the margin was not very large." *Id.* at 2.

38. *Id.* at 18–19, 26–29, 50–51, 59, 116, 138, 142; Economic Report of the President 170 (1960).

39. Butters *et al, op. cit. supra* note 31, at 28–29, 76–82, 129. See further c. V.

40. Economic Report of the President 2, 171 (1960).

41. In December, 1929, there was a special tax reduction for that year. The top individual rate was temporarily set at 24 instead of 25 per cent, and the corporate rate at 11 instead of 12 per cent.

42. Houston, *Taxation and the Investor,* in Proc. Nat. Tax Ass'n 254, 259 (1951); Report of the Special Tax Study Committee, *supra* note 1, at 5; 104 *Cong.* Rec. 8164 (1958).

43. See Economic Report of the President 155, 220 (1960); H. R. Rep. No. 1274, *supra* note 19, at 8, 13; Sen. Rep. No. 1013, *supra* note 19, at 13.

44. H. R. Rep. No. 1274, *supra* note 19, at 1, 10–12, 16; Sen. Rep. No. 1013, *supra* note 19, at 12–13, 16. For a later statement of the same views, see H. R. Rep. No. 586, 82d Cong., 1st Sess. 147 (1951).

45. See H. R. Rep. No. 180, *supra* note 19, at 10–11.

46. See *id.* at 11; Sen. Rep. No. 173, *supra* note 19, at 1, 9–10.

47. In 1958 Representative Curtis developed a kindred rationalization. He reasoned that the recession of that year was due to a faulty tax structure. See 104 Cong. Rec. 8163, A2497 (1958).

48. Federal Reserve Bulletin 1139, 1140, 1143, 1145 (Nov. 1953).

49. The Budget of the United States Government for the Fiscal Year Ending June 30, 1955, m15 (Jan. 21, 1954); H. R. Rep. No. 1337, 83d Cong., 2d Sess. 1 (1954); Sen. Rep. No. 1622, 83d Cong., 2d Sess. 1

(1954); Smith, *Two Years of Republican Tax Policy: An Economic Appraisal,* 8 Nat. Tax J. 2, 7 (1955).

50. Speech of Secretary of the Treasury George M. Humphrey before the Illinois Republican Committee on November 23, 1953; Yntema, *Our Long-Run Internal Problems,* Saturday Review 18, 22 (Jan. 17, 1959); 96 Cong. Rec. 9287 (1950). See also 104 Cong. Rec. 14474 (1958). Compare some recent reasoning by the Research and Policy Committee of the Committee for Economic Development. The Policy Committee points out that in 1958, amid very high rates, three families out of five had incomes of $4,000 or more after all taxes. In 1929, "up to that time the most prosperous era in American history," only one family out of four enjoyed such an income. The figures for both years are in terms of 1956 prices. Yet a number of pages later the Policy Committee sadly infers, in accordance with the ideology of barriers and deterrents, that the same high rates "adversely affect economic growth, and tend in the long run to diminish incomes of all groups in the society." CED, Economic Growth in the United States—Its Past and Future 12, 50 (Feb. 1958).

5. By Incentives Possessed

1. Pollock v. Farmers' Loan & Trust Co., 157 U.S. 429 (1895), *rehearing,* 158 U.S. 601 (1895). See p. 18.
2. 157 U.S. at 450, 452, 497–498.
3. This portion of Choate's rhetoric does not appear in the U.S. report. It may be found in the printed copy of his argument on file with the Supreme Court. See 19 Sup. Ct. File Copies of Briefs, Closing Argument of Mr. Choate, at 60. See also 39 L. Ed. 807.
4. 157 U.S. at 549–550.
5. *Id.* at 443–449, 550.
6. *Id.* at 596–597.
7. 50 Cong. Rec. 3840 (1913).
8. On the dangers of being "locked in," compare Brown, *The Locked-In Problem,* in Federal Tax Policy for Economic Growth and Stability, Joint Committee on the Economic Report, 84th Cong., 1st Sess. 367 (1955), with Heller, *Investors' Decisions, Equity, and the Capital Gains Tax,* in *id.* at 381.
9. H. R. Rep. No. 2333, 77th Cong., 2d Sess. 29 (1942); Sen. Rep. No. 1567, 75th Cong., 3d Sess. 6 (1938); Sen. Rep. No. 1631, 77th Cong., 2d Sess. 49 (1942).

10. H. R. Rep. No. 350, Pt. 1, 67th Cong., 1st Sess. 10–11 (1921); Sen. Rep. No. 275, Pt. 1, 67th Cong., 1st Sess. 12 (1921).

11. See, *e.g.,* Carl S. Shoup, in *Hearings before the Subcommittee on Tax Policy of the Joint Committee on the Economic Report,* 84th Cong., 1st Sess. 319, 322 (1955); Surrey, *The Federal Income Tax Base for Individuals,* 58 Col. L. Rev. 815, 819 (1958).

12. H. R. Rep. No. 1388, 67th Cong., 4th Sess. 1–2 (1923). See also 1 Report of the Staff of the Joint Committee on Internal Revenue Taxation 42 (1928).

13. 61 Cong. Rec. 6575–6576 (1921).

14. Sen. Rep. No. 1567, 75th Cong., 3d Sess. 6 (1938). See also H. R. Rep. No. 1860, 75th Cong., 3d Sess. 7 (1938).

15. See Statement of Merle H. Miller, in *2 Hearings before the Committee on Ways and Means on General Revenue Revision,* 85th Cong., 2d Sess. 2310, 2312, 2317 (1958).

16. *Id.* at 2312–2313, 2317–2318. More recently Mr. Miller has become less skeptical. See Miller, *Taxation of Capital Gains,* in 2 Tax Revision Compendium on Broadening the Tax Base Submitted to the Committee on Ways and Means 1257 (1959).

17. Jonathan Brown, in *Hearings before the Subcommittee on Tax Policy, supra* note 11, at 307–309, 341; Klem, *The Stock Exchange Point of View on Capital Gains Transactions,* in Proc. Nat. Tax Ass'n 138, 141 (1953); Letter of Robert B. Dresser, 32 Taxes 88 (1954); 104 Cong. Rec. 15650 (1958).

18. Houston, *Taxation and the Investor,* in Proc. Nat. Tax Ass'n 254, 256 (1951). Cf. Eustace Seligman, in Tax Institute, Capital Gains Taxation 57 (1946); Representative Thomas B. Curtis, in *Hearings before the Subcommittee on Tax Policy, supra* note 11, at 589.

19. See 104 Cong. Rec. 15650 (1958); Smith, *The Philosophy of Tax Policy,* in Proc. Nat. Tax Ass'n 540, 542 (1953).

20. Klem, *supra* note 17, at 143.

21. Hayek, *The Case Against Progressive Income Taxes,* 4 The Freeman 229, 231 (1953).

22. See *Hearings before the Subcommittee on Tax Policy, supra* note 11, at 308; *Hearings before a Subcommittee of the Committee on Ways and Means on Technical Amendments to the Internal Revenue Code,* 84th Cong., 2d Sess. 428 (1956); Burgess, *Federal Taxes and Business Investment Policies,* in Federal Tax Policy for Economic Growth and Stability, *supra* note 8, at 119, 125; 105 Cong. Rec. A672, A674, A1346 (1959).

23. See H. R. Rep. No. 2319, 81st Cong., 2d Sess. 60 (1950); Sen. Rep. No. 2375, 81st Cong., 2d Sess. 55 (1950). See also Klem, *supra* note 17, at 143; *2 Hearings before the Committee on Ways and Means on Revenue Revi-*

sion, 83d Cong., 1st Sess. 963 (1953). The president of the New York Stock Exchange is more logical about the problem. He contends that the present "discrimination" against speculators "is unwise" because they, too, "make a valuable contribution to the development of our country and to the liquidity of our market." *2 Hearings before a Subcommittee of the Committee on Ways and Means, supra* note 22, at 963.

24. 104 Cong. Rec. 15650, A7313 (1958).

25. See Professor Walter J. Blum, in *Hearings before the Subcommittee on Tax Policy, supra* note 11, at 271; Henle, *Taxes From the Worker's Viewpoint,* in 1 Tax Revision Compendium, *supra* note 16, at 119, 132–133. On the other hand, Harry J. Rudick says that the present rate of 25 per cent is a satisfactory mode of averaging the tax on capital gains received by high-bracket individuals. He would only lengthen the holding period to at least one year. See Tax Institute, Capital Gains Taxation 29, 47, 98 (1946).

26. See Surrey, *Definitional Problems in Capital Gains Taxation,* in Federal Tax Policy for Economic Growth and Stability, *supra* note 8, at 417; Surrey, *The Federal Income Tax Base for Individuals, supra* note 11, at 820, 830; *Hearings before the Subcommittee on Tax Policy, supra* note 11, at 313–314, 318–321, 344.

27. The number of taxable returns filed for 1958 was 45,652,134. Of this total, 2,791,712 returns reported net gains from sales of capital assets. The aggregate net long-term capital gains were $8.3 billion. Of this sum, $4.6 billion appeared on 340,353 returns filed by taxpayers reporting adjusted gross incomes of about $20,000 or more; and $2 billion on 16,172 returns filed by taxpayers reporting adjusted gross incomes of $100,000 or more. See Internal Revenue Service, Statistics of Income—Individual Income Tax Returns for 1958, 31, 62, 63 (1960). See further *Hearings before the Committee on Ways and Means on Revenue Revision of 1951,* 82d Cong., 1st Sess. 11 (1951).

28. The exclusion reduces total taxable income by about $275 million. Pechman, *What Would a Comprehensive Individual Income Tax Yield?* in 1 Tax Revision Compendium, *supra* note 16, at 251, 265.

29. See The Budget of the United States Government for the Fiscal Year Ending June 30, 1955, m 18 (Jan. 21, 1954); Representative Thomas B. Curtis, in *Hearings before the Subcommittee on Tax Policy, supra* note 11, at 524; H. R. Rep. No. 1337, 83d Cong., 2d Sess. 6 (1951); Sen. Rep. No. 1622, 83d Cong., 2d Sess. 6 (1954).

30. H. R. Rep. No. 1337, *supra* note 29, at 5–6; Sen. Rep. No. 1622, *supra* note 29, at 5–6. See also H. R. Rep. No. 2319, 81st Cong., 2d Sess. 149 (1950); The Budget of the United States Government for the Fiscal

Year Ending June 30, 1955, m 18 (Jan. 21, 1954); *1 Hearings before the Committee on Finance on H. R. 8300,* 83d Cong., 2d Sess. 90 (1954): Smith, *Two Years of Republican Tax Policy: An Economic Appraisal,* 8 Nat. Tax J. 2, 8 (1955). Cf. H. R. Rep. No. 1274, 80th Cong., 2d Sess. 13, 15–16 (1948); Sen. Rep. No. 1013, 80th Cong., 2d Sess. 13–16 (1948).

31. See H. R. Rep. No. 1337, *supra* note 29, at 6; Sen. Rep. No. 1622, *supra* note 29, at 6; 100 Cong. Rec. 3433–3434, 3440, 8996, 9275 (1954); Humphrey, How New Tax Bill Can Promote Prosperity, Life, March 15, 1954, pp. 37, 38. For the thoughts of Representatives Reed and Martin, see 96 Cong. Rec. 9283, 9386 (1950). See also *id.* at 9369, 9390, 9397. The Wall Street Journal is of the same opinion as the two Congressmen. It has no doubt that corporations pass their taxes on to the consumer. "The simple fact is that they must do so because there is no one else to pay the tax." The Wall Street Journal, June 3, 1954, p. 6, col. 1.

32. Burnet v. Guggenheim, 288 U.S. 280, 289 (1933).

33. Representative Thomas B. Curtis, in *Hearings before the Subcommittee on Tax Policy, supra* note 11, at 523. At times the Republican ideologists have stated that the corporate tax may be partially absorbed by the corporation itself through reduced profits, or by the stockholders through reduced dividends. But, on the whole, when the corporate tax is involved, they are inclined to insist that most of the burden, if not all, is passed on to consumers. See H. R. Rep. No. 2319, 81st Cong., 2d Sess. 146 (1950); H. R. Rep. No. 586, 82d Cong., 1st Sess. 148 (1951). Cf. *Hearings before the Committee on Finance on H. R. 8920,* 81st Cong., 2d Sess. 25 (1950). For variations among the Democrats, see 96 Cong. Rec. 9398 (1950); 100 Cong. Rec. 3259, 3364, 9165–9167, A4609 (1954); 105 Cong. Rec. 11871, 11889–11890 (1959); 106 Cong. Rec. 111 (daily ed. Jan. 7, 1960); *Hearings before the Committee on Finance on H. R. 7523,* 86th Cong., 1st Sess. 105 (1959).

34. *Hearings before the Subcommittee on Tax Policy, supra* note 11, at 128–129, 212, 510. The Republicans in the Treasury, however, refused to yield. They continued to insist that "one of the major purposes of the credit" was to reduce the burden of "double taxes." *Hearings before the Committee on Finance on H. R. 7523,* 86th Cong., 1st Sess. 37 (1959).

35. *Hearings before the Subcommittee on Tax Policy, supra* note 11, at 212, 507, 523–524. See also *id.* at 128–130, 212.

36. *Id.* at 525. However, at times Congressman Curtis still contends that the supply of equity capital has not kept pace with the demand. 104 Cong. Rec. A2497 (1958).

37. See *Hearings before the Subcommittee on Tax Policy, supra* note 11, at 526, 589; 104 Cong. Rec. A2497 (1958); Butters, Thompson and Bollinger,

Effects of Taxation: Investments by Individuals 242–246, 250–252 (1953). See also pp. 63, 81–82.

38. *1 Hearings before the Committee on Finance on H. R. 8300, supra* note 30, at 143.

39. H. R. Rep. No. 1337, *supra* note 29, at B7.

40. See 105 Cong. Rec. 11893 (1959); 100 Cong. Rec. 3362, 3423, A5807 (1954); *1 Hearings before the Committee on Finance on H. R. 8300, supra* note 30, at 90–91; The Wall Street Journal, March 18, 1954, p. 2, col. 2.

41. 100 Cong. Rec. 3418, 3434 (1954). See also *id.* at 3362.

42. See Butters *et al, op. cit. supra* note 37, at 23–26, 399–400, 440; Butters, *Effects of Taxation on the Investment Capacities and Policies of Individuals,* in Federal Tax Policy for Economic Growth and Stability, *supra* note 8, at 126, 127; Perlo, *"People's Capitalism" and Stock Ownership,* 48 Amer. Econ. Rev. 333, 336, 338–340 (1958); Henle, *Taxes From the Worker's Viewpoint, supra* note 25, at 123–124, 136; *1 Hearings before the Committee on Finance on H. R. 8300, supra* note 30, at 91–93. The cited figures on stockholdings cover only shares that are individually owned.

43. H. R. Rep. No. 2319, *supra* note 33, at 149, 151.

44. Smith, *supra* note 30, at 9–11.

45. H. R. Rep. No. 1337, *supra* note 29, at 6–7; Sen. Rep. No. 1622, *supra* note 29, at 6–7; 100 Cong. Rec. 3423, 3440, 3455, 3458 (1954); 105 Cong. Rec. 11892–11893 (1959); *1 Hearings before the Committee on Finance on H. R. 8300, supra* note 30, at 93–94.

46. See Smith, *Objectives of United States Tax Policy,* 105 J. of Acc. 35, 36 (1958). See also Sen. Rep. No. 2375, *supra* note 23, at 5.

47. Cf. Smith, *A Program For Federal Tax Reform,* 50 Amer. Econ. Rev. 470, 474–475 (1960).

48. *1 Hearings before the Committee on Finance on H. R. 8300, supra* note 30, at 90–91; 100 Cong. Rec. 2062, 3423, A1980 (1954); 102 Cong. Rec. A2254 (1956); 104 Cong. Rec. A2497 (1958).

49. *1 Hearings before the Subcommittee on Tax Policy, supra* note 11, at 526. See pp. 55–56.

50. See Remarks by Marion B. Folsom, Under Secretary of the Treasury, before National Petroleum Association, April 15, 1954; 104 Cong. Rec. A2487 (1958). See also 100 Cong. Rec. A1980 (1954).

51. There were 45,652,134 taxable returns for 1958, of which only 3,626,655, or 7.9 per cent, reported dividends. Of the $8.3 billion of total dividends reported, taxpayers with incomes of $20,000 or more filed 513,449 returns reporting dividends of $5 billion, and those with incomes of $100,000 or more filed 20,902 returns reporting dividends of $1.7 billion. See Internal Revenue Service, Statistics of Income—In-

dividual Income Tax Returns for 1958, 3–5, 30 (1960). For the effect of the credit on sales of new issues of stock, see The Federal Revenue System: Facts and Problems 1959, Materials Assembled by the Committee Staff for the Joint Economic Committee, 86th Cong., 1st Sess. 30–31 (1959).

52. See 105 Cong. Rec. 10819, 10955 (1959); *Hearings before the Subcommittee on Tax Policy, supra* note 11, at 212; Smith, *supra* note 47, at 478. The Chamber of Commerce has suggested a dividend credit equal to the entire tax paid by the corporation. See *Hearings before a Subcommittee of the Committee on Ways and Means, supra* note 22, at 420.

53. See Commissioner v. Lo Bue, 351 U.S. 243, 246–248 (1956).

54. Newsweek, Dec. 21, 1959, p. 68. See further Sen. Rep. No. 2375, 81st Cong., 2d Sess. 59–60 (1950); H. R. Rep. No. 2087, 80th Cong., 2d Sess. 4–6 (1948); 94 Cong. Rec. A3893 (1948). But cf. *id.* at 7906–7907 (1948).

55. See 94 Cong. Rec. A3893 (1948); Sanders, Effects of Taxation on Executives 140 (1951); Hall, Effects of Taxation: Executive Compensation and Retirement Plans 15–16 (1951).

56. See example in 105 Cong. Rec. 17063–17064 (1959), which I have somewhat revised because of arithmetical errors. For another example, see Henle, *Taxes From the Worker's Viewpoint, supra* note 25, at 128.

57. Patton, *Annual Report on Executive Compensation*, 36 Harv. Bus. Rev. 129, 131 (Sept.–Oct. 1958). The poll covered 642 companies in 18 major industries.

58. Smith, *Taxation and Executives*, in Proc. Nat. Tax Ass'n 234, 249 (1951); Alexander, *Employee Stock Options and the 1950 Revenue Act*, 6 Tax L. Rev. 163, 166 (1951). But Professor Smith nevertheless wonders why income "received through options" should be more favorably treated than "other forms of income." Proc. Nat. Tax Ass'n at 249–250.

59. *Hearings before the Subcommittee on Tax Policy, supra* note 11, at 192–193.

60. Committee on Postwar Tax Policy, A Tax Program For a Solvent America 14 (1945). See also H. R. Rep. No. 871, Pt. 2, 77th Gong., 2d Sess. 7 (1943).

61. *Hearings before the Subcommittee on Legal and Monetary Affairs of the House Government Operations Committee on Study of the Tax Amortization Program*, 84th Cong., 1st Sess. 73–75 (1955).

6. The Special Deduction for Imaginary Costs

1. These development costs cover between 75 and 90 per cent of the total outlay for a well. See *1 Hearings before the Committee on Ways and Means on*

Revenue Revision of 1950, 81st Cong., 2d Sess. 50, 55–56 (1950); 105 Cong. Rec. 8772, 11911 (1959); Freeman, *Percentage Depletion for Oil—a Policy Issue,* 30 Ind. L. J. 399, 420 (1955); Hellmuth, *The Corporate Income Tax Base,* in 1 Tax Revision Compendium on Broadening the Tax Base Submitted to the Committee on Ways and Means 283, 297 (1959).

2. See Baker and Griswold, *Percentage Depletion—a Correspondence,* 64 Harv. L. Rev. 361, 374 (1951); *3 Hearings before the Committee on Ways and Means on General Revenue Revision,* 83d Cong., 1st Sess. 2002 (1953); Stanley, *The Independent Producer's Position,* in Federal Tax Policy for Economic Growth and Stability, Joint Committee on the Economic Report, 84th Cong., 1st Sess. 474, 482 (1955); Smith, *Tax Policy as Reflected in Statutory Percentage Depletion for Oil and Gas,* in *id.* at 484, 490.

3. See United States v. Dakota-Montana Oil Co., 288 U.S. 459, 462 (1933); F.H.E. Oil Co. v. Commissioner, 147 F.2d 1002, 1003, and 150 F.2d 857, 858 (5th Cir. 1945).

4. 105 Cong. Rec. 11912 (1959). For the cited statistics, see Hellmuth, *supra* note 1, at 295–296; The Federal Revenue System: Facts and Problems 1959, Materials Assembled by the Committee Staff for the Joint Economic Committee, 86th Cong., 1st Sess. 92 (1959). See also 105 Cong. Rec. 8771 (1959).

5. See Hellmuth, *Erosion of the Federal Corporation Income Tax Base,* in Federal Tax Policy for Economic Growth and Stability, *supra* note 2, at 888, 902; Hellmuth, *supra* note 1, at 299–300; 102 Cong. Rec. 1047 (1956); 104 Cong. Rec. 11690 (1958); 105 Cong. Rec. 8786 (1959); *3 Hearings before the Committee on Ways and Means on General Revenue Revision, supra* note 2, at 1996; *2 Hearings before the Committee on Finance on H. R. 8300,* 83d Cong., 2d Sess. 1100–1101 (1954).

6. See *1 Hearings before the Committee on Ways and Means on Revenue Revision of 1950, supra* note 1, at 4, 51, 53, 59, 182. The effective rates of the ten operators ranged from .6 per cent to 63.5 per cent. In four cases the effective rate was under 10 per cent. It was over 50 per cent in only one case—on a net income averaging about $2 million a year.

7. Baker and Griswold, *supra* note 2, at 369, 382. See also 105 Cong. Rec. 17072 (1959). For the Supreme Court's view, see United States v. Dakota-Montana Oil Co., 288 U.S. 459, 461 (1933); Helvering v. Bankline Oil Co., 303 U.S. 362, 367 (1938); Commissioner v. Southwest Exploration Co., 350 U.S. 308, 312 (1956). For Senator Lausche's view, see 105 Cong. Rec. 11,915 (1959).

8. Sen. Rep. No. 617, 65th Cong., 3d Sess. 6 (1918); H. R. Rep. No. 1, 69th Cong., 1st Sess. 6 (1926); Preliminary Report on Depletion, Reports to the Joint Committee on Internal Revenue Taxation From Its

Staff 11 (1930); *1 Hearings before the Committee on Ways and Means on Revenue Revision of 1950, supra* note 1, at 51.

9. Sen. Rep. No. 275, 67th Cong., 1st Sess. 15 (1921); H. R. Rep. No. 179, 68th Cong., 1st Sess. 18 (1924); Sen. Rep. No. 398, 68th Cong., 1st Sess. 20 (1924).

10. See Sen. Rep. No. 52, 69th Cong., 1st Sess. 18 (1926); Conf. Rep. No. 356, 69th Cong., 1st Sess. 31 (1926); 67 Cong. Rec. 3018–3019 (1926). Sometimes the ideologists of percentage depletion offer novel explanations for its origin. Senator Long, for instance, is under the impression that the rate of 27½ per cent is supposed to represent the risk of drilling dry holes. As he puts it, "My understanding of the manner in which the proposal for a 27½ per cent depletion allowance arose is that it was found that over a period of time, if one attempts to drill new wells, about 27½ per cent of the attempts to drill wells are unsuccessful. Based upon that calculation, it was felt that that would be the proper depletion allowance to offset the risk factor when wells go dry and one attempts to drill new wells." 100 Cong. Rec. 9304 (1954). This explanation should even puzzle others who are devoted to percentage depletion.

11. 67 Cong. Rec. 3762 (1926).

12. 65 Cong. Rec. 2799 (1924); 78 Cong. Rec. 6182 (1934).

13. See H. R. Rep. No. 704, 73d Cong., 2d Sess. 25 (1934); Sen. Rep. No. 558, 73d Cong., 2d Sess. 30 (1934); 105 Cong. Rec. 8773 (1959). See also 102 Cong. Rec. 1043 (1956); *2 Hearings before the Committee on Ways and Means on General Revenue Revision,* 85th Cong., 2d Sess. 1295 (1958). In Colorado alone the available shale oil is at least three time as large as the estimated petroleum reserves for the entire United States. 104 Cong. Rec. 15512 (1958).

14. The five doctrines and related rationalizations may be conveniently found in Baker and Griswold, *supra* note 2; Lambert, *Percentage Depletion and the National Interest,* in Federal Tax Policy for Economic Growth and Stability, *supra* note 2, at 449; Smith, *supra* note 2.

15. See 78 Cong. Rec. 6181 (1934); 105 Cong. Rec. 8771, 11813 (1959); Baker and Griswold, *supra* note 2, at 362, 366, 378; The Federal Revenue System: Facts and Problems 1959, *supra* note 4, at 88–89.

16. See Freeman, *supra* note 1, at 418, 422, 426; 104 Cong. Rec. 11691 (1958); Baker and Griswold, *supra* note 2, at 370.

17. See 78 Cong. Rec. 6182 (1934); 105 Cong. Rec. 8771, 11813, 11919, 17075, 17246 (1959); Scott C. Lambert, in *Hearings before the Subcommittee on Tax Policy of the Joint Committee on the Economic Report,* 84th Cong., 1st Sess. 358 (1955); Baker and Griswold, *supra* note 2, at 362, 372.

18. 104 Cong. Rec. 16922 (1958); 105 Cong. Rec. 8418, 11912, 11919,

11923, 17073, 17240 (1959); *1 Hearings before the Committee on Ways and Means on Revenue Revision of 1950, supra* note 1, at 52–59; *3 Hearings before the Committee on Ways and Means on Revenue Revision of 1951,* 82d Cong., 1st Sess. 1702–1703 (1951); *Hearings before the Subcommittee on Tax Policy, supra* note 17, at 361; The Federal Revenue System: Facts and Problems 1959, *supra* note 4, at 88, 206; Gray, *Percentage Depletion, Conservation, and Economic Structure,* in Federal Tax Policy For Economic Growth and Stability, *supra* note 2, at 430, 437; Freeman, *supra* note 1, at 412, 418, 422. Between 1926 and 1952 the over-all percentage of dry holes varied between 23.5 and 39.9 per cent a year. The average for the period was 30.7 per cent. *3 Hearings before the Committee on Ways and Means on General Revenue Revision, supra* note 2, at 2012, 2018.

19. 105 Cong. Rec. 8771–8772 (1959). See also *Hearings before the Subcommittee on Tax Policy, supra* note 17, at 408. Cf. 105 Cong. Rec. 17075 (1959).

20. See Baker and Griswold, *supra* note 2, at 362, 369, 378; 103 Cong. Rec. 7631 (1957); 105 Cong. Rec. 11813 (1959).

21. See *1 Hearings before the Committee on Ways and Means on Revenue Revision of 1950, supra* note 1, at 50; *3 Hearings before the Committee on Ways and Means on Revenue Revision of 1951, supra* note 18, at 1715–1716; *3 Hearings before the Committee on Ways and Means on General Revenue Revision, supra* note 2, at 1996; *2 Hearings before the Committee on Finance on H. R. 8300,* 83d Cong., 2d Sess. 1102 (1954); Sen. Rep. No. 1631, Pt. 2, 77th Cong., 2d Sess. 5 (1942).

22. Baker and Griswold, *supra* note 2, at 368–369.

23. See *id.* at 362, 366, 378, 379; 100 Cong. Rec. 9308 (1954); 105 Cong. Rec. 11927, 17071 (1959). At times the ideologists seem unable to decide whether the deduction represents depleted capital or replenished capital. See, *e.g.,* Representative Curtis, in *Hearings before the Committee on Ways and Means on Mineral Treatment Processes for Percentage Depletion Purposes,* 86th Cong., 1st Sess. 18–19 (1959).

24. Baker and Griswold, *supra* note 2, at 379.

25. *Id.* at 372–375, 382. See further discussion in 100 Cong. Rec. 9308 (1954); 105 Cong. Rec. 8771 (1959); Stanley, *supra* note 2, at 474, 476, 478; Smith, *supra* note 2, at 487.

26. Baker and Griswold, *supra* note 6, at 380.

27. The dispensation to encourage sales was originally bestowed in 1919, when discovery depletion was also granted. The surtax was limited to 20 per cent of the sales price "to stimulate prospecting and exploration." Sen. Rep. No. 617, 65th Cong., 3d Sess. 6 (1918). In 1921 it was limited to 16 per cent. In 1934 the dispensation was repealed as no longer necessary in "the present state of overproduction." H. R. Rep.

No. 704, 73d Cong., 2d Sess. 25 (1934); Sen. Rep. No. 558, 73d Cong., 2d Sess. 30 (1934). However, two years later the Finance Committee restored it at 30 per cent because individuals had "been discouraged" from looking for oil. The return of the dispensation would "stimulate" them "to develop oil and gas properties, and to sell." Sen. Rep. No. 2156, 74th Cong., 2d Sess. 18 (1936). For the two arguments which I have just considered, see *3 Hearings before the Committee on Ways and Means on Revenue Revision of 1951, supra* note 18, at 1710–1711; 100 Cong. Rec. 9309 (1954); 105 Cong. Rec. 11814 (1959); Baker and Griswold, *supra* note 2, at 373; Stanley, *supra* note 2, at 477–478.

28. 105 Cong. Rec. 11926 (1959); Baker and Griswold, *supra* note 2, at 362; Smith, *supra* note 2, at 492–493; *3 Hearings before the Committee on Ways and Means on General Revenue Revision, supra* note 2, at 2003; 104 Cong. Rec. 16922 (1958). See also 100 Cong. Rec. 9303, 9308, 9318 (1954).

29. 105 Cong. Rec. 8773 (1959). See also *3 Hearings before the Committee on Ways and Means on General Revenue Revision, supra* note 2, at 2003–2004. Cf. The Federal Revenue System: Facts and Problems 1959, *supra* note 4, at 90.

30. Cf. *Hearings before the Subcommittee on Tax Policy, supra* note 17, at 403; 105 Cong. Rec. 17240–17241 (1959).

31. See *Hearings before the Subcommittee on Tax Policy, supra* note 17, at 403–404, 406.

32. See 105 Cong. Rec. 11813, 11927–11928, 11930, 17071, 17075–17076 (1959); 104 Cong. Rec. 16923 (1958); 100 Cong. Rec. 9301–9302, 9306 (1954); *3 Hearings before the Committee on Ways and Means on Revenue Revision of 1951, supra* note 18, at 1702, 1718; *Hearings before the Subcommittee on Tax Policy, supra* note 17, at 362–363; Baker and Griswold, *supra* note 2, at 362–363. Senator Carlson fears that a reduction of percentage depletion will bring on a depression. 100 Cong. Rec. 9303 (1954). The adherents of percentage depletion often claim that it is responsible for lower prices to consumers. But studies show that percentage depletion has little to do with the price of oil. See Freeman, *supra* note 1, at 423.

33. *Hearings before the Subcommittee on Tax Policy, supra* note 17, at 363; 105 Cong. Rec. 17075 (1959). See further pp. 147–148.

34. See Baker and Griswold, *supra* note 2, at 366–367; 103 Cong. Rec. 7631 (1957). Cf. *Hearings before the Committee on Ways and Means on Mineral Treatment Processes, supra* note 23, at 18–19, 21. Another ideologist prefers to say that percentage depletion merely treats the oil industry equally with others by removing "what I term a 'disincentive.'" See *Hearings before the Subcommittee on Tax Policy, supra* note 17, at 375.

For further variations on the same theme, see 105 Cong. Rec. 17072 (1959); *2 Hearings before the Committee on Ways and Means on General Revenue Revision, supra* note 13, at 1299, 1308. Recently a new view of percentage depletion has appeared—that it does not reduce taxes but only postpones their payment. See 105 Cong. Rec. 17074 (1959). However, some adherents of the deduction are unable to follow this explanation. See *id.* at 17239.

35. 105 Cong. Rec. 11912, 11920 (1959). See also, in regard to coal, 75 Cong. Rec. 10418–10419 (1932).

36. *Id.* at 10419.

37. H. R. Rep. No. 586, 82d Cong., 1st Sess. 30 (1951); Sen. Rep. No. 781, 82d Cong., 1st Sess. 37 (1951). See also H. R. Rep. No. 2319, 81st Cong., 2d Sess. 64 (1950). The gold mining industry, among others, is also seeking a higher rate of depletion because it needs a helping hand. See *Hearings before the Committee on Finance on H. R. 8381,* 85th Cong., 2d Sess. 101–105 (1958).

38. See Cary, *Pressure Groups and the Revenue Code: A Requiem in Honor of the Departing Uniformity of the Tax Laws,* 68 Harv. L. Rev. 745, 758, 762 (1955).

39. National Coal Association, *Percentage Depletion Allowance for Coal,* in Federal Tax Policy for Economic Growth and Stability, *supra* note 2, at 917–921. See further 104 Cong. Rec. A786 (1958). Domestic coal reserves are estimated at nearly two trillion tons. See *2 Hearings before the Committee on Ways and Means on General Revenue Revision, supra* note 13, at 1295. But some determined ideologists still speak about the mining of coal as if it were a quest for oil. See, *e.g.,* Fernald, *Distinctive Tax Treatment of Income from Mineral Extraction,* in Federal Tax Policy for Economic Growth and Stability, *supra* note 2, at 419.

40. 105 Cong. Rec. 11920 (1959).

41. See H. R. Rep. No. 586, 82d Cong., 1st Sess. 29–30 (1951); Sen. Rep. No. 781, 82d Cong., 1st Sess. 37 (1951); H. R. Rep. No. 2319, 81st Cong., 2d Sess. 64 (1950); *Hearings before the Committee on Finance on H. R. 8920,* 81st Cong., 2d Sess. 32 (1950).

42. 96 Cong. Rec. 9358 (1950). But cf. *id.* at 9400.

43. See H. R. Rep. No. 586, *supra* note 41, at 29–30; Sen. Rep. No. 781, *supra* note 41, at 37–38.

7. The Wondrous Ways of Equity

1. 104 Cong. Rec. 16919 (1958). For a few other statements of the generality, see Blough, The Federal Taxing Process 387 (1952); Paul, *Fiscal*

Priorities For Our Growing Economy, 2 How. L. J. 173, 181 (1956); Heller, *Appraisal of the Administration's Tax Policy,* 8 Nat. Tax J. 12, 25 (1955); Groves, *Special Tax Provisions and the Economy,* in Federal Tax Policy for Economic Growth and Stability, Joint Committee on the Economic Report, 84th Cong., 1st Sess. 286 (1955).

2. Proc. Nat. Tax Ass'n 569, 572 (1953). Cf. H. R. Rep. No. 708, 72d Cong., 1st Sess. 9 (1932). See Cahn, The Sense of Injustice 40 (1949), for the suggestion that a general sales tax expresses, "not quite perfectly," the kind of "elementary equality among individuals that obtains in respect to their civil rights."

3. Simons, Personal Income Taxation 30, 139, 184 (1938). See also *id.* at 152, 157, 170, 184, 204–205, 210 n. 2.

4. Director, *Capital Gains and High Rates of Progressive Taxation,* in Proc. Nat. Tax Ass'n 144, 145 (1953); Groves, *supra* note 1, at 290; Blough, *op. cit. supra* note 1, at 387.

5. *Hearings before the Subcommittee on Tax Policy of the Joint Committee on the Economic Report,* 84th Cong., 1st Sess. 232–233 (1955). See also Senator Douglas, in *Hearings before the Committee on Finance on H. R. 7523,* 86th Cong., 1st Sess. 60–61, 64 (1959); Surrey, *The Congress and the Tax Lobbyist—How Special Tax Provisions Get Enacted,* 70 Harv. L. Rev. 1145, 1146 (1957); Surrey, *Do Income Tax Exemptions Make Sense?* in 102 Cong. Rec. A3053 (1956); 105 Cong. Rec. 8437, 11910 (1959); 106 Cong. Rec. 1271 (Jan. 27, 1960); AFL-CIO, Federal Taxes 1 (1960).

6. The Federal Revenue System: Facts and Problems 1959, Materials Assembled by the Committee Staff for the Joint Economic Committee, 86th Cong., 1st Sess. 12–13 (1959); Sen. Rep. No. 98, 86th Cong., 1st Sess. 7 (1959).

7. H. R. Doc. No. 523, 80th Cong., 2d Sess. 1–2, 5, 11, 22–23, 33 (1947).

8. *Hearings before the Subcommittee on Tax Policy, supra* note 5, at 597–598.

9. See The Budget of the United States Government for the Fiscal Year Ending June 30, 1955, m 15 (Jan. 21, 1954); H. R. Rep. No. 1337, 83d Cong., 2d Sess. 74 (1954); *Hearings before the Subcommittee on Tax Policy, supra* note 5, at 602, 627–628; 100 Cong. Rec. A1980 (1954). See also 105 Cong. Rec. A77, A1440 (1959).

10. 103 Cong. Rec. 270 (1957). For a few of the many observations on behalf of small business, see Sen. Rep. No. 1310, 84th Cong., 2d Sess. 9–11 (1956); H. R. Rep. No. 2198, 85th Cong., 2d Sess. 2–3 (1958); The Federal Revenue System: Facts and Problems 1959, *supra* note 6, at 32; 102 Cong. Rec. 4804 (1956); 104 Cong. Rec. 14471 *et seq.* (1958); 105 Cong. Rec. 15380–15386 (1959). But cf. Thompson and Silberman, *Can Anything Be Done About Corporate Taxes?,* Fortune, May, 1959, pp. 121, 267–268.

11. See 105 Cong. Rec. 8771 (1959).

12. *Id.* at 8771–8772.

13. Sen. Rep. No. 781, 82d Cong., 1st Sess. 50 (1951).

14. Surrey, *supra* note 5, at 1147 n. 4; Steele, *Our Income Tax Sieve,* in the Washington Daily News, Jan. 14, 1958, p. 14, col. 1.

15. See Sen. Rep. No. 1622, 83d Cong., 2d Sess. 115, 444 (1954). See also the related plea for equity in *4 Hearings before the Committee on Finance on H. R. 8300,* 83d Cong., 2d Sess. 2002–2003 (1954).

16. See Leo Sanders, 21 T. C. 1012 (1954), *aff'd,* 225 F.2d 629 (10th Cir. 1955), *cert, denied,* 350 U.S. 967 (1956).

17. Conf. Rep. No. 2253, 84th Cong., 2d Sess. 5 (1956).

18. For further examples, see Surrey, *supra* note 5, at 1147n. 4, 1163, 1177–1178; Cary, *Pressure Groups and the Revenue Code: A Requiem in Honor of the Departing Uniformity of the Tax Laws,* 68 Harv. L. Rev. 745, 747–757 (1955).

19. Cary, *supra* note 18, at 780.

20. *Hearings before the Subcommittee on Tax Policy, supra* note 5, at 272. Sgt. Alvin C. York, a hero of World War I, is among the many who have failed to evoke the attentive sympathy that Mr. Mayer induced. A number of years ago he received a substantial sum from a motion picture based on his life, and now owes a tax of $85,000. Like Mr. Mayer, he desires to have his income taxed as a capital gain. Even the House of Representatives of Tennessee has interceded in his behalf. But Congress refuses to respond. The Washington Post and Times Herald, Feb. 18, 1959, p. 1, col. 7.

21. See pp. 43–46.

22. H. R. Doc. No. 523, *supra* note 7, at 2.

23. Sen. Rep. No. 173, 80th Cong., 1st Sess. 14–15 (1947).

24. 96 Cong. Rec. 14090–14091 (1950).

25. See pp. 32–34.

26. See H. R. Rep. No. 1337, *supra* note 9, at 7–8; Sen. Rep. No. 1622, *supra* note 15, at 7–8.

27. Memorandum to the Press by Treasury Secretary Humphrey, Feb. 17, 1954.

28. See Fahey, *"Relief" Provisions in the Revenue Act of 1943,* 53 Yale L. J. 459, 478 (1944); Sen. Rep. No. 627, 78th Cong., 1st Sess. 25–26 (1943).

29. See H. R. Rep. No. 1337, *supra* note 9, at 4, 82, A280; Sen. Rep. No. 1622, *supra* note 15, at 113, 439; 100 Cong. Rec. 8423, 8996 (1954). Cf. Sen. Rep. No. 2375, 81st Cong., 2d Sess. 44 (1950).

30. *Hearings before the Committee on Finance on H. R. 2,* 80th Cong., 1st Sess. 49 (1947). Professor Surrey, who supported income splitting, felt that the Senator was overly concerned. *Ibid.*

31. See H. R. Rep. No. 586, 82d Cong., 1st Sess. 11 (1951); Sen. Rep. No. 781, *supra* note 13, at 8, 10–11; Conf. Rep. No. 1179, 82d Cong., 1st Sess. 68 (1951).

32. See H. R. Rep. No. 586, *supra* note 31, at 11.

33. H. R. Rep. No. 1337, *supra* note 9, at 4–5, B2–B3. President Eisenhower had come to the same conclusion as the Republican majority. See The Budget of the United States Government for the Fiscal Year Ending June 30, 1955, m 16 (Jan. 21, 1954).

34. Sen. Rep. No. 1622, *supra* note 15, at 5; 100 Cong. Rec. 9172 (1954). For further observations to the same effect, see *id.* at 9481 *et seq.* (1954).

35. *Id.* at 9482, 9485–9486.

36. H. R. Rep. No. 2319, 81st Cong., 2d Sess. 54 (1950); Sen. Rep. No. 2375, *supra* note 29, at 44; Conf. Rep. No. 3124, 81st Cong., 2d Sess. 27 (1950).

37. *3 Hearings before the Committee on Finance on H. R. 8300, supra* note 15, at 1612.

38. See pp. 94–95.

39. Sen. Rep. No. 781, *supra* note 13, at 42; *Hearings before the Subcommittee on Tax Policy, supra* note 5, at 267, 271. In a true spirit of equity Congress has refused to distinguish between cattle and other livestock, such as sheep and hogs. See Conf. Rep. No. 3124, *supra* note 36, at 28; Sen. Rep. No. 781, *supra,* at 41.

40. See pp. 134–137.

41. Magill, *The Impact of Income Tax Leakages—A Postscript to Randolph Paul,* 12 Tax L. Rev. 1 (1956).

42. See *Hearings before a Subcommittee of the Committee on Ways and Means on Technical Amendments to the Internal Revenue Code,* 84th Cong., 2d Sess. 150 (1956).

43. Cahn, The Sense of Injustice 14 (1949).

8. What Is a Loophole?

1. I am referring to a married individual. If he is single and head of a household, the figure is $28,000. If he is merely single, it is $18,000.

2. These figures are derived from Musgrave, *How Progressive Is the Income Tax?* in 3 Tax Revision Compendium on Broadening the Tax Base Submitted to the Committee on Ways and Means 2223, 2224, 2226 (1959). See also Henle, *Taxes From the Worker's Viewpoint,* in 1 *id.* at 119, 121–122.

3. *Hearings before the Subcommittee on Tax Policy of the Joint Committee on the*

Economic Report, 84th Cong., 1st Sess. 468 (1955); 105 Cong. Rec. 11910 (1959); Mills, *Our Taxes: A Mess and a Gyp*, Life, Nov. 23, 1959, pp. 51, 52. See also 104 Cong. Rec. 17094 (1958).

4. Century Dictionary (2d ed. unabridged).

5. See Magill, *The Impact of Income Tax Leakages—A Postscript to Randolph Paul*, 12 Tax L. Rev. 1, 9–10 (1956); Mills, *supra* note 3, at 52. I am not suggesting that Magill is always concerned with the needs of consistency. On some occasions he argues that special dispensations cannot be viewed as loopholes because they are deliberately granted. See Magill, *Federal Income Tax Revision*, in 1 Tax Revision Compendium, *supra* note 2, at 87, 100–101.

6. Humphrey, Tax Loopholes 10 (Public Affairs Institute, 1952).

7. See The Budget of the United States Government for the Fiscal Year Ending June 30, 1955, m 15 (Jan. 21, 1954).

8. Compare pp. 45–47, *supra*, with 100 Cong. Rec. 9153 (1954); Sen. Rep. No. 1310, 84th Cong., 2d Sess. 13 (1956); *Hearings before the Subcommittee on Tax Policy*, *supra* note 3, at 111; Humphrey, *supra* note 6, at 11, 15. See also Paul, *Fiscal Priorities For Our Growing Economy*, 2 How. L. J. 173, 191 (1956).

9. See H. R. Rep. No. 2319, 81st Cong., 2d Sess. 54 (1950); p. 172.

10. Compare pp. 119–20, *supra*, with Griswold, *The Blessings of Taxation: Recent Trends in the Law of Federal Taxation*, 36 A.B.A.J. 999, 1057 (1950). For further unkind words, see Griswold, *The Mysterious Stock Option*, 2 Tax Revision Compendium, *supra* note 2, at 1327.

11. Compare Baker and Griswold, *Percentage Depletion—A Correspondence*, 64 Harv. L. Rev. 361, 369 (1950), with 104 Cong. Rec. 9967, 11692, 16918 (1958); 105 Cong. Rec. 8418, 8771, 11911, 17239, 18212 (1959); *1 Hearings before the Committee on Ways and Means on Revenue Revision of 1950*, 81st Cong., 2d Sess. 4 (1950); *Hearings before the Subcommittee on Tax Policy*, *supra* note 3, at 111; Humphrey, *supra* note 6, at 11, 12.

12. Compare pp. 106, 117, *supra*, with 100 Cong. Rec. 9160 (1954); 104 Cong. Rec. 17094 (1958); 105 Cong. Rec. 11896, 12065 (1959); *Hearings before the Subcommittee on Tax Policy*, *supra* note 3, at 111; *Hearings before the Committee on Finance on H. R. 7523*, 86th Cong., 1st Sess. 63 (1959).

13. Reports of the Special Tax Study Committee to the Committee on Ways and Means 5, 53 (1947).

14. For Congressional concern over colleges, see *1 Hearings before the Committee on Ways and Means on Revenue Revision of 1950*, *supra* note 11, at 4–5, 18–19, 165–166; H. R. Rep. No. 2319, *supra* note 9, at 36; Sen. Rep. No. 2375, 81st Cong., 2d Sess. 26 (1950). The Treasury has tried to ex-

plain the difference in treatment on the ground that "religious organizations as such" have not indulged in any "abuse" of their exemption. See *Hearings, supra,* at 171–172. Cf. *Hearings before a Subcommittee of the Committee on Ways and Means on Technical Amendments to the Internal Revenue Code,* 84th Cong., 2d Sess. 46, 57 (1956).

15. See H. R. Rep. No. 1, 69th Cong., 1st Sess. 7 (1925); Sen. Rep. No. 1631, 77th Cong., 2d Sess. 54 (1942); Sen. Rep. No. 781, 82d Cong., 1st Sess. 52–53 (1951). Compare discussion at pp. 122–23.

16. H. R. Rep. No. 2333, 77th Cong., 2d Sess. 50 (1942). See also Sen. Rep. No. 52, 69th Cong., 1st Sess. 20–21 (1926); Sen. Rep. No. 665, Pt. 1, 72d Cong., 1st Sess. 15 (1932).

17. *1 Hearings before the Committee on Ways and Means on Revenue Revision of 1950, supra* note 11, at 74, 158; H. R. Rep. No. 2319, *supra* note 9, at 46.

18. *Id.* at 153; 96 Cong. Rec. 9286, 9378, 9391 (1950). See also Sen. Rep. No. 2375, *supra* note 14, at 50.

19. H. R. Rep. No. 1337, 83d Cong., 2d Sess. 14 (1954); 100 Cong. Rec. 3426 (1954); Sen. Rep. No. 1622, 83d Cong., 2d Sess. 15 (1954).

20. Smith, *Two Years of Republican Tax Policy: An Economic Appraisal,* 8 Nat. Tax J. 2, 7 (1955).

21. See *Hearings before the Committee on Ways and Means on H. R. 10,* 84th Cong., 1st Sess. 49 *et seq.* (1955); *2 Hearings before the Committee on Ways and Means on General Revenue Revision,* 85th Cong., 2d Sess. 1759 *et seq.* (1958); H. R. Rep. No. 2277, 85th Cong., 2d Sess. 2 (1958); 103 Cong. Rec. A6584 (1957); 104 Cong. Rec. 15450–15453, 16515, 17063 (1958); 105 Cong. Rec. 15495, A5347 (1959).

22. See 103 Cong. Rec. A6583, A6585, A7256 (1957); 104 Cong. Rec. 15450–15451, 15453–15455, 17063 (1958); 105 Cong. Rec. 4266, 4273, 15495 (1959).

23. 104 Cong. Rec. 15453 (1958); 105 Cong. Rec. 4268 (1959); *Hearings before the Committee on Ways and Means on H. R. 10, supra* note 21, at 41; *Hearings before the Committee on Finance on H. R. 10,* 86th Cong., 1st Sess. 32, 42–43, 45–47, 57, 106 (1959).

24. See 104 Cong. Rec. 9272, 15449–15451, 15454, 16515, 17063 (1958); 105 Cong. Rec. 4266 (1959).

25. Smith, *General Policy Problems of Tax Differentials,* in Tax Institute, Income Tax Differentials 3, 8 (1958). For similar reasoning, see Magill, *Federal Income Tax Revision,* in 1 Tax Revision Compendium, *supra* note 2, at 87, 99.

26. See pp. 125–27.

27. Cary, *Pressure Groups and the Revenue Code: A Requiem in Honor of the Departing Uniformity of the Tax Laws,* 68 Harv. L. Rev. 745, 747 (1955); Sur-

rey, *The Congress and the Tax Lobbyist—How Special Tax Provisions Get Enacted,* 70 Harv. L. Rev. 1145, 1148, 1149 (1957).

28. Surrey, *supra* note 27, at 1146.

29. See Mills, *supra* note 3; and pp. 38–39, 41, 44–45, 142–144.

30. See *Hearings before the Subcommittee on Tax Policy, supra* note 3, at 333, 335–336, 377, 591, 593; 103 Cong. Rec. 7631 (1957). Cf. Secretary of the Treasury Snyder, in *Hearings before the Committee on Finance on H. R. 1,* 80th Cong., 1st Sess. 103 (1947).

31. *Hearings before the Subcommittee on Tax Policy, supra* note 3, at 591, 593. Compare the critical comments of Senator Douglas, in *id.* at 335.

32. Sen. Rep. No. 98, 86th Cong., 1st Sess. 35 n. 6, 40 (1959).

33. See, *e.g.,* 100 Cong. Rec. 3421 (1954); *Hearings before a Subcommittee of the Committee on Ways and Means on Technical Amendments, supra* note 14, at 95.

9. The Pursuit of the Public Interest

1. For leading examples of this mode of reassurance, see Cary, *Pressure Groups and the Revenue Code: A Requiem in Honor of the Departing Uniformity of the Tax Laws,* 68 Harv. L. Rev. 745 (1955); and Surrey, *The Congress and the Tax Lobbyist—How Special Tax Provisions Get Enacted,* 70 Harv. L. Rev. 1145 (1957).

2. See Redlich, *Taxes and Politics: The Lessons of 1952,* 8 Tax L. Rev. 381, 396–398 (1953); Griswold, *The Blessings of Taxation: Recent Trends in the Law of Federal Taxation,* 36 A.B.A.J. 999, 1057 (1950); Surrey, *supra* note 1, at 1166, 1172, 1182; Cary, *supra* note 1, at 776–778; 96 Cong. Rec. 5003–5004 (1951).

3. Sutherland, *Responsibilities of the Bar in the Tax Field,* in U. of So. Calif. Tax Institute 419, 424 (1948). See also Mellon, Taxation: The People's Business 9–10 (1924).

4. See 100 Cong. Rec. 9507–9510, 9591–9602 (1954); 104 Cong. Rec. 17007–17008 (1958); 105 Cong. Rec. 19409 (1959). See also 100 Cong. Rec. 12538–12539 (1954) (Senator Morse); 103 Cong. Rec. 5869 (1957); 105 Cong. Rec. 9059–9060 (1959) (Senator Neuberger). Cf. Lanning, *Some Realities of Tax Reform,* in 1 Tax Revision Compendium on Broadening the Tax Base Submitted to the Committee on Ways and Means 19, 58 (1959), where dispensations are distinguished in terms of whether the benefits are in the lower brackets or the upper brackets.

5. See *Panel Discussions before the Committee on Ways and Means on Income Tax Revision,* 86th Cong., 1st Sess. (1959); Press Release, May 18, 1959.

6. Mellon, *op. cit. supra* note 3, at 9.

7. See 102 Cong. Rec. A2253–2255 (1956); Mills, *Our Taxes: A Mess and a Gyp*, Life, Nov. 23, 1959, pp. 51, 52, 60. See further 104 Cong. Rec. A3315 (1958), where the late Representative Simpson asked for an income tax that would provide an "equitable distribution" of the burden and simultaneously "encourage economic expansion."

8. See, *e.g.*, Cary, *supra* note 1, at 773 *et seq.; Surrey, supra* note 1, at 1182. The three exhortations are at times combined with an intimation that lobbying is deplorable behavior. See, *e.g.*, Cary, *supra* note 1, at 745. Evidently some adherents of ability are insufficiently aware that the Constitution guarantees the right of petition. U.S. Const. Amendment I; and see United States v. Harriss, 347 U.S. 612 (1954); Eastern Railroad Presidents Conference v. Noerr Motor Freight, Inc., 29 U.S. Law Week 4191 (1961). Under our system of government even the well-to-do are constitutionally entitled to be heard.

9. See Griswold, *supra* note 2, at 1002.

10. See Surrey, *supra* note 1, at 1171–1173.

11. 26 A.B.A. Rep. 262 (1903); 31 A.B.A. Rep. 339 (1907); 71 A.B.A. Rep. 77 (1946); Section of Taxation, Program and Committee Reports 25 (1948); Sutherland, *supra* note 3, at 424, 425; 39 A.B.A.J. 44, 692–693, 766 (1953); Webster, *The Section of Taxation: The People's Tax Attorney*, 39 A.B.A.J. 29 (1953).

12. Mason, Brandeis: A Free Man's Life 489 (1946).

13. Blough, The Federal Taxing Process 28, 29, 477 (1952); Surrey, *supra* note 1, at 1170. Surrey qualifies his complaint with a note of "hope for a more objective attitude." *Ibid.*

14. Apparently the Section considers income splitting its outstanding achievement in the "public interest." Splitting supposedly illustrates what the Section can do "on a basis of fairness and equity to the whole country." Sutherland, *supra* note 3, at 423–425. Single people, it seems, are not part of our country. Compare my discussion at pp. 37–38, 134–37.

15. For recent versions of the amendment, see H. J. Res. 16, 86th Cong., 1st Sess. (1959); S. J. Res. 25, 85th Cong., 1st Sess. (1957). See further 78 A.B.A. Rep. 445, 448 (1953). The Association, in fact, derived its proposed limitation of 25 per cent from Mellon. See *Hearing before a Subcommittee of the Committee on the Judiciary on S. J. Res. 23*, 83d Cong., 2d Sess. 183–184 (1954).

16. See 77 A.B.A. Rep. 578, 587 (1952); *Hearing, supra* note 15, at 136, 139, 149; *Hearing before a Subcommittee of the Committee on the Judiciary on S. J. Res. 23*, 84th Cong., 2d Sess. 73 (1956); Dresser, *The Reed-Dirksen Amendment: Developments in the 83d Congress*, 39 A.B.A.J. 206, 207 (1953);

Dresser, *The Case for the Income Tax Amendment: A Reply to Dean Griswold*, 39 A.B.A.J. 25, 28, 84, 87 (1953). For further fruits of Mr. Dresser's meditations, see *The Reed-Dirksen Amendment: A Reply to Professor Cary*, 40 A.B.A.J. 35 (1954). Compare, along similar lines, Packard, *The Dirksen Amendment: A Reply to Theodore R. Meyer*, 43 A.B.A.J. 423 (1957). For Mr. Coolidge's view, see Mellon, *op. cit. supra* note 3, at 220.

17. See 76 A.B.A. Rep. 423 (1951); *Hearings before the Committee on Ways and Means on Postponement of Income Tax on Income Set Aside for Retirement*, 82d Cong., 2d Sess. 27 (1952); *Hearings before the Committee on Ways and Means on H. R. 10*, 84th Cong., 1st Sess. 65 (1955); *Hearings before the Committee on Finance on H. R. 10*, 86th Cong., 1st Sess. 69 (1959).

18. See Surrey, *supra* note 1, at 1174–1175; Cary, *supra* note 1, at 779; Darrell, *Internal Revenue Code of 1954—A Striking Example of the Legislative Process in Action*, in U. of So. Calif. Tax Institute 1, 17 (1955); Surrey, *The Income Tax Project of the American Law Institute*, 31 Taxes 959, 961 (1953). In quoting Darrell I do not intend to imply that he is an adherent of ability. I am merely referring to him as an acknowledged authority on the Institute's labors.

I should add that recently Cary has become disenchanted with the Institute. "An immense intellectual investment," he writes, "has been made in the *status quo*"; and a "better structure has been provided for slipping in special provisions at the behest of interest groups." Cary, *Reflections Upon the American Law Institute Tax Project and the Internal Revenue Code: A Plea For a Moratorium and Reappraisal*, 60 Col. L. Rev. 259, 264–265, 277 (1960).

19. See Surrey, *supra* note 18, at 959–960; Darrell, *supra* note 18, at 2–3, 15–17, 20. The staff of the Institute has prepared an elaborate study on the taxation of capital gains. ALI, Discussion Draft of a Study of Definitional Problems in Capital Gains Taxation (1960). However, the approval of the Institute "was neither given nor asked for." And the study "assumes the continuance of a preferential statutory treatment of capital gain." *Id.* at iii, 1.

20. See Surrey and Warren, *The Income Tax Project of the ALI: Gross Income, Deductions, Accounting, Gains and Losses, Cancellations of Indebtedness*, 66 Harv. L. Rev. 761, 764–765 (1953); Surrey and Warren, *The Income Tax Project of the American Law Institute: Partnerships, Corporations, Sale of a Corporate Business, Trusts and Estates, Foreign Income and Foreign Taxpayers*, 66 Harv. L. Rev. 1161–1164 (1953).

21. See Surrey, *supra* note 1, at 1175.

22. Griswold, *supra* note 2, at 1057.

23. Surrey, *supra* note 1, at 1164–1166. See also Cary, *supra* note 1, at 777;

Hearings before the Subcommittee on Tax Policy of the Joint Committee on the Economic Report, 84th Cong., 1st Sess. 240 (1955).

24. See pp. 145–146, 155–156, 159–161.

25. *1 Hearings before the Committee on Finance on H. R. 8300,* 83d Cong., 2d Sess. 96 (1954); The Budget of the United States Government for the Fiscal Year Ending June 30, 1959, m 10 (Jan. 13, 1958); Humphrey, *How New Tax Bill Can Promote Prosperity,* Life, March 15, 1954, pp. 37, 43; Remarks by Secretary of Treasury George M. Humphrey at the 41st Annual Meeting of the Associated Industries of Massachusetts, Oct. 25, 1956; *Hearings before the Committee on Finance on H. R. 4725,* 83d Cong., 2d Sess. 4 (1955); *Hearings before the Committee on Finance on H. R. 8381,* 85th Cong., 2d Sess. 31 (1958); *1 Hearings before the Committee on Ways and Means on General Revenue Revision,* 85th Cong., 2d Sess. 1097 (1958); 6 J. of Taxation 281 (May, 1957).

26. Compare Senators Humphrey and Douglas, in 100 Cong. Rec. 9608 (1954).

27. See *Statement by Under Secretary Folsom before the Subcommittee No. 2 of the Select Committee on Small Business of the House of Representatives,* 83d Cong., 1st Sess. 299, 301 (1953); *Hearing before a Subcommittee of the Committee on the Judiciary, supra* note 15, at 122. For other examples where the Treasury deferred to budget considerations, see *Hearings before the Committee on Ways and Means on H. R. 10, supra* note 17, at 6, 14, 34, 41–43; *Hearings before the Committee on Finance on H. R. 10, supra* note 17, at 12–14, 38, 40, 42, 48, 50; *Hearings before the Committee on Ways and Means on H. R. 5,* 86th Cong., 1st Sess. 37–40, 56–57, 68, 74, 76–77 (1959).

28. See Cary, *supra* note 1, at 778; Surrey, *supra* note 1, at 1168, 1182.

29. 103 Cong. Rec. 6356 (1957).

30. H. R. Rep. No. 1337, 83d Cong., 2d Sess. 1, B6 (1954); Sen. Rep. No. 1622, 83d Cong., 2d Sess. 1 (1954); 100 Cong. Rec. 3439, 3450, 3528, 3535, 9160, 9436, 9477 (1954).

31. 103 Cong. Rec. 6356 (1957). See also 100 Cong. Rec. 9436 (1954). Now and then the committees do not even furnish a formal analysis of the proposed legislation. There may be too little time to struggle with explanations. See, *e.g.,* H. R. Rep. No. 2087, 80th Cong., 2d Sess. 36 (1948).

32. 104 Cong. Rec. 3606–3607 (1958).

33. See 104 Cong. Rec. 1204, 14473 (1958); 105 Cong. Rec. 3418, 3564, 4268 (1959); The Wall Street Journal, Jan. 29, 1958, p. 9, col. 1. Cf. 99 Cong. Rec. 9523–9527 (1953).

34. See, *e.g.,* Representative Jenkins in 100 Cong. Rec. 3439–3440 (1954).

35. If Illinois is viewed as an oil state, then Senator Douglas is the excep-

tion that proves the general rule. For the quoted observations of Representative Curtis and Senator Douglas, see *Hearings before the Subcommittee on Tax Policy, supra* note 23, at 130.

36. The New York Times, July 24, 1952, p. 16, cols. 4–5; *id.,* Oct. 1, 1952, p. 26, col. 6; 100 Cong. Rec. 3457, 3556 (1954); 105 Cong. Rec. 11880 (1959). Republicans also like to dwell on alleged differences between the parties. See, *e.g.,* 104 Cong. Rec. A8313 (1958); 106 Cong. Rec. 1084 *et seq.* (daily ed. Jan. 25, 1960). For an instructive discussion of party politics and taxation, see Redlich, *supra* note 2.

37. See *Hearings before the Subcommittee on Tax Policy, supra* note 23, at 127–128, 130, 181, 212; 102 Cong. Rec. A3696 (1956); 105 Cong. Rec. 4268, 11893 (1959); NAM, Facing the Issue of Income Tax Discrimination 11, 14, 15, 22 (rev. and expanded ed. 1956); The Wall Street Journal, October 21, 1959, p. 6, col. 3. Cf. 102 Cong. Rec. A3672 (1956); Mills, *supra* note 7, at 52; Morag, *Reflections on Progressive Taxation,* 11 Nat. Tax J. 219, 228 (1958).

38. Magill, *The Impact of Income Tax Leakages—A Postscript to Randolph Paul,* 12 Tax L. Rev. 1, 13 (1956). See also Magill, *Federal Income Tax Revision,* in 1 Tax Revision Compendium, *supra* note 4, at 87, 90.

39. Humphrey, Tax Loopholes 9 (Public Affairs Institute, 1952); Surrey, *The Federal Income Tax Base for Individuals,* 58 Col. L. Rev. 815, 829 (1958). See also Surrey, *supra* note 1, at 1149–1150; *Hearings before the Subcommittee on Tax Policy, supra* note 23, at 313; 102 Cong. Rec. A3053 (1956). Along similar lines, see further Simons, Personal Income Taxation 16, 219 (1938); Director, *Capital Gains and High Rates of Progressive Taxation,* in Proc. Nat. Tax Ass'n 144, 145 (1953); Groves, *Special Tax Provisions and the Economy,* in Federal Tax Policy for Economic Growth and Stability, Joint Committee on the Economic Report, 84th Cong., 1st Sess. 286, 289 (1955); Henle, *Taxes From the Worker's Viewpoint,* in 1 Tax Revision Compendium, *supra* note 4, at 119, 132.

40. See Surrey, *supra* note 39, at 830; Surrey, *supra* note 1, at 1150–1151; 102 Cong. Rec. A3053–A3055 (1956). Randolph Paul also succumbed to this view. See Paul, *Fiscal Priorities For Our Growing Economy,* 2 How. L. J. 173, 186 (1956); *Hearings before the Subcommittee on Tax Policy, supra* note 23, at 234.

41. See Pollock v. Farmers' Loan & Trust Co., 157 U.S. 429, 583–586 (1895); 50 Cong. Rec. 508 (1913).

42. See pp. 51–53. Cf. 103 Cong. Rec. 4719 (1957).

43. H. R. Rep. No. 2319, 81st Cong., 2d Sess. 146–147 (1950).

44. See *Hearings before the Committee on Ways and Means on Revenue Revision of 1932,* 72d Cong., 1st Sess. 218–219 (1932).

45. See 100 Cong. Rec. 2167, 3445 (1954); *Hearings before the Subcommittee on Tax Policy, supra* note 23, at 129–130. See also 100 Cong. Rec. 3418, 3445, 3452, 3455, 3523, 3528, A1979 (1954).

46. See 2 *Hearings before the Committee on Ways and Means on General Revenue Revision,* 83d Cong., 1st Sess. 1185–1194 (1953); Sen. Rep. No. 1622, *supra* note 30, at 81; *Hearings before the Subcommittee on Tax Policy, supra* note 23, at 164, 498, 628.

10. A Restrained Conclusion

1. Cary, *Pressure Groups and the Revenue Code: A Requiem in Honor of the Departing Uniformity of the Tax Laws,* 68 Harv. L. Rev. 745, 746 (1955); *Hearings before the Subcommittee on Tax Policy of the Joint Committee on the Economic Report,* 84th Cong., 1st Sess. 270 (1955).

2. The New York Times, Oct. 14, 1960, p. 21, cols. 4, 5.

3. See pp. 110–11, 116.

4. Hurst, The Growth of American Law 374 (1950).

5. Seligman, *Income Tax,* in 7 Encyc. Soc. Sciences 626, 637 (1932); Paul, Taxation in the United States 153–154 (1954).

6. See pp. 45–46, 53.

7. See p. 5.

Index